Producing Good Citizens

D1452416

PITTSBURGH SERIES IN COMPOSITION, LITERACY, AND CULTURE

David Bartholomae and Jean Ferguson Carr, Editors

Producing Good Citizens

Literacy Training in Anxious Times

Amy J. Wan

UNIVERSITY OF PITTSBURGH PRESS

Published by the University of Pittsburgh Press, Pittsburgh, Pa., 15260
Copyright © 2014, University of Pittsburgh Press

10 9 8 7 6 5 4 3 2 1

Parts of this book were previously published as "In the Name of Citizenship: The Writing Classrooms and the Promise of Citizenship," *College English*, copyright 2011 by the National Council of Teachers of English, reprinted with permission, and as "Pushing the Boundaries of Citizenship: Undocumented Workers and Temporary Work Policies in the United States," in *Entertaining Fear: Rhetoric and the Political Economy of Social Control*, copyright 2009 by Peter Lang Publishing, reprinted with permission.

Library of Congress Cataloging-in-Publication Data

Wan, Amy J.
Producing Good Citizens: Literacy Training in Anxious Times / Amy J. Wan.
    pages cm. — (Pittsburgh Series in Composition, Literacy, and Culture)
Includes bibliographical references and index.
ISBN 978-0-8229-6289-2 (paperback: acid-free paper)
1. Literacy—Political aspects—United States—History—20th century. 2. Citizenship—United States—History—20th century. 3. Immigrants—United States—History—20th century. 4. Acculturation—United States—History—20th century. 5. Americanization—History—20th century. 6. Labor unions—United States—History—20th century. 7. Education, Higher—United States—History—20th century. 8. United States—Social conditions—1865–1918. 9. United States—Social conditions—1918–1932. 10. United States—Ethnic relations—Political aspects—History—20th century. I. Title.
LC151.W28 2014
302.2'244—dc23   2013048537

For Donovan and Elliott

CONTENTS

ACKNOWLEDGMENTS

While writing a book about citizenship, I've learned that the virtues of a single citizen are shaped by the citizenship of others. In that spirit, I must acknowledge the importance of those around me who have helped make this book possible. They should take all of the credit and none of the blame.

I am grateful for the collegiality and generosity of colleagues in the field of writing studies. Deb Brandt, Cathy Chaput, John Duffy, Jess Enoch, Bruce Horner, Asao Inoue, Connie Kendall Theado, and Morris Young probably don't realize it, but they have all been kind in ways that have encouraged this work. Linda Adler-Kassner, Juan Guerra, John Schilb, and a reviewer for *College English* all provided valuable feedback when I was still in the conceptual stages of this project. Kirk Branch and John Trimbur provided careful and honest responses to an earlier draft of this book and clarified my thinking in immeasurable ways. I am especially thankful for their contributions.

The City University of New York's pre-tenure release time allowed me to finish this book, and I thank my union, PSC-CUNY, for their tireless efforts to guarantee research leave and parental leave for all faculty at CUNY. My research has also been supported by grants from the CUNY Research Foundation and release time and writing support from the CUNY Faculty Fellowship Publication program.

The CUNY composition and rhetoric faculty have made a welcoming intellectual home. Kelly Bradbury, Leigh Jones, Mark McBeth, Tim McCormack, Corey Mead, Rebecca Mlynarczyk, Sondra Perl, and Cheryl Smith, along with Kate O'Donoghue, Lisa Vaia, and Dominique Zino, are just a few who are integral to the work of composition at CUNY.

My colleagues in the English department at Queens College have created a lively, supportive, and shockingly sane community for junior faculty. I am grateful for the tireless efforts of chairs Glenn Burger and Nancy Comley to make that possible. Ryan Black, Duncan Faherty, Kevin Ferguson, Gloria Fisk, Caroline Hong, Sian Silynn Roberts, Kim Smith, Eric Song, Jason Tougaw, Andrea Walkden, and Karen Weingarten have been significant to my life, both inside and outside of Klapper Hall. I know how lucky I am to be in their company.

This book is graced with amazing cover art. Thank you to Marc Fasanella for suggesting it and to Sara Harari from the Andrew Edlin Gallery for working out the details.

Special thanks to Josh Shanholtzer and Alex Wolfe from the University of Pittsburgh Press, who have been steadying and encouraging throughout this process. Kathy Meyer's careful eye has been invaluable. I am also indebted to Jay Barksdale at the New York Public Library for providing such warm support for scholars.

Never underestimate the enduring influence of a graduate program. The Center for Writing Studies at the University of Illinois at Urbana-Champaign produced a community of scholars that continues to challenge and nurture me. Over the years, Elizabeth Baldridge, Patrick Berry, Kory Ching, Melissa Girard, Christa Olson, Kim Hensley Owens, Jim Purdy, and Janine Solberg have given me their time, their insights, and most importantly, their friendship, all of which have made this project better. I am particularly thankful for Patrick Berry and Janine Solberg, who have read every word of this book, many times.

Debbie Hawhee, Gail Hawisher, Peter Mortensen, and Cathy Prendergast have been model mentors. Thanks to them for allowing me to continue taking advantage of their unflagging guidance. Peter Mortensen deserves special acknowledgment. Everyone should be lucky enough to have an advisor and friend as intelligent, generous, encouraging, and hilarious as Peter.

I am fortunate enough to be related to people, including my grandparents and the rest of my extended family, who give me much needed perspective for all of my research. My parents, Sam and Chun Wan, might be confused about how an engineer and an accountant produced a writing teacher, but they have given me unconditional parental encouragement and lots of free childcare. Special thanks to Debby Wan, who has been my ally, co-conspirator, and cheerleader for a lifetime.

I could not conjure up a better partner than Donovan Finn. His love, support, and commitment to an equitable household have enabled me to do this work. He and Elliott deserve the biggest thanks of all for sustaining me, for being such good sports, and for making it all worthwhile.

Producing Good Citizens

INTRODUCTION

I f you want to take the temperature of a nation, just turn to its discussions about citizenship. In 1916, in the midst of the First World War and a spike in immigration from countries outside of northern Europe, the United States Bureau of Naturalization sponsored a Citizenship Convention in Washington, DC. Various stakeholders, including teachers, labor leaders, and congressional representatives, were called together to discuss how to shape the citizenship of new immigrants. This convention synthesized a host of disparate lessons already circulating across the United States in workplaces, community groups, and schools about how to communicate with your boss, how to dress for work, how to read and write, and many other topics, all designed to produce versions of the good citizen. Similar conversations can be tracked throughout the twentieth century and into the twenty-first, a time when even the president of the United States can have the authenticity of his citizenship questioned as evidenced by the "birther" movement that sought to discredit President Barack Obama's citizenship. How a nation defines, constructs, and produces citizens communicates not only the ideals of that nation, but also its anxieties, particularly in moments of political, cultural, and economic uncertainty.

Defining citizenship can be both absolutely clear and seriously tricky business. If we stick to legal aspects, a citizen is a person who is a member of a nation-state, either by birthright or by fulfilling the requisite duties required by the state in order to have the status of citizenship conferred. In the eyes of the law, you are either a citizen or you are not. But, of course, a nation is not made up of only legal citizens. In the United States, there are permanent residents and temporary workers and undocumented immigrants and international students who also make up the fabric of the nation. While people in these different categories are welcome, to varying degrees, to work or study in the United States, they are not legally citizens and do not have full access to the privileges of citizenship. Even some who have legal citizenship status are still disenfranchised—politically, culturally, and economically—and cannot be said to have access to what is often called "full citizenship," in which all rights and privileges of citizenship are available.

This is where defining citizenship becomes tricky business. Attempts to do so are not merely explicit discussions about the nuances of these legal categorizations, but also implicit debates about the processes through which people move in and out of legal categories and attain culturally recognizable versions of citizenship. Citizenship beyond strict legal definitions is most often described as cultural citizenship, which Aihwa Ong defines as the "dual process of self-making and being made" and the "cultural practices and beliefs produced out of negotiating the often ambivalent and contested relations with the state and its hegemonic forms" (738). This *process of cultural citizenship production* provides a useful framework through which to interrogate practices in many learning situations, most certainly because citizenship is such a persistent theme in education and also because it is so intertwined with student preparation. Peruse any document that articulates the purpose of an educational institution—a university website, its strategic plans, a course syllabus, a program's learning goals, the K–12 Common Core State Standards—and quite often, producing good citizens is invoked as a goal.

Citizenship assumes such prominence in education; it was a learning outcome before there was such a thing. Consider John Dewey, Horace Mann, Thomas Jefferson, Aristotle—all of whom argued for citizenship as part of the educational endeavor. Education trains citizens. And it eases anxieties about citizenship because it offers structured, institutionalized, and routinized spaces for the widespread production of citizens and communication of citizenship ideals. The need to cultivate a more participatory democratic citizenship, a more literate citizenship, a more active citizenship—these are all common refrains. But what are the practices and definitions of good citizenship beyond the common platitudes? What do teachers, particularly those who teach literacy, teach as citizenship? And why is literacy so often at the center of citizenship production? *Producing Good Citizens: Literacy Training in Anxious Times* examines these questions by historicizing the role of literacy within the broader processes of citizenship instruction and citizen-making and by examining the enduring appeal of citizenship in literacy training spaces.

While current educational discourse often celebrates literacy as a necessary pathway to citizenship, U.S. history is filled with examples of literacy's restrictions on citizenship (e.g., literacy tests for voting in the Jim Crow South and for immigration in the 1917 Immigration Act). Addressing the complex historical relationships between literacy and citizenship, I connect these two strands—the wholly expected outcome of citizenship for literacy instruction and the troubled use of literacy as a measurement of personhood—to uncover the interplay between literacy and citizen-making efforts, particularly in the context of labor and work preparation. Drawing on literacy studies, composition history, and citizenship theory and situating them alongside historical evidence of U.S. immigration and labor practices in the early twentieth century (1910–29), this book constructs a history of work-oriented citizenship in literacy learning spaces, thus complicating the liberatory and participatory notions of citizenship commonly taken up by contemporary educators, particularly literacy teachers.

By focusing on the intersections between literacy training and contested citizenship production that coincided with changes in notions of U.S. democracy and national identity, *Producing Good Citizens* locates the roots of contemporary assumptions about citizenship and literacy for our current information and service economy much further back in the citizenship crisis of the early twentieth century. At that time, multiple immigration reforms such as the 1917 Literacy Test Act unfolded alongside profound economic changes brought on by the proliferation of mass manufacturing. In order to construct a genealogy of how literacy instruction takes up (or attempts to take up) demands for citizenship, particularly in the U.S. context, I analyze the literacy and citizenship lessons embedded in immigrant citizenship programs and worker education programs with an adjacent examination of the proliferation of the university writing classroom. The early decades of the twentieth century were marked by changes in immigration law, labor unrest, and the rise of a mass manufacturing economy, a world war, an international Communist threat, and U.S. imperialism, all of which created anxieties about citizenship and a desire for a sturdy sense of what it meant to be an American citizen in order to contrast against those who were not. In this period of contested citizenship, these educational spaces attempted to define and construct their students as the "right" kind of citizen with the "right" kind of literacy.

Considering citizenship at this previous historical moment offers a view of how the connections between teaching literacy and teaching citizenship have been drawn. While not a neat parallel, what the previous moment and our current one share is profound economic change and the uses of education through literacy as a mass strategy to shape citizenship. These kinds of recurrent citizenship questions can be one way of tracing the nation's history. Contemporary discussions about citizenship are built on these previous moments, often compressing a variety of citizen rights and obligations with civil, political, and social elements into an uncomplicated and unrealized version of citizenship that is attainable to all, while sidestepping the economic and cultural factors that might preclude it. Rather than assuming literacy's absolute connection to citizenship, *Producing Good Citizens* investigates how this association has been constructed, with literacy often used to cultivate a brand of citizenship defined by an individual's productivity and work habits as opposed to more explicitly civic activity.

To that end, this book studies how sites of citizenship training in the early twentieth century, such as those organized by unions, community groups, and the government, constructed certain conceptions of the citizen through literacy training. I am particularly interested in how legal battles over drawing boundaries of citizenship—real boundaries with both legal and material consequences—shape definitions of citizenship and the evolving paths of who has access to it. What kind of force is being exerted not just legally but rhetorically as a result of these legal battles? And how does evidence of good habits or good behavior seemingly provide opportunities to push against those boundaries?

In order to examine the implications of these efforts to redefine citizenship, I examine three pedagogical spaces designed to help people attain citizenship during the 1910s and 1920s: Americanization and citizenship programs sponsored by the federal government and community organizations; union-sponsored literacy programs such as those organized by the International Ladies' Garment Workers' Union and the Workers' Education Bureau; and first-year writing programs, which proliferated widely at colleges and universities in the United States during this period. With these three sites, the book historicizes literacy's role in the construction of U.S. citizenship and, conversely, how concepts of citizenship have been embedded in literacy practices (Heath, Street), specifically the historical and cultural context that surrounds literacy training and distribution. I pay particular attention to how working conditions and opportunities shape certain expectations for what a literacy training site—such as a citizenship class, union education program, or first-year writing class—promises to deliver. The book undertakes the critical task of understanding how such programs positioned literacy not only as a barrier (e.g., literacy tests for immigrants, African Americans, and other often marginalized populations), but also as a *habit of citizenship* that would extend opportunities. Habits of citizenship such as literacy are less explicit than civic activity such as voting but are not necessarily a less influential marker of citizenship. I direct attention to the institutions that supported literacy as a habit of citizenship through literacy training and the ways their conversations, rationales, and reasonings for literacy simultaneously imagined opportunities and revealed the limited spheres of citizenship available to certain classes of laborers.

Current anxieties about citizenship are influenced prominently by access to work opportunities, as seen in late twentieth- and early twenty-first-century debates over immigration policies such as temporary worker programs and the DREAM Act, in which the boundaries of citizenship rely on academic success as a key to economic success and, by extension, citizenship. Literacy training often eases these anxieties by certifying individuals as acceptable and providing a marker of cultural citizenship. An understanding of how anxieties were mitigated during the early-twentieth-century shift into a mass manufacturing economy could enlighten the current shift out of it, as well as the dual economic and citizenship anxieties prevalent in the United States in both eras. During the early decades of the twentieth century, profound changes in the American work experience (such as unionism, rise of office work, professionalism through college education and training, routinization and Taylorism, loss of power over working conditions) transformed the lives of citizens and potential citizens. Even though industrialization actually took place over the course of the nineteenth century as well, historian Herbert Gutman specifically describes the post-1893 United States as a "mature industrial society," in which industrialism eclipsed previous agrarian and craft-oriented economies (13).[1] As part of this process, work moved away from craft production of an object toward a more abstract process of working for an employer simply for wages. David Montgomery suggests that this increase in personnel management and scientific management is characteristic of the change in the nature of work toward a mass manufacturing posture (32–33). I refer to this shift to a mass manufacturing economy throughout the book, marking not just an industrial shift in the way work was organized but a cultural one as well.

One consequence of this mature industrial society was a shift in the nature of work itself. Daniel Nelson depicts this change as the expansion of a system in which bosses increasingly made decisions about who was qualified for particular jobs, a system that "gradually substituted managerial direction and controls for the informal, ad hoc methods of the past" (10). As a result of this loss of autonomy, workers were judged and appraised for their work skills and potential through traits such as literacy. The advent of mass manufacturing and the rise of office work (Diner 156) established an economy in which certification, often impersonal, became a necessary part of doing business. In educative spaces, literacy was being used as a way to certify and then direct students into particular roles in the emerging mass-manufacturing economic system. The mantle of citizenship production was imposed onto this process, helping to create societal requirements for literacy (basic, advanced, university-styled, cultural, or otherwise). An accompanying imperative to be productive became acceptable, even patriotic.

Following the citizenship theories put forward by Danielle Allen, Barbara Cruikshank, and Bryan Turner, I posit citizenship as more than just a construct or political institution that determines who can vote; as a membership structure, it works to determine who is acceptable and who is not. Like literacy, like a university diploma, like unaccented English, citizenship acts as a kind of credential with legal and cultural purchase. Citizenship is produced in more than just the moments when a person fills out the proper paperwork, passes a test, has lived in the country for the required amount of time, and then takes an oath of citizenship. Production of citizenship, of course, does occur in the legal realm, but also in cultural and material spaces such as classrooms, workplaces, and community spaces. The university represents one such training ground for particular kinds of literacy and citizenship, but *Producing Good Citizens* includes other training sites such as union education programs sponsored by the Workers' Education Bureau and federal Americanization programs to gain a broader sense of how literacy training was used in the service of citizenship production, particularly at a heightened moment of anxiety about citizenship when questions about U.S. imperialism, immigration, and communism mingled with changing economic conditions.

By examining a range of spaces where those hoping to acquire citizenship might have encountered literacy training, I ask how the everyday practices of producing citizenship through literacy have resulted in these practices being mutually but often contradictorily implicated for disenfranchised individuals, creating a situation in which the allure of democratic citizenship in the United States obscures its inequities. While I agree that the production of a democratic citizenry is a worthwhile goal for literacy instruction, I focus on demonstrating how literacy simultaneously influences the creation of worker-citizens in addition to participatory citizens. This comparative approach reveals how and why literacy teachers so often position literacy as a tool for students' social and economic mobility in their quests for citizenship, whether the students are immigrants, laborers, or college students (or all three), and locates that positioning in a long history of contested citizenship.

Good Citizens and the Literacy Myth

With the publication of *The Literacy Myth* in 1979, Harvey Graff set into motion a way of thinking about literacy that debunked common assumptions associating literacy with progress and viewed it as a "measure of modernity" (8). In doing so, Graff emphasized how literacy was "more central to the training, discipline, morality, and habits it accompanied and advanced than to the specific skills it represented" (321). As Graff describes it, the literacy myth perpetuates a belief that literate skills yield certain benefits and progress. Yet faith in literacy, a kind of literacy hope, still remains the backbone of much literacy instruction, not because those who believe in it are naïve, but because there are material, legal, and political effects of literacy that merit attention. As Deborah Brandt argues in *Literacy in American Lives*, "literacy skill is treated primarily as a resource—economic, political, intellectual, spiritual—which, like wealth or education, or trade skill or social connections, is pursued for the opportunities and protections that it potentially grants to its seekers" (5). Literacy instructors often play a role in the process of imbuing hope and value in literacy, even if only by reinforcing literacy's importance by teaching it. Though many of us recognize, thanks to Graff, that literacy is not a panacea, those of us who teach literacy often continue to believe that the skills we teach are useful and can have a positive impact on the lives of students, whether in other classrooms or the world at large.

In this book, I strive to understand the role of literacy hope in citizenship production and the implications of using literacy as a measure of citizenship. Such implications are clear in events such as the literacy test for immigrants of the early twentieth century or literacy requirements for suffrage, but perhaps less clear in spaces like Americanization programs, union education programs, or even university writing classes from this same time period, where literacy is seen as a means to extend opportunity and cultivate citizenship. Sharon Crowley warns against "conflat[ing] economic inequality and racial discrimination with a literacy problem" (234) because addressing the latter does not automatically solve the former. Yet this conflation perseveres because of literacy hope, a belief in the power of literacy to cure these larger societal problems. This literacy hope is so powerful because literacy appears to reconcile existing inequalities by helping to provide access to certain privileges of citizenship and their attendant societal resources. But too often, inequalities remain. For example, as discussed in chapter 2, immigrants who learned English in federal Americanization programs also learned lessons about productivity and good work habits embedded in stories that taught workers how to disagree with their boss (don't do it), how to call in sick (only if there is a danger of infecting the rest of the workforce), how to question paycheck errors (politely because it is probably an "honest mistake"), and how to gain a promotion (obey the rules of the factory and go to night school). These texts used literacy teaching as a way to cultivate specific definitions of the good worker-citizen, while simultaneously reinforcing the idea that citizenship and all of its benefits were earned through individual behavior. In his study of rhetorical approaches to literacy,

John Duffy argues that literacy practices must be framed within "arguments about such topics as race, language, history and the place of the Other" (227). Citizenship provides one such frame. When literacy acts as a measure of citizenship in this way, it perpetuates the possibility of equal footing for all individuals. In turn, the will to citizenship in writing classes operates as an extension of the literacy myth.

The desire to use literacy to mitigate inequality flourishes because literacy acts as a mechanism for citizenship: if citizenship is defined by characteristics that can be cultivated and achieved, then literacy instruction can serve as the process through which to attain these markers of citizenship. As educators, when we see ourselves as part of the citizen-making enterprise, it is often connected to the seemingly benign desire to increase the participatory efficacy of students; however, our will to citizenship holds other values and messages. In the context of literacy learning, the definition of citizenship in more specific legal and cultural terms reveals the civic values that are being supported and promoted. For example, an instructor who sees citizenship as primarily an enterprise in growing liberty and another who views citizenship as participatory would approach literacy's role in citizenship differently. While each imagines using literacy to promote or define a distinct definition of citizenship, the citizenship promoted is almost always imagined to liberate, rather than restrict. Morris Young describes how "discourse about literacy" is "often a coded way to talk about race, citizenship, and culture in America" (6). Following Young's approach, coercive examples of citizenship production through literacy, such as the productivity imperatives found in Americanization programs set in motion by the Bureau of Naturalization in 1916 or the push for political power in union education around World War I or the arguments about the utility of English as a discipline forwarded by a newly formed NCTE in the 1910s and 1920s, can be placed alongside today's current liberatory scenarios and can help us better understand how literacy acts as a mechanism in the process of citizenship production, and conversely how conceptions of citizenship shape literacy and literacy training.

Citizenship and literacy are often used together as credentials to gain access to society's resources. This literacy and citizenship-conferred credential has become most prevalent and influential in the context of securing employment where one's citizenship status and literate ability has tangible and material gains. This focus on distribution of societal resources through work reveals how workers and immigrants positioned literacy as a tool for social and economic mobility in their quests for full citizenship, and as a result how such positioning of literacy defines citizenship through these terms. Literacy, and the ideological freight that accompanies it, is created by and perpetuates these other inequalities and reframes them in citizenship terms. While literacy as an attained skill may not necessarily guarantee specific advances for an individual, having such a skill (or not having it) marks that individual as *worthy of* certain kinds of resources. So while literate ability does not inherently make resources and opportunities available, one often follows the other.

Understanding literacy as a mechanism of citizenship that appears to reconcile inequality can help to reveal the limitations of a model of citizenship disproportionately focused on participation (a prevalent model in educational circles), and to overlook the importance of legal and cultural boundaries to citizenship. As Catherine Prendergast contends in *Literacy and Racial Justice: The Politics of Learning after Brown v. Board of Education*, claims to equal legal rights in the realm of education have not always resulted in equality in the material world. In that same vein, despite the theoretical and legal possibility of conferral of equal citizenship rights to individuals, the resulting equality narrative that accompanies discourses around rights, privileges, and obligations obscures the fact that full citizenship itself cannot be realized equally by all. While citizenship theorist T. H. Marshall acknowledges the ongoing presence of inequality, he also imagines the conferral of rights as creating a "uniform status of citizenship," in which equal access to rights would equalize the other disparities among citizens. In literacy instruction, a space or tension exists between equality and individualism, where a citizen might gain a kind of equality through increasing literate skills but would still need to rely on personal success in developing certain citizenship practices to gain full access to citizenship. With a focus on an individual's literacy, the burden of realizing citizenship remains on individual acquisition of these practices rather than a larger system of inequality.

The role of literacy in providing access to citizenship is simultaneously coercive and empowering, perpetuating a tension between a definition of citizenship rooted in equality and one rooted in individualism. In *The Will to Empower* (1999), Barbara Cruikshank defines technologies of citizenship as "participatory and democratic schemes . . . for correcting the deficiencies of citizens" (4), calling attention to the idea that regulation is embedded in the making of participatory citizens. For example, contemporary pedagogical practices such as critical literacy or letter-to-the-editor assignments or public writing can be viewed as both offering a way of empowering students, but also providing a space for citizen dissent that is unthreatening. The citizenship and literacy training of the early twentieth century also functioned in this dual role. Administrators of union education programs, for instance, hoped that literacy learning could be used as a way to turn workers into good citizens of the country and good citizens of the union, yet the lessons promoted in this space often limited participants to narrow ways that good citizens would use their literacy. Citizenship production spaces like the ones discussed in this book promoted literacy learning as a way to achieve good citizenship, but that citizenship was often restricted to certain narrow definitions, while simultaneously offering vague liberatory and equalizing possibilities. Such possibilities, whether or not ever fully realized, are what continue to perpetuate hope in literacy.

Citizenship in the Writing Classroom and Beyond

In recent years, a spate of publications has questioned the efficacy of higher education.[2] Such publications represent millennial anxiety about the relevancy of education; hand wringing over whether students are learning enough or doing the right kinds of learning; whether institutions of higher education are taking the necessary steps to produce "good citizens"; and whether the citizenship being produced should be defined through a framework of productivity, liberal humanism, or globalization (or perhaps all three simultaneously). For those who teach or administer writing classes, these assessments of the efficacy of higher education reflect our own questions about what we imagine students are doing with literacy once they leave the classroom, which in turn informs curricula and teaching practices.

Literacy and education are often conflated but with good reason. Literacy frequently stands in for education, in a similar way that it acts as a measure of citizenship. Literacy, the most basic of skills, provides a measureable way to decide whether someone is educated. If someone cannot speak, read, or write in a dominant language, then they are perceived as unworthy of having access to society's resources. If someone cannot pass a first-year composition class, they often are not allowed to move through the rest of a curriculum. The contemporary United States might not have a formal literacy test for citizenship, but evidence of literacy is necessary. In the context of literacy instruction, the power to certify someone as literate—and as this book explores, as a citizen—often relies on individual responsibility when it comes to success in educative spaces.

With their focus on the role of writing within the development of the university in the United States, historians of the field of rhetoric and composition such as James Berlin, Robert Connors, Sharon Crowley, David Gold, Charles Paine, and Kelly Ritter have done much of the critical background work on the early twentieth century to analyze implicit connections between the college writing requirement, often viewed as a microcosm of the values of the larger university, and beliefs about the production of an American citizenry. Berlin's *Rhetoric and Reality: Writing Instruction in American Colleges, 1900–1985* makes clear that changes in the writing requirement were related to other social, economic, and political developments: "the college writing course, a requirement for graduation for most students throughout the century, responds quickly to changes in American society as a whole, with literacy (as variously defined by the college curriculum over the years) serving as the intermediary between the two—between the writing course and larger social developments" (5).

Similarly, Connors sets up his *Composition-Rhetoric* by drawing a connection between literacy skills and citizenship as defined by an individual's productivity, explaining, "there is a new rhetorical tradition that arose in the United States during the nineteenth century to try to inform an ever increasing demand for literacy skills for the professional and managerial classes" (4). Following Berlin and Connors, I take up the idea that literacy becomes defined, shaped, and distributed in ways that mediate the relationship between the sponsoring institution and larger social trends. That is, literacy becomes a tool to shape citizenship in response to societal shifts, such as the changes in work explored in my subsequent chapters. Berlin and Connors limit considerations of the citizen to the college-educated segment of the population, but these university-centric debates over writing requirements and standards reveal how notions of literacy are informed by general societal concerns about the health of the American citizenry, as expressed in early-twentieth-century public debates and proposed solutions to improve the state of citizenship. For instance, deliberations about immigration laws, the rise of public schooling, and the Americanization movement, to name a few, took place in a wide variety of spaces, including the academy, community groups, the media, the government, and unions.

Invocations of "citizenship" or "the citizen" in educational spaces often imply a cultivation of ideals through civic habits such as voting and participation. However, attributes such as productivity and hard work have also always been crucial characteristics of the U.S. brand of citizenship, particularly in spaces designed to prepare students for employment. Nowhere do we see this more than times of economic change, in which both formal and informal education become antidotes to broader societal anxieties and crises. When the influx of immigrant workers in the 1910s typically landed mass manufacturing jobs, Americanization programs could do the simultaneous work of teaching them English and teaching them how to function and behave in their new workplaces, all in the name of citizenship training. At the center of this connection between citizenship and literacy is the obligation to make curricula relevant in specific learning situations and in the face of beliefs about what literacy can and should help an individual to achieve.

This book has been inspired by the many projects in writing studies that explore the "extracurricular," as Anne Ruggles Gere describes learning spaces outside of formal school settings. In order to gain a better understanding of citizenship and the ways it is activated in service of literacy training, I have brought together nonschool literacy training sites with the first-year composition classroom, focusing on these sites of extracurricular study for two main reasons. First, I want to illustrate how nonschool instantiations of literacy and citizenship worked together to influence the value of each. And second, I unpack the consequences of acquiring literacy for students who were not "mainstream" college students. Such an approach facilitates an examination of the many ways that literacy—emerging out of Americanization programs, defined by unions, or university-styled literacy born out of writing classrooms—was used to respond to anxieties surrounding changes in the occupational sphere as well as shifting demographics, with a certain kind of citizenship constructed for the students of each type of program.

Producing Good Citizens is based primarily on an examination of documents that played a role in the literacy and citizenship training of workers and immigrants in the early-twentieth-century period—limited circulation publications such as citizenship training books or factory training manuals, policy documents on educational programs, and public deliberations on such training—providing a better understanding of the ways citizenship and literacy converged across purposes for these often disenfranchised populations. I rely on sources that reveal the goals and rationales for teaching literacy, how teachers and architects of programs imagined students acquiring citizenship and literacy through their courses, and what these designers thought students would do with that citizenship and literacy once they left the classroom. The documents examined—labor newspapers, federally produced citizenship textbooks, conference proceedings, hearings, journals—came into contact with teachers or students and reveal rationalizations of the connection between literacy and citizenship in the practices of different literacy training sites. By following a number of citizenship training spaces, I examine how literacy training telegraphs an individual's citizenship potential and subsequently, his or her access to a society's resources.

This historical and theoretical investigation reveals how themes of work and productivity have been integral to how we imagine the citizen and also addresses how fluctuating concepts of citizenship have been embedded in practices of literacy training by examining literacy's role in the distribution of societal resources during periods of economic restructuring such as those explored here. The good citizen constructed by this training is one who participates but must also meet eligibility criteria that speak to an individual's potential for productivity, often defined through educational background and along race, class, and gender lines, in order to become a full citizen. Analysis of citizenship training for immigrants and workers during a period of heightened citizenship anxiety also allows for comparison between the citizenship training of those with more tenuous citizenship status vis-à-vis the citizenship-producing mechanisms of the university, as well as a deeper understanding of how literacy is implicated in these different situations. Through a close examination of disciplining mechanisms like citizenship and work, I examine how economic opportunities and expectations (in the form of jobs and other resources) of those trying to gain citizenship status shape the credentialing potential of literacy in the pursuit of citizenship and, likewise, how literacy is used to mark a citizen's potential for productivity.

The first chapter provides the theoretical and historical framework for an investigation of this credentialing process in relation to literacy training in the United States. I introduce several key concepts from citizenship theory, such as Danielle Allen's "habits of citizenship," to illuminate how literacy training is a form of citizen-making and to lay the groundwork for the major questions addressed in the following chapters: In the classroom setting, is there a consistent idea of what is meant by citizenship or are there different ideas? What is the danger in letting these definitions remain unspoken? Why is citizenship such an appealing goal, and why is literacy often positioned as a means to acquire it? How is literacy imagined to extend the opportunities afforded by citizenship?

Chapters 2 through 4 address these questions by examining three sites of citizenship production—federal Americanization programs, union education, and university English classes, all from the period 1910–29. The literacy training documents analyzed reflect a worker-defined citizenship as developed by several different groups—the nation, the university, the union, the factory, and the community. Chapter 2 investigates the role of literacy training in immigrant Americanization programs during the early twentieth century, revealing a number of cultural lessons about citizenship. This chapter focuses on how the term "good citizen" became equated with productivity in emerging citizenship and literacy classes for immigrants as well as federal and community-produced training documents such as textbooks and guidebooks provided to immigrants by Americanization programs. Literacy training was used to promote a particular construction of citizenship to new immigrants, one that emphasized work habits in order to make *potential* citizens into *productive* citizens. An analysis of publications like federal Americanization textbooks, for instance, illuminates literacy's influence beyond the literacy test in the immigration debates of the era. The heightened stakes and impact of literacy during this moment of economic change are also examined, such as in the move from a craft-producing and agricultural economy to a mass manufacturing one, as described by labor historians Herbert Gutman and David Montgomery. In this context, equating good work habits with characteristics such as productivity provides insights about the economic expectations and opportunities for potential citizens, with immigrants expected to internalize these habits in order to gain access to opportunities and to full citizenship.

Chapter 3 takes up literacy as it was used in worker education programs organized by the Workers' Education Bureau and the International Ladies' Garment Workers Union (ILGWU) during the same time period. Unions such as the ILGWU and groups such as the Workers' Education Bureau used the concept of the citizen to produce a version of literacy intended to level the ground between workers and management. If government-sponsored literacy programs equated literacy with productivity, union-sponsored programs attempted a more liberatory approach, focusing on the creation of good citizens *of the labor movement* while employing the rhetoric of cultivating good citizens *of the country.* By examining at the motives behind literacy training for workers, I underscore the unions' belief in a kind of literacy hope. Authors of these documents consistently imagined citizens who acted intelligently, collectively, and on behalf of workers' conditions. By cultivating more educated, rhetorically savvy, and literate workers, unions wanted its members to gain the practical and intellectual tools to negotiate for labor reform within growing mass industry.

Chapter 4 examines higher education through histories of the teaching of college writing. Analyzing the development of the first-year writing class through the lens of work, this chapter explores how students' prospective work opportunities impacted the writing requirement's connection to the fulfillment of citizenship. Literacy training in higher education illustrates how the concept of citizenship was used to help construct a burgeoning middle class that took up the lessons of productivity for individual social mobility and stability. Teachers and administrators, particularly at public institutions, positioned university-styled literacy as a crucial component of a college education and, thus, of social mobility. The chapter examines literacy distribution through higher education, particularly how universities articulated the "usefulness" of literacy at the same time as they were developing into comprehensive institutions.

In chapter 5, I connect the historical context for the literacy training discussed in previous chapters with contemporary studies of citizenship and literacy. By focusing on the present, when citizenship production and economic change are still in play, I track how twenty-first-century trends in general education curricula, strategic plans in higher education, and education-oriented immigration policy such as the DREAM Act are connected to current ideals of citizen production. Extending the study of literacy teaching for citizenship production into the present underscores how changing economic opportunities affect our current expectations for productive citizenship and, subsequently, how educators manage those expectations as they attempt to create literate citizens.

Taken together, the training at these various sites reveals how literacy operates in negotiations of the terms of citizenship, not just for voting rights but also for access to a range of other citizenship practices in the form of resources such as education or power over working conditions. Citizenship and literacy operate together to persuasively categorize, sort, and credential individuals. The material effects of these categorizations are critical, especially when considering the impact and role education and literacy can play in a person's enactment of citizenship. Not only are education and literacy viewed as predicting the potential a person has to access citizenship, they also guide the kind of training that potential citizens receive, shape their understandings of the meaning of citizenship, and influence whether that citizenship can be fully realized or not. Particularly when the actualization of citizenship is seen solely as the responsibility of the individual, persistent inequalities among citizens can be justified despite an increasing access to literacy and other habits of citizenship.

At its core, *Producing Good Citizens* is an investigation of how various literacy educators attempt to produce good citizens within the auspices of training and education. By considering the implications of these conversations on our own practices of citizen-making through the teaching of literacy, this book is intended to create a sense of possibility. By making concrete aspirations for a more robust citizenship, rather than just a routine call to action, we can think about the habits of citizenship being cultivated through our practices. And we can respond to continuing changes to how citizenship is being defined, whether that definition is dependent on shifting boundaries from globalization, legal restrictions, public policy decisions, or an individual's economic contribution. In doing so, we acknowledge the limits of what citizenship can do for students and the limitations put upon students by the idea of citizenship, while simultaneously considering how educators engage those restrictions. Understanding such limitations helps students and teachers move beyond impoverished notions of citizenship and allow richer, more politically and materially situated notions to take root.

IN THE NAME OF CITIZENSHIP

> Citizens should know what their status implies; and they should understand when politicians abuse the term by according the whole concept only a partial range of attributes. It is, moreover, important to understand the complexity of the role of citizen and to appreciate that much needs to be learned if civic rights are to be exercised, civic duties are to be performed and a life of civic virtue is to be pursued. The citizen, in short, must be educated; and no teacher can properly construct the necessary learning objectives if semantic confusion surrounds the very subject to be studied.
>
> —Derek Heater, *Citizenship*, vii

The charge of producing citizens has long been an integral part of the mission of education in the United States. From Thomas Jefferson's linking of an "educated citizenry" to "our survival as a free people" to educational reformer Horace Mann's common school movement through John Dewey and other Progressive era pragmatists, from the New Left–era education movements of the 1960s (e.g., Students for a Democratic Society) to the rhetoric of the 2006 Spellings Commission report, education in the name of citizenship endures. Yet as educational historian Derek Heater explains, citizenship—what it means, what kind of behavior it describes, what resources are afforded through it—often suffers under "semantic confusion" in which a "partial range of attributes" stands in for the whole. While Heater tasks the teacher with sorting out the confusion, the realm of education often perpetuates this confusion by labeling so many educational aims as citizenship. Encompassing civic, intellectual, cultural, and vocational goals, the production of the citizen remains an uncontroversial leitmotif in the rhetoric surrounding educational objectives.

Citizenship—not just the legal status, but the cultural certification—takes on heightened importance in moments of anxiety, whether economic, social, or national. And often education is used as a way to alleviate these anxieties, playing a role in shaping individuals based on a model deserving of that cultural certification. While citizenship has always been produced in multiple spaces (e.g., federal government, adult education, community groups), the increase in mass formal education, first in K–12 and more recently in higher education,[1] has been justified, in part, by its crucial role in the fulfillment of citizenship. *Higher*

Education for Democracy, a report from the President's Commission on Higher Education[2] published in 1947, drove a national education policy around the production of citizens and advocated "increased access to college" (Hutcheson, "Truman Commission" 107) as a way of addressing societal concerns during the post–World War II era and at the beginning of the Cold War. By increasing the number of college-educated Americans and through a more fully articulated general education, institutions of higher education would guide "the transmission of a common cultural heritage toward a common citizenship" (United States, *Higher Education* 88). Along with the G.I. Bill of 1944, the Truman report "marked the beginning of a substantial shift in the nation's expectations about who should attend college" (Hutcheson, "Truman Commission" 107), thus connecting increasing higher education rates with generating citizenship. While educative spaces have always been positioned as crucial elements of citizenship production, the continued increasing importance of formal education means these institutions now have more of an influence on how citizenship is being produced and defined and, to some degree, has resulted in a definition of good citizenship that is disproportionally focused on success in education.

A definition of citizenship in the context of rising standards for literacy and education challenges the seemingly central importance of citizenship to education in general, and, for writing teachers, the influence of citizenship in literacy learning. To this end, I must ask two crucial questions: First, why is citizenship a faithful goal of literacy instruction? In turn, why is literacy so often used to cultivate citizenship? Literacy is supposed to yield a more democratic and participatory citizenship, a more educated citizenship, a more active citizenship—all familiar refrains in the field of rhetoric and composition and beyond. Yet despite assuming that successful writing instruction plays a key role in making good citizens and that the classroom space can reinvigorate democratic and participatory citizenship, the terms and boundaries used to define citizenship are vague at best and often go uninterrogated. Although citizenship has become a superterm that can encompass many definitions, the resultant lack of specificity that often accompanies it allows us to elide crucial concerns about the access to, impact, and exercise of citizenship.

For instance, scholarship in the contemporary field of rhetoric and composition often promotes the idea that successful writing instruction plays a key role in the preparation of good citizens, situating the classroom as a space that can reinvigorate democratic and participatory citizenship (see Campbell; Eberly; Ervin; Flower; Gilyard; Simmons and Grabill; and Weisser, to name just a few). Writing teachers often see citizenship-building as an integral part of the classroom mission, and scholarly investigations about writing classrooms take up the compelling concept of citizenship in a variety of ways, offering some familiar configurations: a potential antidote for students' impoverished citizenship through the transfer of skills to engage critically (as with critical pedagogy), a space to encourage participation in the outside world (such as service learning and ethnography), or a way to cultivate the use of writing skills to participate in citizen discussions (e.g., public writing, letter to the editor assignments, and blogs). What goes unarticulated in these configurations is how writing skills and other literate practices actually make citizens—that is, what kinds of citizens are cultivated in relation to literacy.

In this way, the "semantic confusion" around citizenship that Heater describes in this chapter's epigraph is actually productive because the confusion is masked by educational skills and other signs of improvement such as literacy. Citizenship theory as a body of work can help articulate literacy's role (and thus the role of literacy teachers) in citizenship production, such as the will to make citizenship central in literacy learning spaces and the "ideological freight" (Brandt 20) accompanying the widespread attainment of literacy. Doing so locates the pervasive use of citizenship in its malleability and its capacity to carry a broad set of potential values and beliefs. This capacity is further amplified alongside a societal imperative that education is necessary to becoming a full citizen and that one must collect as much education as possible. The persistence of education as a means of acquisition, which exists outside of all legal definitions of citizenship, is evident in the contemporary setting of the writing classroom, a familiar (but not the only) space through which to begin to understand both how literacy is used to produce citizens and which theoretical questions about citizenship endure in our current landscape.

In scholarship about the goals of the college writing classroom and policy documents (such as Kathleen Yancey's "Writing in the Twenty-First Century" for the NCTE), college-level literacy and citizenship are intertwined. Citizenship, namely its flexibility as a term, can imbue the work of higher education—and more specifically, the writing classroom—with a sense of its larger societal impact while at the same time its ambiguity allows for unspoken and sometimes conflicting beliefs about what citizenship is. In order to counteract what I call the *ambient* nature of the use of the term "citizenship," I analyze three key factors that have helped to establish "citizenship" as a superterm and underlie its unspoken assumptions in literacy learning spaces: the infinite flexibility that comes from shifting definitions of citizenship; the belief that citizenship is an achievable status by individuals who have the will for it; and the implicit understanding that equality and social mobility are synonymous with and can be achieved through citizenship.

These three influences on our thinking about citizenship have allowed citizenship to serve as shorthand for a variety of objectives such as productivity, usefulness, or transformation in literacy learning, whether in the contemporary writing classroom or in spaces such as federal Americanization programs and union education classes of the early twentieth century, which are discussed in later chapters. Unspoken assumptions about how citizenship is being defined and produced through literacy are not endemic to contemporary writing classrooms, as the historical inquiry in the following chapters examines through literacy learning inside and outside of formal schooling during the late Progressive era around World War I. The contemporary uses of citizenship and the role of education as an embedded element of citizenship production demonstrate the continuing influence of factors—such as a changing ecnomy and shifting immigration patterns—on citizenship expectations, both now and in the early twentieth century.

Literacy is often implicated in the work of citizenship production. Despite extensive scholarly research that historicizes and problematizes the connection between literacy and citizenship (e.g., H. Graff, Street, Young), engaging citizenship as an educational goal remains a murky undertaking with the potential to undermine aspirations for the democratizing aspects of literacy. The capacious nature of the term "citizenship" contributes to a lack of attention to concrete civic goals and allows for the term's too-infinite flexibility, allowing the public good of citizenship to stand in for any number of values that are more economically than critically motivated. A citizenship premised on equality—economic, legal, social, cultural—must incorporate the multiplicity of its definitions, and uncovering such assumptions in its production can help to clarify literacy's role in the production of citizenship and the impact of citizenship as a commonplace term in literacy learning spaces.

The Cultivation of Ambient Citizenship in Writing Classrooms

While American education has been steeped in the job of creating citizens, citizenship is often relegated to an unspecific rhetorical flourish in policy and practical discussions with regard to how one achieves citizenship through classroom practices. Especially when civic behavior is in the foreground, as in classes focused on service learning and public writing, the assumptions, implications, and consequences of cultivating civic behavior in the classroom setting go largely unexamined. Citizenship becomes an easy trope because of its immediate associations with positive civic activities such as voting. Pervasive and nonthreatening, citizenship provides a convenient and agreeable greater goal for literacy instruction, intimately connecting it with democracy. Perhaps citizenship plays such a central role because it facilitates political activity in the classroom without an overtly political charge. Or perhaps its prominence can be explained via Joseph Harris's critique of the term "community"—without a negatively charged opposite, "citizenship" becomes completely and unquestionably acceptable ("Idea"; "Beyond Community"). In his landmark 1976 book, *English in America*, Richard Ohmann succinctly explains the reasons why democratic citizenship, education, and literacy are often viewed together: "Democracy can't work unless citizens are literate and informed" (124). Who would disagree? Yet while citizenship or a more robust enactment of the citizen is a worthwhile goal for writing instruction and other educative endeavors, a closer investigation of the term can help writing teachers and scholars better understand the concept's limitations and even obfuscations.

Although a handful of contemporary writing textbooks (see Berndt and Muse's *Composing a Civic Life*, Delli Carpini's *Composing a Life's Work*, Ford and Ford's *Citizenship Now*) address the issue of citizenship directly, more often than not the term is left largely underexamined. Two general approaches to engaging citizenship are common in scholarly conversations about writing instruction—one is a reference to citizenship in a general list of student goals in syllabi or pedagogical studies (and on a larger scale, departmental and institutional goals and outcomes). Such casual references to citizenship often pepper pedagogical discussions. This move should be quite familiar; by briefly invoking citizenship or the citizen in service of a particular research or teaching agenda, the work becomes connected to an external motive and broader significance.

For example, Yancey focuses on using twenty-first-century "composings" to "foster a new kind of citizenship" (7) and refers to the "citizen writers of our country, of our world, and the writers of the future" (1) in order to encourage a more engaged, informed, and literate citizen through the teaching of writing. The citizen writer is expected to use writing skills toward action, particularly in a "Web 2.0 world" in which technology enables all writers to share, dialogue, and participate (5). Yet while Yancey does much to advance new technologically inflected models of literacy, she also depends on an assumed connection between producing writers and producing a particularly participatory brand of citizenship. By doing so, Yancey yokes citizenship to a kind of political action, suggesting that "through writing, citizens might exercise their own control" (2) over their lives and produce a sense of empowerment. While Yancey's report is meant as more of public document designed to effect changes in policy and public opinion rather than in scholarship, the uses of citizenship here are implicit but powerful because they are used to underscore a primary motivation for writing and teaching writing in the twenty-first century. For Yancey, the trope of the citizen writer works to demonstrate the urgency of this task.

The second approach takes on this same association but is more focused in its attention to citizenship and the production of participatory action through writing. In this configuration, scholars give more explicit attention to how the classroom can serve as a "protopublic" space for public discourse and participation, which Rosa Eberly describes as a "means of reinvigorating public life and citizenship" (168),[3] where citizenship's impoverished state can be nourished through a cultivation of public sphere participation. Similarly, Christian Weisser expresses wanting to "help my students become active citizens who are capable of using language to defend themselves, voice their opinions, and take part in the public debates" (94). Other scholars such as Kermit Campbell, Ellen Cushman, Elizabeth Ervin, and Michele Simmons and Jeffrey T. Grabill, among many others, have also written about the writing classroom as a training ground for active and participatory citizenship. Calls for increased public discourse and public engagement are seen as a way to cultivate a richer sense of citizenship, seemingly in the face of a dearth of civic activity. This deficit model of citizenship, drawing from Susan Wells's critique of the deficit model of public discourse, imagines the student subject as "needing more."[4] The writing classroom with its transfer of advanced literacy skills is situated as a space that can reinvigorate democratic and participatory citizenship through writing that relates to the public. Underlying this approach is a belief in using the classroom as a space to cultivate the ability and desire to "read the world" critically (Freire), to participate in the public sphere as a marker of good citizenship, and to build the community necessary for a strong citizenry. This training engages the public with varying levels of directness, from positioning the writing classroom as a space where students hone their writing and therefore, citizenship skills (e.g., Eberly; Gilyard; Weisser) to putting students into situations in which they are involved with a particular nonschool community (e.g., Cushman; Flower; Goldblatt).

Important work has been done in the areas of public writing, participatory writing, citizen journalism, citizen rhetoric, and service learning. But using "citizenship" as shorthand to describe all of these different goals obscures the distinctions among them because it assumes citizenship is synonymous with the most overt of these civic activities. Instead of letting, for example, "deep democracy" (Gilyard) or "community literacy" (Flower) stand in for the kind of citizenship cultivated in the writing classroom, different shades of meaning need to be articulated. By overlooking these distinctions, the casual reference to citizenship and the more specific attention to participation work together to create an "ambient awareness" of citizenship in writing instruction that obfuscates the range of a citizen's rights, obligations, and privileges. This phrase was originally used to describe the casual awareness of another person's life through electronic media (Thompson), but I see it as a fitting concept to describe compositionists' "awareness" of citizenship. Journalist Clive Thompson describes "ambient awareness," namely through Facebook updates, as "insignificant on its own, even supremely mundane. But taken together, over time, the little snippets coalesce into a surprisingly sophisticated portrait of your friends' and family members' lives, like thousands of dots making a pointillist painting" (2). The application of ambient awareness to citizenship is apt, describing both the frequency and the surface nature of dealings with citizenship in writing instruction, but simultaneously acknowledging the cumulative impact of these small bits of civic activity to form a more complicated understanding of citizenship. Yet, as Thompson acknowledges, ambient awareness has its limits because it amplifies "weak ties" (4) rather than deeper social relationships.

An "ambient awareness" of citizenship might be similarly tenuous, especially if the message is often the same or similar: citizenship is participation in a public achieved through the literacy learned in educative spaces. These moments of implication and inference about citizenship in scholarship can both make this citizenship unspecific and obscure the assumptions and values that animate a definition (or definitions) of citizenship. The many references to citizenship raise awareness of its importance to literacy learning, but the ambient nature of the conversations, these fleeting moments, maintain these references as simply impressions rather than as a force. This allows an easy ignorance of the complexities and contradictions in the experience and practice of citizenship, which should be attended to if the expectation is a more potent citizenship through literacy learning.

Teachers, whether implicitly or explicitly, play a role in shaping the citizenship produced in educative spaces, not only by issuing calls to adopt active citizenship, but also because often the desired skills—public writing, public engagement, citizen critique, critical literacy, or technology—become inextricably, although often silently, linked to the imagined ideal of the "good citizen." What is significant about the teaching of citizenship through writing is that arguments for a particular skill are also implicit arguments for what a person needs (or needs *to be*) in order to be prepared for a future and to act as a citizen: a good citizen is one who participates, who is engaged, who can critique society, and who is a productive, satisfied member of the nation, using advanced literacy skills as a means to achieve these civic acts. All of these skills fall under the umbrella of the citizen, and as a result the term acts as a kind of shorthand with an unspoken and assumed meaning that conceals other ways of being a citizen. In these instances, scholars use citizenship as a way to imagine students as agents beyond the institution, understanding that student subjectivity is transient and temporary and replacing that transience with a citizen-oriented subjectivity.

Such work is critical in recognizing the role that literacy instruction can play in students' public actions in both the classroom and the world beyond, but these invocations are premised upon unspoken, casual, or ambient assumptions about citizenship itself: the belief that one only needs to act as a citizen through participation in a community or society in order to become a citizen, or the resulting wholesale acceptance of citizenship as a meaningful product of effective writing instruction. This is not sufficient, particularly when the tenuous certification of citizenship has both material and cultural consequences. Citizenship is an appealing yet slippery term. A necessary step toward making the efforts effective in public writing, participatory writing, citizen journalism, citizen rhetoric, and service learning is understanding the meaning behind the citizenship that is invoked, acknowledging citizenship beyond participation. An examination of the struggles over defining citizenship, its historical development as an achieved status, and its role in providing access to resources can help us understand how literacy is imagined to contribute to citizen-making and the limits of this imagination.

Struggles over Defining Citizenship

Responding to the ambient use of citizenship as a term requires examining its multiple definitions in order to sort out how and why citizenship is used in conjunction with institutions' sponsorship of literacy. Citizenship has become a common term in relation to education, mainly because the concept of citizenship can be formed to fit any kind of outcome. But citizenship at its most basic is defined legally as membership in a particular nation-state. Strict legalists might be puzzled by debates over definitions of citizenship or even discussions of citizenship in educative spaces because of their view of citizenship as a legal category, with conferral of status occurring in the legal realm and certainly outside of the classroom or other social institutions. But citizenship theorists in fields such as political theory, sociology, and history have expanded thinking about citizenship beyond legal status to understanding citizenship as cultural identity, standing and status, civic virtue, everyday habits, and participatory action, such as T. H. Marshall, who developed a rights-oriented perspective of citizenship in the mid-twentieth century (categorizing certain practices into civil, political, and social rights), and more recently, scholars such as Danielle Allen, Eamonn Callan, Derek Heater, Judith Shklar, and Bryan Turner.

Such discussions confirm the view that citizenship must be understood as more than simply conferral of membership by a government, and that the process of creating the citizenry of a nation involves a number of practices other than simply granting legal status. For example, political theorist Shklar argues for the importance of moving beyond the idea of citizenship as purely legal standing by defining citizenship as "nationality, as active participation or 'good' citizenship, and finally, ideal republican citizenship" (3) and thereby underscoring engagement and representation in a nation. Legal scholar Linda Bosniak echoes Shklar by categorizing citizenship in four different ways: legal status, "fundamental rights," "a state of active engagement in the polity," and identity (241). Using identity, Bosniak expands citizenship to include a cultural orientation, demonstrating how citizenship functions to give an individual entry into a particular society or social group. She explains that "in psychological or cultural terms, the term citizenship is invoked to refer to an experience of identity and solidarity that a person maintains in collective or public life" (241). There are, of course, many variations on these definitions, but both Shklar's definition and Bosniak's categories allow for different approaches that incorporate a more qualitative element into how citizenship is produced through rights, involvement in public life, or identification with other citizens. The sum of these ideas is implied through phrases like "full citizenship," which represent the cultural dimensions and acceptance of an individual's citizenship and identity in addition to the legal rights afforded to citizens.

These foundational discussions often highlight the struggles over definitions; building a more complex taxonomy as Bosniak or Shklar have done is a common starting point among citizenship theorists, not only to get a sense of the variations that are possible, but to name those variations and the values inherent in the different categories and viewpoints. Multiple political theories ground the range of definitions in these different taxonomies—communitarian, republican, liberal democratic, and more. The varied political tradition of the United States draws from Jeremy Bentham, Edmund Burke, Alexis de Tocqueville, John Dewey, John Locke, J. S. Mill, John Rawls, and Jean-Jacques Rousseau, among others, and the distinctions among them can, of course, be quite large. As political theorist Eamonn Callan points out, "A Millian education for liberal individuality and a Deweyan education for democratic competence and fidelity are not the same thing" (11). Educational historian Derek Heater talks specifically about Bentham, de Tocqueville, and Mill as "political thinkers who struggled to accommodate the growing idea of democratic citizenship in the prime political value of liberty" (73), foregrounding the idea of liberty in contrast to other theorists who draw from Dewey's ideas about democratic participation and the possibility for individuals to contribute to public discourse. Each of these theorists emphasize certain principles over others that establish boundaries and possibilities for citizenship—whether liberty, democratic participation, the public good, social equality, or some other value.

For instance, Peter Kivisto and Thomas Faist discuss the distinction between the republican and liberal traditions: "The republican tradition is particularly concerned with activities that contribute to the public good and thus is prepared to ask a considerable amount from the citizenry, while counterpoised to it and with an emphasis on the individual, the liberal tradition seeks a more minimalist set of duties on the part of citizens" (50). These two approaches make the distinction between a societal contribution that prioritizes the larger public good of the republic and one that values self-sufficiency above all else. These goals—one that considers a contribution to the larger public good, and one that emphasizes individuality—have purchase when thinking about literacy learning in relation to citizenship. For example, literacy learning at the college level tends to shape certain civic behaviors such as participation in civic life or in academic discourse and the building of a collective through public writing assignments or even an activity such as peer review. But the individual, or their literate skill, is also emphasized through grading and evaluation, as well as through changes in the curriculum that may reflect external or institutional pressure to guide individual academic and economic success. Along with these different curricular goals, the definition of citizenship shifts.

These varied and sometimes conflicting expectations demonstrate different approaches to cultivating citizenship within the scope of literacy learning. Applying a more critical lens to citizenship in connection to teaching writing, literacy teachers and researchers could expose the various ways they envision the citizens being created, whether the term "citizen" is used explicitly or not, and clarify the implications, responsibilities, differences, and rationales that accompany citizenship. In many ways, citizenship training within formal education perpetuates the idea that citizenship is shaped beyond its legal boundaries through institutions such as literacy training spaces; simply put, educators believe that these spaces can have an impact on the citizenship of students. But a transparent display of values and the material and legal consequences of citizenship status would mean articulating a specificity of terms that describes citizenship beyond its ambient definition. Legal scholars T. Alexander Aleinikoff and Douglas Klusmeyer explain that citizenship should be understood beyond its legal status as a set of institutionalized policies and that how a group administers citizenship is "a powerful measure of its core commitments" (1), reminding us of certain unarticulated commitments expected of students in different kinds of classrooms. A classroom that emphasizes critical thinking, argumentation, Web 2.0, and service learning, to name just a few, reveals a teacher's commitment to a particular approach to citizenship; each of these different skills encourages specific civic behaviors. It is essential to be articulate about such commitments if we want to think deeply about the consequences that literacy teaching has on citizenship; to take up this project, it is necessary to see what is happening with citizenship outside the classroom door, both legally and theoretically. In order to make room for ideological influences on definitions of citizenship, one must understand that the "good citizen" is one who effectively reflects the values of a particular community.

For example, the widely shared goal of increased civic participation within a particular community should be seen as more than a singular approach and could have many different meanings. If we follow the logic equating literacy with civic behavior, then improved literacy skills mean an individual is better equipped to participate. Of course, literacy can bolster the participatory elements of citizenship with possibility and potential. But I wonder if conceptions of citizenship are incomplete if we limit possibility or make assumptions in the way that we conceive of citizenship as participatory, not only because there are multiple approaches and definitions, but also because what is meant by *participation* is not articulated. A more literate student (however that literacy may be defined) is assumed to be a better citizen because of his or her ability to participate more effectively (however that effectiveness may be defined). But even if someone evokes participatory citizenship, the terms of that participation must be considered: What counts? What is most effective—voting, critical reading skills, letters to the editor, public writing on blogs and wikis, measurable societal change? What kind of citizenship is being produced and promoted? Most importantly, does everyone have access to the same types of citizenship? These questions often go unasked and unanswered when we talk about the citizen, but those answers need to be clear to us as teachers if we hope for them to be clear to students.

Because participation seems to be the most prominent civic value connected to literacy, I question the ambient approach to participatory citizenship, which assumes an unspoken agreement about its definition and the possibility of using the literacy classroom to distribute politically neutral participation skills. This assumption of a neutral "goodness" elides citizenship's other definitional possibilities as *status* or *standing*, possibilities not easily accessible for all students merely through participation. Enhancing participation does not necessarily mean enhancing equality, yet literacy skills and associated participation skills often perpetuate the illusion of equality. This has dangerous implications when we affably state citizenship's importance in university strategic plans, the K–12 Common Core State Standards, or in goals for a particular program or class without acknowledging the different kinds of meanings that correspond to ideas about work, productivity, status, and access to resources, in addition to one's ability to participate. Historically, literacy's relationship with citizenship is fraught with consequences such as the literacy test within the 1917 Immigration Act (King 76), yet citizenship is often used as a way to ground the work done in the classroom or legitimize work outside of it by providing a kind of national endorsement. By not being specific about the goals and motivations for cultivating literacy in the name of citizenship, we risk being in unspoken agreement about these definitions and don't seem to acknowledge how burdened this association between literacy and citizenship is. The difficulty in this acknowledgment arises from a foundational belief that citizenship is a status that simply can be achieved and entered into at will.

Citizenship as Achievable Status

While citizenship's multiple definitions evoke feelings of possibility, assumptions about the achievability of citizenship gloss over the spectrum of potential meanings. In the broadest strokes, citizenship can be acquired legally in a variety of ways: by birth, by naturalization, or by blood (parentage). But the path to acquire full citizenship—citizenship *beyond* the legal status to include cultural citizenship and access to all of society's resources—is not as clear-cut. Yet this cultural realization of citizenship is often at work in literacy education and the writing classroom. Those who profess to teach citizenship, such as writing teachers or institutions like universities or public school systems, rely on a foundational belief that citizenship is not just a legal status, but a state of being that can be cultivated and shaped by literacy teaching. In this view, citizenship is not just a static status, but a standing that one can change through behavior and desire. The United States has cultivated the idea that citizenship is not just a birthright, but an achievable status, which has resulted in a citizenship based on individual actions and behavior. This fundamental value of U.S. citizenship means that it is not simply a conferred legal status, but cultivated through a number of civil, political, and social rights and obligations, which, as Marshall explains in *Citizenship and Social Class*, have become layered onto the status of legal citizenship over the past two centuries. Literacy skills intertwined with the realization of these rights and obligations influence the role of the literacy teacher as civic educator. The thought that citizenship is an achievable standing rather than something born into undergirds the connection between citizenship and literacy, implying that it is possible to activate the civic behavior of an individual through activating his or her critical literacy. Citizenship becomes a state that can be cultivated in the classroom through the encouragement of habits of citizenship.

The foundations of U.S. citizenship as an achievable status lie in what James Kettner describes as the "idea of volitional allegiance" (173), a result of American colonialism in which (white and European) individuals voluntarily moved to a territory and built allegiances in their new homes.[5] This identity shift from subject of a monarch to citizen of a country brought with it a subsequent movement from dependence to independence and the belief that citizenship was something to be learned or achieved. The dependent subject relied on the monarch for care and rule, but the independent citizen took on these responsibilities himself (and at the time, it was *him*self). United States citizenship became defined through its sovereignty in contrast to that of the monarchies of England and to France's own quest for sovereignty and the development of its *citoyen*. In order to make use of this sovereignty, those deemed citizens were required to participate, to take an active role in the shaping of government. This shift in thinking about an individual's relationship to larger society highlights the ability to rule one's self, with education becoming such an important part of fulfilling this status.

The achievement of citizenship through "individual choice," one's own volition, and self-responsibility can reflect potentially complicated beliefs about individual responsibility for behavior and life situations. Historian Michael Katz describes the availability of the rights of citizenship for those with a preexisting status compared to those who earn a citizenship in which rights are deemphasized "in favor of obligations or merit; [which] is earned through contributions to society" (344). This emphasis on earning citizenship demonstrates the importance of personal responsibility, which underscores the expectations that educators might have about what students do with the skills taught in their classrooms. When citizenship is earned partially through literacy, students' ability to self-govern and achieve citizenship also becomes dependent on their literacy and how they may contribute to society; as a result, educative spaces that take on this goal implicitly promote an ability to self-govern and the cultivation of this ability. Although the dynamic process of achieving citizenship is critical to a nation open to immigrants, some implications of this process should give us pause.

The attainment of U.S. citizenship, and therefore the citizenship attained in many writing classrooms, is consistent with a belief that any individual has the ability to access citizenship, at least in theory. This results in a classroom in which citizenship becomes a fixed object to be created and attained, or a situation entered into easily or provided at will. Literacy instructors such as myself who view the citizenship-making project as an integral part of their work hold an implicit belief that citizenship and its associated civic behavior can be influenced or achieved; in turn, acquisition of literacy then becomes embedded in the achievement of that status of full citizen. The belief that writing class-rooms can create spaces for the cultivation of better citizenship (or rather, the particular model of citizenship that the teacher or the curriculum identifies as "better") prevails, but this individualized and fixed orientation of citizenship embeds two potentially problematic assumptions.

First, if literacy comes with responsibility, then also it is implied that there is a right way and a wrong way to employ it, especially if such literacy is used in service of a particular brand of citizenship. If, as Callan claims, the encourage-ment of certain kinds of civic behavior means cultivating "public virtue" (3), then might educators also think about literacy as a way to cultivate public vir-tue? Is morality being invoked? Or, as educational historian Heater describes, do educators desire "a sense of justice and a moral and rational conscience: the true citizen seeks the realization of the General Will, the common good, not the satisfaction of his own selfish interests" (41). Or is this version of citizen-ship consistent with some other (unspoken) definition? When we think about literacy as shaping a sense of morality or virtue, we uncover the inherent value embedded in how such traits are defined through teaching situations. But in many ways, citizenship is just that—a code of behavior that affects interaction with one another, whether that code translates to participation, individual lib-erty, responsibility, or other civic virtues through critical literacy.

Second, an individualized conception of citizenship does not fully ac-knowledge the process of cultivating citizenship or the idea that students come to an educative space with differing opportunities for cultural and legal forms of citizenship and with the varied definitions of and points of access to cit-izenship. Often absent from citizenship cultivated in the university writing classroom, unlike other literacy learning spaces, are the overt connections to economic and personal gains of citizenship, particularly related to how higher education contributes to the citizen-making process. Citizenship and associ-ated civic behavior seems to be available simply to anyone who wants it. As a result, the term becomes merely palliative and there is a risk of people ignoring issues of inequality.

The achievability of citizenship through volition plays a crucial element in the constellation of beliefs about citizenship and the processes through which it can be attained. Along with it comes the importance of self-fulfillment and individual responsibility, complicating the more commonly known citizenship traits defined through literacy—the cultivation of the civic and a sense of re-sponsibility to participate. Emphasis on personal responsibility brings with it the importance of will in the achievement of citizenship, which can be seen in, for example, efforts in the writing classroom to get students to participate; literacy as an ability to read and write doesn't inherently offer that will, but it may be expected, despite an individual's desire or access. By understanding these different assumptions and using them as a framework for thinking about literacy as it relates to citizenship, we begin to grasp the logic of why citizenship is valued as a goal of literacy and what formal literacy learning spaces can or cannot do to cultivate it without disregarding the limitations of an individual student's will. Within a classroom, we might imagine that every student's access to citizenship is equal and that one simply activates a desire to practice that citizenship, but that is not always the case. In fact, this inequality is an important, but ignored, facet of how we might think about citizenship.

The Function of Inequality and the Access to Resources

Literacy has long been linked to an equality project, such as in the college writing classroom and its development of basic writing pedagogy, as described in Patricia Bizzell's "Composition Studies Saves the World!," and reflected in the casual references to citizenship discussed above. Judith Shklar traces the roots of these ideals about the equality of U.S. citizenship to the "participatory aristocracy" of ancient Greece. Instead of a "perfect form of democratic activity" for a privileged few, Shklar argues that disenfranchised Americans have strived for a configuration of citizenship that is "equally distributed, so that their standing might also be recognized and their interests be defended and promoted" (30). Yet while citizenship in itself seems to imply the guarantee of a certain equality in its distribution of rights and obligations, the realization of citizenship brings with it inequalities, such as the varying levels of access to education. This desire for equal distribution of citizenship (along with the role that literacy plays in it) lies at the heart of the expansion of higher education and the middle class in the twentieth century. In this context, individuals believe in a narrative of equality against the realities of restricted access to resources such as certain jobs or education. Aspirations for equality motivate much of the way citizenship is invoked in service of literacy, but behind these aspirations remains an ever-present inequality that conflates a definition of citizenship as cultivated status with one of citizenship as access to societal resources.

If the fully produced citizen is one who has gained multiple attributes of citizenship (that is, has access to all of the rights and privileges of citizenship and has the ability to easily perform the obligations of citizenship by choice), then in what ways can literacy cultivated in formal school settings help students gain this access, and in what ways can it not? Perhaps the most obvious of the rights and privileges of citizenship is voting, which can be impacted by a critically literate approach to one's voting choices; another might be using one's literacy skills toward participatory action. While these practices bring with them a sense of the quotidian nature of citizenship, it is important to consider how these habits intersect with an individual's access to societal resources, often a motivating factor behind the establishment of rights in the first place, not to mention a common incentive to gain education. But access to society's resources, such as certain jobs or education, is also a privilege of citizenship that educators influence, and it, in turn, influences teaching practices. The pervasive approach to citizenship produced by literacy as a status accessible by all within the classroom setting stands in sharp contrast to literacy scholars such as Deborah Brandt, who describes how "literacy skill is treated primarily as a resource—economic, political, intellectual, spiritual—which, like wealth or education, or trade skill or social connections, is pursued for the opportunities and protections that it potentially grants to its seekers" (5). We imagine that as literacy teachers we are helping to distribute this resource, yet literacy as a skill integral to citizenship does not lie solely in learning civic activity, as has been configured by many classroom spaces that address citizenship. Although the participatory aspect of citizenship plays a role in easing certain inequalities (e.g., the civil rights movement), it's not a guarantee of equality. Enduring faith in the equality of citizenship perpetuates the belief that literacy of all kinds will secure both participation in society and the achievement of personal and economic success.

Continued inequality and the desire for access to resources often activates the work done in literacy learning spaces, particularly with the imperative for increasingly more formal education in the United States, as discussed earlier. Over the course of the twentieth century, college educations have shifted in purpose from the maintenance of an upper-class privilege to the creating and sustaining of a middle class after the GI Bill, the Truman report, and onward. That expansion has continued in the twenty-first century with the growth of community colleges, for-profit colleges, and regional institutions. The creation, maintenance, and administration of writing curricula, which is often at the center of most general education programs, simultaneously respond to and cultivate the assumed influence of writing and literacy instruction on social mobility and equality. The civic habit of literacy affords different possibilities for different kinds of students, most obviously those who are marked as "other" either linguistically or visually, such as international students, naturalized citizens for whom English is a second (or third) language, and nonwhite students. Participation through literacy skills allows for the sense of being equal, maybe even the illusion of equality. But I wonder if it is possible that an investment in this narrative is dangerous because we imagine that equality and full citizenship can be accessed via classroom-cultivated literacy. If literacy is a resource and the classroom a point of access to that resource, then citizenship becomes another measurable skill distributed by literacy instructors, rather than a cultural and, importantly, legal status. At the same time, we must also acknowledge that the writing classroom represents a space where not just participatory potential develops but also cultural practices that signal one as an acceptable, competent, and productive citizen. Put bluntly, gaining access to resources is what gives individuals the ability to enjoy these rights and to live as full citizens. Access to resources (or lack of it) highlights the inequality among people's citizenship and the inadequacy of literacy as a sole solution. Yet the hope U.S. society has for literacy does not seem to wane.

Literacy and the Good Citizen

I highlight these three ideas about citizenship—the malleability of its definition, the belief in it as an achieved status, and the view that it provides equal political standing and access to resources—because these ideas aid in both explaining and analyzing how literacy has played a role in producing good citizens. Integrating these theories about citizenship into the practices of literacy teaching and literacy research is crucial if we are to understand how and why literacy has come to be seen as an inextricable component of citizenship's cultivation. These theories underscore the importance of specifying what citizenship (and literacy's role in it) can be beyond a mere metaphor or universal shorthand for being a good person; there are, as the rest of this book will describe, both material and political effects that have influenced the belief that literacy helps to activate an individual's citizenship. In an effort to bring together the theoretical good of citizenship with the material and the political and to examine the effects of an unfailing belief in the achievability of an ambient brand of citizenship, I propose looking at literacy as *a habit of citizenship* and considering how literacy teaching helps to construct this habit.

When political theorist Danielle Allen defines citizenship as "basic habits of interaction in public spaces" (5), she recognizes that these habits are not always the most explicit or obvious activities in the enactment of citizenship, such as those with legal guarantees like the right to vote. In her deliberations on anxieties around citizenship after *Brown v. Board of Education*, she reaches beyond the idea of citizenship as consisting primarily of rights and duties by examining a photo of Elizabeth Eckford, who is African American, being taunted by Hazel Bryan, who is white, at the start of desegregation in Little Rock, Arkansas, on the first day of school, 4 September 1957. Allen explains the habits of citizenship demonstrated through the photo, using the concept of habits to account for the spatial distance and demeanor between black and white, male and female citizens. She describes how "political order is secured not only by institutions, but also by 'deep rules' that prescribe specific interactions among citizens in public spaces" and help guide "political tasks" beyond duties like voting that help to shape the order of public life (10). For Allen, habits of citizenship influence what "political tasks" and the corresponding behaviors are deemed "appropriate" for interaction (or lack of interaction) with other citizens. In the Little Rock example, these tasks vary from protecting Hazel Bryan to taunting her. Allen contends that these deep rules, or habits of citizenship, promote a feeling of unity among certain groups of citizens, who must imagine themselves as part of a whole. And with this desire for wholeness "come[s] also particular *practices*" (17; emphasis in original) that overcome individuals.

For Allen, these habits of citizenship are cultivated by people's interactions with one another. Thus, habits of citizenship take on more subtle meanings, not simply defined as explicit civic activity through participatory action, nor just legal boundaries. Rather, citizenship needs to be understood as located in everyday activities that may be mediated through habits and practices, such as the literate skill learned in classrooms and beyond. Perhaps one consequence of making this shift in thinking, for those teachers who hope to be more mindful of how to integrate citizenship into literacy instruction, is a shift in scale: rather than only trying to amplify those citizenship habits that seem most obvious, we should also consider the multiple ways that habits of citizenship are encouraged through literacy learning. So, although literacy can certainly help improve an individual's ability to be a participatory citizen through the improvement of critical and communicative skills, thinking about literacy as a habit of citizenship can reflect its wider impact. And, as Allen suggests, habits, as practices that have been ingrained into a person's behavior, are shaped by both institutions and deep rules.

Literacy as a habit of citizenship that works in concert with other habits of citizenship reveals the more specific ways that literacy produces the good citizen, both directly and indirectly. Our study of literacy's direct influence on the production of citizenship provides a sense of what kinds of habits of good citizenship literacy can enforce, such as civic participation and the ability to engage in political dialogue or malleable behavior like good work habits. An understanding of literacy's more indirect influence as a habit of citizenship considers the effects of being literate and educated, namely, how certain privileges of citizenship can be accessed through literacy. For example, while the literacy test in the 1917 Immigration Act, which based entrance to the country on an individual's literacy, is certainly a historical example of how literacy directly allowed for access to possible legal citizenship, literacy obtained through a union hall, community center, or university also helped individuals gain indirect access to aspects of cultural and economic citizenship through "wholeness," as Allen would say, with groups or communities.

The question of who has access to what kind of citizenship is foundational to any conversation about citizenship. Sociologist Bryan Turner describes how access is shaped by "that set of practices (juridical, political, economic, and cultural) which define a person as a competent member of society, and which as a consequence shape the flow of resources to persons and social groups" (2). The idea of citizenship as a status that helps society direct the flow of its resources becomes particularly important when thinking about the role of literacy—basic, advanced, or university-styled—in the determining and credentialing of who is a full citizen and who is not. So literacy as a cultural practice, for example, might provide access to certain educational opportunities, which would then allow for a job that would have greater access to other societal resources like healthcare or home ownership. Therefore, a habit such as literacy works in tandem with other practices of good citizenship that credential an individual as a competent member of society; a literate person who has economic advantages, mainstream cultural citizenship, and the opportunity to learn appropriate work habits would have greater access to resources compared to someone who does not.

In this way, the designation of "citizen" acts as a gateway to societal resources, but not all citizens have equal access, contradicting the implication of equality in the concept of citizenship. Despite theoretical and legal conferral of equal citizenship rights to individuals, the resulting equality narrative that accompanies discourses around rights, privileges, and obligations obscures the fact that citizenship itself cannot be realized equally by all. Marshall characterizes this contradiction within the logic of citizenship as "equal with respect to the rights and duties," acknowledging the persistence of inequality despite the development of these equal rights for citizens. Citing the growth of these civil, political, and social rights simultaneous to the growth of capitalism, Marshall explains that the conferral of rights creates a "single uniform status of citizenship," but does not necessarily distribute power, which "provide[s] the foundation of equality on which the structure of inequality [can] be built" (21). So while citizenship appears to be a status that confers equality among those who have it, it is equality defined in terms of rights only, which have grown in number as inequalities have become apparent.

With resources and inequality as part of the equation, literacy and citizenship do not just mutually define one another. Instead, the importance of literacy can be seen as a specific response to the inequalities of citizenship that are obscured by the appearance of equal footing for all individuals. Literacy can be used as a way to explain inequalities because an individual can gain literacy, can gain access to resources, or not. An immigrant who learned to read and write in a federal Americanization program learned habits of citizenship, but then it became his or her responsibility to actually enact them. But literacy is also used as a way to respond to inequalities, as in how a group or government or community organization uses literacy to create good citizens out of those whose citizenship is in flux or possibly suspect. In this way, literacy is used as a tool for intervention to reconcile existing inequalities. An understanding of the limitations of literacy as a means to reconcile inequalities can serve as an important complement to the easy access model of citizenship so prevalent in educational spaces. We so often believe that the literacy we teach can be only good, can only help students achieve their goals, succeed in school, and ultimately gain access to society's resources if they would just do well in our classes.[6] But literacy not only brings about healthier citizenship; it can also reinforce the legal, economic, and cultural exclusions that already exist, which can go unacknowledged and should be made more visible in citizenship-producing efforts.

For my purposes, I would explain this inequality by also acknowledging an equally present narrative of individualism as part of citizenship production in the United States. Literacy represents a way to mediate the space or tension between these two narratives of equality and individualism, which is particularly useful in thinking about citizenship practices and how they develop. When the focus is only on an individual's literacy, the burden of realizing citizenship remains on the individual rather than locating that burden within a larger system of inequality. Allowing this inequality to persist when individuals fail to be seen as literate, the citizenry that imagines itself as legitimate for legal or cultural reasons then has a category of noncitizens against whom they define themselves, with some dominating others. Understanding the function of inequality in definitions of citizenship is crucial, particularly because efforts to bolster citizenship through education are pervasive. In order to make these efforts more effective, or even to understand the complexities in attempting to do so, rethinking, theorizing, and historicizing citizenship must be incorporated into our deliberations. Lack of discussion about these uncontested and unspoken narratives of equality, competition, and the distribution of resources in writing classrooms only compounds this burden.

As literacy teachers, the desire to bolster citizenship needs to be read against the backdrop of ever-present inequality among citizens. Ideas about definitions, achievability, and accessibility of citizenship should be significant to literacy teachers; in particular, ambient definitions of citizenship allow for the conflation of citizenship and equality that helps to drive many of the narratives around literacy's role in producing good citizens. Shklar reminds us of the importance of making the distinction between one who is a citizen and one who is equal: "In spite of all the obstacles thrown in its way by injustice and discrimination in all its many forms, the vote was won, but not that other emblem of equal citizenship, the opportunity to earn one's livelihood" (61). While earning power is hardly the goal of literacy educators, the impact of earning— or rather, the anxieties produced by the fear of not having access to resources— cannot be ignored. In fact, such concerns are already shaping the practices of literacy teaching, as the following chapters indicate. Literacy learning, in other words, can shape earning potential and the possibility of equal earning power through the enforcement of certain work habits and has long done so.

Turner views these practices of citizenship, the ones that help to shape the flow of resources, as particularly important because they help "us to understand the dynamic social construction of citizenship which changes historically as a consequence of political struggles" (2). Seen in this way, citizenship can be defined not just as rights and obligations for citizens, a conferral of legal status, but also in light of dynamic, changing, and sometimes contested citizenship practices and boundaries that emerge from a particular set of laws. For instance, the citizenship through basic literacy that allowed someone access to permanent residency in 1917 is not the same citizenship through literacy that individuals must demonstrate in the current version of the Development, Relief, and Education for Alien Minors Act (also known as the DREAM Act), in which minors must have high school diplomas or GEDs to be rewarded with permanent residency after two years of military service or college (thus, education works as both evidence of your citizenship and reward). Policies reflect the changing requirements of literacy along with literacy and literacy practices; in 1917, evidence of literacy was being able to write your name and answer a handful of questions, while today's DREAM Act sets the bar at college success for those who do not wish to serve in the military. But while these practices change along with historical conditions, proof of literacy, in its variety of definitions, continues to function as evidence of one's potential for productivity. The DREAM Act, which I discuss in more detail in chapter 5, is a potent example of how citizenship is made up of both a number of habits and practices, but also shows the lack of a guarantee yet strength of faith put into the enactment of these habits, whether connected to literacy or not. The proposal codifies the encouragement of particular habits and practices of citizenship as part of the path to citizenship. Habits and practices become measures of commitment, either by service or education, in contrast to other possible measures, such as number of years living in the country or work habits, community involvement, or contribution.

Ultimately, what I'm interested in is the way these two ideas come togeth-er—the everyday habits of citizenship and the citizenship practices that emerge from laws and policies to certify individuals as good citizens. During anxious times, whether negotiating the passage of the DREAM Act today or training immigrant laborers in 1920, the intersection of the everyday habits and the legal practices in the production of citizens demonstrates that what makes a good citizen can change over time and is deeply reflective of historical and econom-ic conditions. An understanding of these recurrent and foundational beliefs about citizenship production can provide a fuller sense of not only the influ-ence of teachers and programs, but also how policies and economic structures can shape how those habits came to be and how they are are then interpreted as good citizenship (or not).

Citizenship is certification, a way to demonstrate a willingness to adopt certain values, such as productivity and self-sufficiency. Literacy has proven to be durable evidence of that certification and a means to transmit these values, serving as evidence that an individual will not use already scarce resources and, in turn, that those who can demonstrate these values deserve citizenship rights. Internalized messages about literacy and citizenship, such as how the achievement of one yields the other, are the "ideological freight" Brandt de-scribes, passed along in discussions about and practices of literacy education. We should not regard literacy as having a deterministic association with citi-zenship (in other words, assuming that literacy will always yield citizenship), but at the same time we need to recognize that literacy influences the practices of citizenship. Particularly in times of anxiety, literacy has been used as a way to reorder, redistribute, and recalibrate. The interplay of inequality, participa-tion, and productivity as potential outcomes of literacy should impact our own ideas about citizenship and how they are integrated in literacy training and the distribution of literacy.

LITERACY TRAINING, AMERICANIZATION, AND THE CULTIVATION OF THE PRODUCTIVE WORKER-CITIZEN

> A difficult task is now before the man or woman who has not even learned to hold a pencil in his hand. Their hands are stiff from hard labor and they are not able to control the arm movement in a regular way. The thing they long to do is to be able to write their own names. . . . The teacher of immigrants has a greater task than simply the teaching of a new language. He must also interpret to them the real America they have never known.
>
> —Lillian P. Clark, *Teaching Our Language to Beginners*, 27, 1.

In the 1922 *Federal Textbook on Citizenship Training*, an aptly titled lesson called "The Good Citizen" begins with Mr. Brown telling Mr. White, "I have been reading that they intend to build some school buildings." Their conversation moves through issues of cost ("it will take a great deal of money") and benefits ("we must give our children the best chance for an education") and eventually lands on voting for a certain candidate for the school board. The reader is told, "On the day of the election Mr. Brown voted. He was very busy, but he thought every voter should do his duty by voting." As the lesson ends, Mr. Brown informs his wife that even when taxes get higher, the benefits of being part of a citizenry outweigh the monetary cost, telling her, "we will get so much in return. My tax alone would not give me this. The city serves us well because we all work together" (48). This single-page lesson from one of a series of federal citizenship textbooks published in the 1920s illustrates some habits of the "good citizen"—one who reads current events, supports education for children, pays taxes, works together with fellow citizens, and votes. National Americanization efforts as represented by federal textbooks reveal how literacy learning was used to cultivate a certain kind of citizenship in new immigrants.

New immigrants in the late 1910s and throughout the 1920s may have encountered "The Good Citizen" and similar lessons in *Teaching Our Language to Beginners* or any of the other versions of the *Federal Textbook on Citizenship Training*[1] in federally sponsored citizenship classes, which had the dual purpose of teaching students to become citizens and to become proficient in the English language. These textbooks, produced by the Bureau of Naturalization with help from the Department of Education, are filled with lessons such as "The Good Citizen," which telegraphs the imagined habits of good citizenship that immigrants could access by becoming literate in English and additionally, offer a glimpse into a larger body of citizenship training documents produced during this period. Seen together, these citizenship training documents—federally produced textbooks for the teaching and learning of English, legislative and conference proceedings about immigration, and booklets from community groups intended to aid immigrants—provide ways to understand how literacy was used as a tool in citizenship training to transform early twentieth-century immigrants to the United States into "good citizens."

These textbooks and the citizenship training programs that produced them were the product of an explicit citizenship movement in the early twentieth-century United States. An anxiety about the state of the citizenry, which historian John Higham attributes to nativism motivated by U.S. imperialism (109), changing demographics of immigration (159), and the threat of Bolshevism (222), fueled debates around immigration during the late nineteenth and early twentieth centuries. The era produced numerous pieces of immigration legislation, including a literacy test to determine who among potential immigrants could enter the country that passed in 1917 after twenty years of heated debate,[2] and the Americanization movement, which developed on the cusp of World War I. While the literacy test for immigrants was given in multiple languages to assess an individual's literate ability (and therefore, worthiness to enter the country), government bodies and community groups emphasized English language literacy as a crucial part of the effort to Americanize new immigrants. This chapter focuses on the development of the Americanization movement from the mid-1910s through the 1920s because the cultural effort to produce citizens coincided both with strong legislative efforts to restrict immigration and with changes in work as a result of that era's proliferation of mass manufacturing and big business. Nativist groups such as the Junior Order of American Mechanics, the Immigration Restriction League, and Sons of the American Revolution positioned immigrants as potential threats to the American republic with their cheap labor and foreign (read: Communist) political views that threatened to disrupt mass industrial expansion in the United States.[3] However, nativist groups were not the only proponents of Americanization programs; the Americanization movement was also part of a Progressive Era drive for social reform, a means to confirm citizenship under the threat of World War I, and a federal push to improve the immigration process.

In response to these anxieties, immigrant literacy provided a palatable way to regulate immigration on at least two levels: first, literacy helped to create the legal boundaries of exclusion through the literacy test and then subsequently shaped habits of citizenship of those admitted to the country. Prior to the explicit exclusion of immigration of groups from particular nations, literacy offered a way to rationalize exclusion by basing it on an individualized skill. Second, literacy training offered an avenue through which to introduce habits of American citizenship to newly accepted immigrants with a specific vision of how new immigrants could learn to become good citizens. For example, the federal textbooks, which taught potential citizens through lessons such as "The Good Citizen" with the Mr. Brown/Mr. White scenario, offer explicit evidence of the presence of such citizenship training, which was, moreover, certified by the federal government.

In this chapter, I argue that the citizenship and literacy training of immigrants in the early twentieth century offers a view of literacy's role in citizenship production, one that also helps historicize how literacy has accumulated value in quests for citizenship. In an effort to understand the role literacy plays in the day-to-day acquisition and performance of citizenship, I examine how the literacy training of immigrants during this period—the training texts along with the circumstances surrounding their production—reflected the multiple ways immigrants were imagined to become American citizens by their willingness to be economic entities. The materials produced for such training articulated the connections between literate ability and citizenship, as shown in "The Good Citizen" example, in which an immigrant would learn to become literate through lessons about voting and paying taxes, among other civic behaviors. The connection between these two concepts, however, went beyond the explicit associations of citizenship and literacy—for example, with literacy tests for immigrants—in which literacy acted as a boundary to physical access to the country. A deeper understanding of this association is crucial in order to understand how citizenship has been constructed in connection to literacy and how one gets mobilized for the other.

Citizenship and literacy training of immigrants during the early twentieth century employed both the liberatory and regulatory potential of literacy to construct a "good citizen," a literate citizen who would be particularly beneficial to the economic mechanisms and needs of the country during the development of a mass manufacturing economy. Following political theorist Danielle Allen, who describes "habits of citizenship" cultivated in the ways people interact with one another, I argue that these programs specifically equated good citizenship with worker-oriented traits such as economic productivity and compliant work habits. By forwarding an economically inflected interpretation of citizenship's influence on literacy requirements, I examine the "habits of citizenship" developed through literacy training during this period. Most relevant to my discussion in the rest of the chapter are the ways that the imperative for literacy was layered onto, came to stand for, and became associated with a number of other citizenship habits such as productivity, good work attitudes, individuality, and democratic participation. As a crucial component of citizenship, literate ability served to enforce a particular kind of productivity that benefited the economy and put immigrants into a specific place in the social structure.

Through an emphasis on productivity and economic survival in literacy training, immigrants were taught the importance of literacy as a habit of citizenship and as a marker of productivity. The promise of economic survival in the training of immigrants, especially those who came to the U.S. for better economic opportunities, shows how literacy's coercive force could be gently and implicitly persuasive to students and teachers who took up this imperative. Literacy itself, and all of the privileges (namely, economic privileges) that accompany it, became available to certain groups of immigrants through participation in organized literacy training. Building on Bryan Turner's concept of citizenship as a status marker that helps to direct the flow of society's resources (2), I examine how certain groups of immigrants were persuaded to participate in these programs because of the promise of citizenship and its privileges. The training books taught that when people became literate, they gained economic stability. Immigrants were deemed eligible for citizenship in a legal sense by taking the classes, but also were given a tacit promise of access to a wider number of jobs and other economic opportunities by performing the habits of good citizenship taught in the texts. While Harvey Graff's *The Literacy Myth* asserts that these kinds of gains are not inherent to literacy on its own, training such as this perpetuates the idea that literacy facilitates access to employment and other citizen resources. Immigrant literacy training programs offered one avenue through which literacy became a valuable component of citizenship and, perhaps more importantly, institutionalized the perceived yield of material benefits.

The training of immigrants demonstrates how, even when work was not directly dependent on literate skill, literacy played an important role in the creation of worker-citizens. Taking up Deborah Brandt's "economies of literacy" (19) and her concept of sponsorship, I see the parties involved in the literacy training of immigrants—students, teachers, government officials, community organizations—as benefiting from the distribution of literacy in certain immigrant populations. For example, immigrants demonstrated their productive potential by learning English, a sign to potential employers that they were practicing all of the habits of good American citizenship, while employers and government officials saw literacy as a marker of potential for assimilation and commitment, of legitimacy in the immigrant.

Brandt's sense of sponsorship is central to understanding how literacy training produced a particular kind of citizen (and worker) in the transition from a craft-producing and agricultural economy to a mass manufacturing one. Through this perspective, citizenship habits equaled good work habits and brought the promise that good citizenship would translate to economic success for the individual. This equation benefited both societal harmony (those employers who sponsored literacy gained workers and citizens who complied with the existing system) and the material health of individuals (those who acquired literacy training were able to get jobs). The use of literacy in conjunction with citizenship to enforce work habits created a palatable rationale for the acceptance of certain immigrants over others; while laws kept out groups or individuals who were not desirable, this kind of training was designed for those with the potential to be integrated easily and to satisfy the labor needs of mass manufacturing.

When literacy, and the training that accompanied it, was allowed to stand in as a symbol of an individual's or an ethnic group's potential to contribute to the nation's economy, the skill began to represent a good faith effort on the part of the worker, symbolizing a certain commitment to the country and to habits of citizenship beyond voting and participating in self-government. And this presumption of a good faith effort continues to resound in how literacy and citizenship are entangled today. While literacy acquired meaning by demonstrating a commitment to the country, it also operated to mask inequities or even true parity in economic opportunity; literacy's individualized ethos allowed immigrants and members of other marginalized groups to shoulder the work of citizenship on their own. At the same time, those immigrants who were considered "too literate" were also suspect, as seen in the Red Scare of the 1910s and 1920s. In addition to discussing the general lessons about the importance of productivity and the view of these potential citizens as workers, I also analyze how these lessons were designed to close off radical possibilities. Lessons such as "The Good Citizen," which speaks of the importance of working together, contrast with lessons that teach the importance of trusting employers because of the resources and jobs they provide for employees.

Through behavioral instruction embedded in literacy training programs for immigrants, literacy became constructed and valued as a crucial facet in the fulfillment of citizenship. The citizenship training described here cultivated an important connection between literacy and the desirability of immigrants. I argue that the emphasis on literacy was not just a legal requirement (i.e., the rejection or acceptance of individuals through the implementation of the literacy test), but a cultural one enforced through programs sponsored by the federal government and the communities that immigrants hoped to join. The cultural requirement of literacy reached beyond decisions about who would take residence in the United States, functioning as a way to sort citizens and potential citizens already in the country into those who were considered "good" Americans and those who were not, those who had access to full citizenship privileges and resources, and those who did not. The stakes and impact of literacy are heightened during this moment of economic change, from a craft-producing and agricultural economy to a mass manufacturing one. In this context, the nature of good work habits described in these documents says much about the economic expectations and opportunities for the potential citizens; immigrants were expected to perform these habits in order to have access to opportunities and to material benefits and full citizenship in the new country.

Anxiety, Legislation, and the Literacy Solution

In 1916, the Bureau of Naturalization[4] brought together public school teachers and Department of Labor administrators in Washington, DC, for a Citizenship Convention. Speakers represented a wide range of stakeholders in the production of citizens, including the chief naturalization examiners from St. Paul, Minnesota, and Pittsburgh, Pennsylvania; Samuel Gompers, president of the American Federation of Labor; superintendents of schools from Portland, Oregon, and Grand Rapids, Michigan; congressional representatives; Secretary of Labor William B. Wilson; Mrs. Cora Wilson Stewart, president of the Kentucky Illiteracy Commission; and Andrew Melville, who served as chief of the bureau of Civic, Commercial, and Community Development at the University of Wisconsin extension division. This diverse group sought to articulate a cohesive approach to shaping the citizenship of incoming immigrants through literacy training and other educative means, hoping to standardize the citizen-making process to ensure that every person was trained in the most effective manner. Seeing the convention as a unifying event, Deputy Commissioner of Naturalization Raymond Crist told the audience in the opening address, "The purpose of this series of meetings is twofold: First, to consider what has been done in the past to profit by the experiences of the past, and, second, to bring out a textbook for the use of the candidate for citizenship who attends the public school" (U.S. Bureau of Naturalization, "Proceedings" 7).

Reflective of broader Progressive-era social reform dynamics that Steven Diner describes as a common struggle to "redefine the meaning of American democracy in the age of corporate capitalism" (12), the convention itself was the culmination of the efforts of the nascent Americanization movement in the early twentieth century.[5] This section examines the legislation and anxiety that helped to elicit the development of training texts and immigrant literacy programs from meetings similar to this one. Americanization efforts gained strength from the convergence of a number of demographic, economic, and cultural shifts within the United States at this time. According to historian Desmond King, among these were growing nationalism as a result of the global tensions leading to the First World War, a growing class stratification in the American population, and eugenics studies that "proved" the higher intelligence of northern and western Europeans. Technical innovations, the rise of corporatization, and the growth of urban communities also produced a sense of rapid transformation that permeated American culture (Diner 3–6).

Out of these shifts, two are especially important to this chapter: (1) a rise in the number of immigrants entering the country,[6] and (2) the growing dominance of a mass manufacturing economy, as agrarian and craft economies had declined over the nineteenth century.[7] Daniel Nelson writes how the war boom between 1915 and 1920 increased wage earners in manufacturing by 29 percent, with new factories appearing and existing ones doubling or tripling in size (153). Both of these changes resulted in focused attention on the American worker and how the immigrant labor pool could be trained to become a productive part of American society. Literacy training could be used to deliberately shape an immigrant's new citizenship around the potential to be a worker who would neatly fit into the American economy in the age of big business. These cultural modes of credentialing citizens and shaping them into productive workers coincided with debates over naturalization and immigration laws determining who had physical access to the United States. Alongside rising nativism, these dual anxieties—about the changing economy and about increasing immigration—contributed significantly not only to legislative activity around citizenship but also to the development of citizenship training and how the Americanization movement imagined the kind of citizens it hoped to produce. By contextualizing literacy and citizenship training within this anxiety-ridden atmosphere and the resultant legislative restrictions and policies, we can better understand how literacy worked alongside multiple legislative and cultural approaches to quell anxiety by fixing immigrants and also what literacy offered that other options, specifically legislative ones, could not.

At the beginning of the twentieth century, immigration was on the rise, having increased steadily since the 1880s. A corresponding increase in the number of countries of origin led to an immigration policy that sought to manage the migration of groups to the United States. Between 1891 and 1928, Congress passed upwards of twenty acts or amendments restricting and regulating immigration, deportation, and citizenship.[8] The 1897 amendment to the 1891 immigration act represented the first attempt to establish a literacy test, which was eventually vetoed by President Grover Cleveland.[9] Congress tweaked immigration policy in 1903 and 1904, establishing additional regulations such as head taxes charged to individuals entering the country. In 1906, President Theodore Roosevelt signed a Naturalization Act, codifying the naturalization processes and creating the Bureau of Naturalization and Immigration, a consolidation of responsibility that spoke to growing fears about the number of immigrants (and their countries of origin) entering the United States. As part of the Immigration Act of 1907, Congress established the Dillingham Commission, a congressional committee dedicated to studying immigration and advising on numerous questions about immigration policy. Over its duration, the Dillingham Commission produced forty-two volumes on various immigration issues, including formally picking up the literacy/illiteracy test debates that had been ongoing since Cleveland's veto in 1897. Twenty years later, after two vetoes by President Woodrow Wilson,[10] the U.S. government imposed literacy tests to determine entry into the United States as part of the 1917 Immigration Act.[11]

Legislative activity around immigration laid the groundwork for development of a federally sponsored Americanization movement and for the use of literacy to produce citizens. Out of this raft of immigration legislation, two important outcomes in particular contribute to the development of citizenship classes that taught civic behavior through the teaching of English literacy. First, codification of the naturalization process in the 1906 Naturalization Act included a provision requiring competency in English as a condition for naturalization (not to be confused with the contentious literacy tests for incoming immigrants). Second, the 1917 Immigration Act (also known as the Burnett Act) formalized exclusion of "truly undesirable" immigrants such as those from the Asia-Pacific triangle. These restrictions were a run-up to quotas on immigration established in 1921 by the Emergency Quota Act (making explicit which groups of immigrants were most desirable) and further restrictions established by the National Origins Act (also known as the Johnson-Reed Act) in 1924. The 1921 restrictions used a formula that based immigration numbers on the proportions of the foreign-born population in 1910; the 1924 restrictions based these numbers on the 1890 census as a way to reduce numbers and restrict certain (non-Anglo) groups even further. Based on these quotas, European immigration could be restricted to "a maximum of about 250,000 and assign most of that total to northwestern Europe" (Higham 311), underscoring the nativist motivations behind much immigration policy.

Despite the installation of quotas and restrictions, there was still a sense that something needed to be done to guide the behavior of those still allowed into the country. The importance of competency in English, combined with growing restrictions on immigration, established the relevance of citizenship training classes and accompanying texts, determining the need for English literacy among immigrants from acceptable (European) countries of origin. These students were considered potential citizens, and the literacy lessons attempted to turn that potential into reality.[12]

I underscore this idea of "potential" because the immigrant education I describe here, as well as restrictions on immigration, was often justified by the belief that the more ethnically diverse immigrants in this wave were not of the same high quality as the immigrants who came before, those mostly northern Europeans who immigrated during most of the 1800s. King reports that "it was the dramatic shift, between the 1880s and 1900s, in the sources of European immigration to the United States, from northwestern countries to southeastern ones that excited sustained public debate and comment" (50).[13] This shift in origin, along with a huge spike in numbers, brought about considerable suspicion and the belief that the new immigrant was fundamentally different than the previous generations and might not assimilate as easily.[14] As Reverend M. D. Lichiter, representing the Junior Order of United American Mechanics (a group that rose out of the remnants of the anti-Catholic Know-Nothings), testified to the Dillingham Commission in 1911,[15] "The immigration of the present is not the immigration of forty years ago. The problem confronting us in this, the opening of the second decade of the twentieth century, is entirely different than at that time, because we are receiving, in the main, a different type of immigrant" (16). Lichiter praised the higher quality of the earlier, mostly Anglo-Saxon, immigrants who, he argued, "were the better part of the nations from which they came—morally, mentally, and physically; in the main they were intelligent, industrious, frugal, law respecting, and liberty loving, and as such assimilated with the native born with marvelous facility" (16). The implication was that the immigrants currently allowed into the country were none of these things. But while there were a number of existing legislative restrictions on immigration, a fundamental belief about the achievability and openness of American citizenship favored assimilation and Americanization strategies for some over a total restriction on immigration. If these "lesser" immigrants were allowed into the country, then at least more explicit citizenship training could help improve them. That said, the potential for change and the belief in the achievability of citizenship was restricted to certain immigrant groups, namely southern and eastern European, as demonstrated by Lichiter's explicit belief that "the moral fiber of the nation has been weakened and its very life-blood vitiated by the influx of this tide of oriental scum" (17). Presumably, some immigrant groups would never have the potential to become true citizens.

Lichiter's attempt to pit immigrant groups against one another and discourage a shared immigrant identity also reflected a perceived need to improve the quality of new immigrants, namely by finding ways to teach them how to be "intelligent, industrious, frugal, law respecting, and liberty loving." While intelligence, abiding the law, and love of liberty were certainly positive traits, many of the lessons taught through citizenship and literacy training were responses to economic concerns about immigrants, such as the belief that they would drive down wages and provide unfair competition to native-born workers. In a statement to the Dillingham Commission, the Immigration Restriction League argued, "what demand there is for free immigration has always come from employers who want to force wages down regardless of the effect upon the community," and "the immigration of cheap labor has just this effect, forcing the workman already here to lower his standard of living and often to lose his job" (Dillingham Commission 106). Their statement later made a distinction between "desirable" immigrants (from certain western European countries) and those who were less desirable: "just so far as immigration of cheap labor injures the status of the native workingmen it prevents the immigration of efficient and desirable foreign workingmen, who will not come here to compete with cheap labor. Labor economically cheap is moreover never socially cheap" (106). The Immigration Restriction League made it clear that desirable immigrants would not bring the labor and social costs that undesirable ones would.

Political concerns about these new immigrants also developed. The potentially radical politics of southern and eastern European immigrants in particular engendered a high level of anxiety. During the period around World War I and the Russian Revolution, many Americans feared that immigrants would import radical or revolutionary ideas, inciting not only other immigrants but also the native-born.[16] Prompted by this anxiety, a 1918 amendment to the Immigration Act of 1917 responded by allowing for deportation of those who support "destruction of property, or anarchy, or overthrow of the United States Government" (qtd. in Recht 4), strengthening a previous act from 1903 that called for deportation of those who supported an overthrow of the government. These pieces of legislation encouraged an atmosphere in which the imperative to "fit in" became part of the immigration process. The combined effect of all of these arguments—the political, racial, and economic—was to foster a heightened and complicated anxiety around the influx of immigrants and to create pressure to find a way to ease that growing anxiety.

Clearly, the United States sought to control immigration through legislative and judicial means, but here I wish to focus on the cultural management that occurred through literacy training during the latter part of this influx of immigration. The use of literacy as a response to deep-seated anxiety over immigrants was, in fact, rooted in one of a number of efforts to regulate their integration into the United States, both legislatively and culturally. Legal restrictions provided one avenue to fight the influx of foreigners coming to the United States, but Americanization efforts offered another—the hope that immigrants who managed to enter the country would become citizens and transform themselves into Americans.

Americanization through literacy presented a solution that could indirectly address a number of these potential problems. Literacy helped to create a culture of self-regulation among new immigrants, which presumably would keep any of the previously mentioned anxieties from coming to fruition, making the Americanization movement a seemingly benign extension of other restrictions on immigrants. John Higham describes how "Americanization served, in fact, as the positive side . . . while anti-radical nativism formed the negative side" (255).[17] Literacy's connection to the production of citizenship is often associated with the literacy test (or illiteracy test[18]), with literacy skills used as a restriction to bar certain people from entering the United States through the various literacy acts.[19] However, as important as the use of literacy as a tool of exclusion, or even evaluation, is the way literacy also served to construct and strengthen a particular kind of citizenship among immigrants who persevered through the gauntlet of restrictions. While the literacy test offered a way to restrict immigrant access to the United States, literacy training was used to fortify and shape developing citizenship habits in order to ensure the productive contribution of immigrants who made it into the country. The fortification of immigrants' newly or nearly acquired citizenship through such training emerged from the same anxieties that produced the literacy test and other immigration restrictions. Citizenship classes offered a space where literacy could transform acceptable immigrants and shape these students into the desired kind of citizen.

Seen broadly, literacy determined access on many different levels, from whether one could enter the country to whether one could be deemed a good citizen. As the legislation described above shows, the issue was not just who got into the country, but what to do with the people who had already been admitted, mainly southern and eastern European immigrants who were viewed as having at least some potential to become American, unlike those who were excluded more overtly through quotas and restrictions such as Asians.[20] The citizenship classes themselves offer a glimpse into one aspect of the complex process of choosing and Americanizing immigrants. By the time students got to these classes, particularly those taught with the standardized federal texts in the 1920s, they had already been sorted by other mechanisms. Students were mostly those who had already been deemed desirable and had "potential" to become good American citizens by their European origins. But that potential was not inherent, and thus, immigrants needed to be shaped deliberately.

Citizenship Textbooks and the Learning of English as Participation and Productivity

Americanization efforts such as citizenship training for immigrants began as an informal mix of classes run by public schools and community groups, in part encouraged by the establishment of the Department of Naturalization in 1906. But Americanization became a much more organized movement with the Department of Naturalization's 1916 citizenship convention, in addition to efforts by the Bureau of Education to provide English language classes in 1914 (becoming the America First program in 1915).[21] These classes were created to train immigrants who had declared an intention for citizenship during the required five-year residency prior to the citizenship test and conferral.[22] Classes were designed to teach immigrants English and educate them about the naturalization process; they were intended to inform, but were also a way of easing the pervasive suspicion of immigrants, ensuring conversion from those deemed to be acceptable immigrants into acceptable citizens. This conversion was meant to prevent immigrants from either becoming political agitators or simply returning to their home countries after earning money in the United States. In this period of anxiety over immigration and in tandem with the implementation of immigration restrictions, the texts used in these classes amplified the importance of becoming a citizen as a symbol of commitment to the country.

After Deputy Commissioner of Naturalization Crist expressed the desire to unify various citizenship classes at the 1916 Citizenship Convention, the Bureau of Naturalization published its series of federal citizenship training texts, the first in 1918, for use in these classes. The first edition of the federal *Student's Textbook* for citizenship training in 1918 was compiled "from material submitted by the State Public Schools"; it is a text-heavy book complete with the full text of the Constitution and detailed descriptions of every government agency, including the Bureau of Soils, the Federal Reserve Board, and the Hydrographic Office. While the density of the text begs the question of whether the intended audience was the student, the teacher, or other concerned parties, the level of details could still be justified under the stated charge of the book, which was to provide "A standard course of instruction for use in the public schools of the United States for the preparation of the candidate for the responsibilities of citizenship." The focus on governmentally determined responsibilities of citizenship implies that the audience was imagined to be potential citizens (naturalization candidates) who possibly already possessed facility with and literacy in English.

However, this imagined audience, along with the content of the text, shifted after the publication of the initial version. Subsequent editions with significant revisions were published throughout the twenties, focusing less on knowledge of federal bureaucracy and more on cultural aspects of citizenship and civic behavior.[23] These later editions even looked different. For example, while the initial 1918 version included lengthy and complicated essays on topics such as the Constitution, editions that followed looked more like elementary school primers with five to ten sentences on each page, each lesson focusing on a specific topic such as opening a bank account, going to the doctor, or calling the fire department. The later textbooks were adapted from a series produced by the Department of Education in Massachusetts for adult immigrant education and consisted of a series of short stories and essays, sometimes accompanied by vocabulary lists and questions, all intended to aid in the teaching of English to naturalization candidates. Lessons covered a wide variety of topics but focused mostly on behavior and demonstrated a less mechanistic and legalistic view of what citizenship training was supposed to accomplish. In the 1922 edition, lessons for beginners included "I Open the Door," "I Read the Paper," "The American Flag," "I Count My Money," and "The Police," while intermediate lessons provided instruction on "What the Flag Stands For," "Our Schools," "The Foreman," "City Government," "Continuation Schools" (for additional education), and "A Mistake in Pay." The first five lessons in part 1 of the 1924 version of the textbook covered how to behave in a classroom ("I walk to the chalkboard . . . I write my name . . . I walk to my seat . . . I sit down" [9]) while lesson 53 was about buying a new suit.[24] These succinct lessons almost exclusively focused on shaping the behavior of immigrants by instructing on habits of a good citizen, as opposed to trying to establish a body of knowledge that all citizens should know, like the earlier citizenship training text.

The development and proliferation of these courses intended to encourage naturalized citizenship among immigrant populations, a goal reflected in the networked structure of the programs. Historian Dorothee Schneider characterizes the organization of Americanization work as "a large network of citizenship programs run by non-governmental agencies (staffed mostly by volunteers) in public schools, clubs and civic organizations" (60). She goes on to describe how "the Bureau wrote up and printed materials and kept tabs on the materials taught in countless citizenship classes with the goal of increasing the number of well-informed naturalized voters" (60). In fact, the Massachusetts system, the same one that produced the first edition of what would become the federal textbooks, provided a model on which the federal system was based. *Adult Immigrant Education in Massachusetts, 1920–1921*, a bulletin from the Department of Education, reported that the classes themselves were held "in public school buildings, in industrial establishments or in such other places as may be approved in like manner. Teachers and supervisors employed therein by a town shall be chosen and their compensation fixed by the school committee, subject to the approval of the department" (7). The state government supplied the materials for the classes but the classes themselves were run through local governments with cooperation from local school committees and industry. The federal classes developed this same structure as evidenced by correspondence in the National Archives for the Bureau of Naturalization. Raymond Crist and the Bureau of Naturalization provided materials and support to hundreds of cities, towns, and villages across the United States.[25] These classes supplemented community-based resource programs for immigrants from organizations such as the American Legion, Daughters of the American Revolution,[26] and the League of Women Voters that sought to educate immigrants and native-born individuals about the duties and responsibilities of American citizenship.[27]

In addition to influencing the citizenship lessons of community organizations, the publication of these federal books offered a carefully controlled valuing of literacy—a way to implicate literacy in other habits of citizenship and of being American. This inculcation through literacy and the view of the good citizen promoted through the citizenship training in these books supported a construction of citizenship that emphasized individuality and individual achievement, democracy through voting (as opposed to other avenues of dissent) and paying taxes, and economic contribution through productivity. By directly addressing the formation of habits of citizenship among immigrants (a process in which many constituencies were invested), these texts shaped how a generation of immigrants learned English and, moreover, learned how to be American. They are particularly illuminating because they lay out some of the primary motives for citizenship instruction, establishing the cultural boundaries of citizenship through the supposedly value-neutral undertaking of literacy training.

While it is not surprising that textbooks for a citizenship class would generate idealized notions about what a citizen can be, it is worthwhile to examine the language used in order to understand how the texts made the connection between citizenship and literacy. At their most explicit, the texts linked learning of English to broader Americanization drives of the 1910s and 1920s, purporting to instill patriotic attitudes and knowledge of the Constitution, civics, and American history. In *Teaching Our Language to Beginners*, a version of the federal citizenship textbook from 1924, the introduction detailed some of the responsibilities and goals of the teacher, giving a glimpse into what the government desired immigrants to learn and teachers to teach:

> The ultimate aim of all citizenship training is to make better American citizens, and this end the teacher must constantly bear in mind. English is only the means to the end, but it is extremely important if we desire to assimilate the immigrants who come to us. They want to know the English language, the customs of the United States, and they want to take part in American life. Our duty as teachers, then, will be to instruct them how to speak, read, and write English as the fundamental step in becoming American citizens. (L. Clark 1)

The introduction goes on to say that "the teacher of immigrants has a greater task than simply the teaching of a new language. He must also interpret to them the real America they have never known" (L. Clark 1), thus revealing an inextricable tie between the learning of English and the transformation of the immigrant into a real American citizen, with the teacher serving as guide and interpreter. While the teaching of English seemed to be the text's primary purpose based on the structure of the lessons and its progressively increasing complexity, the introduction called English "only a means to an end." The texts and the classes (and really, the Americanization movement) were therefore built upon multiple purposes, and one of them was to learn about American life; immigrants came to classes in order to learn English, but they also learned how to become American, how to practice the habits of American citizenship.

Given the goals of these classes, variously stated justifications for why immigrants should learn English seem predictable or at least unsurprising. But what is notable is how language proficiency became connected to other civic habits. In a speech at the First Citizenship Convention in 1916, the Bureau of Naturalization's Crist says:

> If our citizens, native or alien born, are to become real American citizens, it is the ideals of our country that must be put before them. Its Constitution, of course, and reading and writing the English language. Ability to understand one another in speech; that is of the highest importance; that is of the first importance. We must try to build up a common language at any rate—and of course, the English language is the language that has precedence—so whatever our thoughts, from the highest station to the most humble place everyone shall understand through speech and writing what the thoughts of his fellow citizens are. (U.S., "Proceedings" 14)

The ability to speak, read, and write in English, therefore, became associated with how one can participate as a citizen and how citizens can understand one another; here, literacy was specifically implicated in the ability to fulfill the duties of democratic citizenship. Later in the convention, J. M. Berkey, the director of special schools and extension work for public schools in Pittsburgh, told the crowd, "To be intelligent citizens we must know the pending problems, and to know and understand these problems we must come together and discuss them from every angle. Then when election day comes we can vote intelligently" (U.S., "Proceedings" 39). Berkey painted a picture of individual and "intelligent" citizens educating themselves in order to resolve problems as a democratic republic through voting. Fulfilling citizenship duties and being an American became associated with intelligent participation—one cannot have true citizen participation without being educated and informed, and Americanization programs attempted to ensure such.

This sentiment came up repeatedly throughout the proceedings of that first citizenship convention, so it is unsurprising that the idea was reinforced in the introduction of the *Student's Textbook*, the first edition of the federal citizenship textbook in 1918, published two years after the citizenship convention:

> All educational roads lead to the assumption of citizenship responsibilities, and the success with which they are traveled determines their justification. This course is but a step on the road toward the desired standardization and is the joint expression of those engaged immediately in the administration of citizenship matters—the courts, the public schools, and the Bureau of Naturalization. Its purpose is to make possible the ready teaching of the highest of all professions—the profession of self-government—and to create the highest sense of the duties and responsibilities of that profession. (5)

This analogy equating citizenship and self-government as a "profession" enforced an important position for literacy because, according to the texts, proficiency in speaking and reading English was the way that ideas were exchanged between citizens as well as the avenue through which a citizen became informed enough to self-govern. Literacy, therefore, became a vital instrument in the realization of full citizenship for the American citizen. Literacy was positioned to bolster the quality of citizenship by increasing an individual's ability to participate, based on the belief that those who have it would become capable of individual self-government.

Through citizenship training texts, literacy learning became tied both to the progress of the nation and the progress of the individual. Lessons taught that a lack of literacy for immigrants spelled material disaster for them, while a wealth of literacy could often mean employment and financial benefits (and an aggregated benefit to the U.S. economy). But it was not literacy on its own that created this sense of progress but also the value ascribed to it. Part of why I look back at this historical moment of citizenship crisis is to understand how literacy has accumulated value for those members of society whose status is most at the margins, those who have the most to gain not just through the attainment of literate ability, but also through society's *acknowledgment* of such ability. Literate skill, the ability to read and write, clearly provided immigrants access to certain societal resources. But in addition to the instrumental aspects of literacy, it also brought an assurance of an immigrant's ability and willingness to become a good American.

If citizenship training for immigrants was designed to help them become more American, then the subject matter in the training materials appeared to identify the areas in which they were perceived to need the most help— hygiene, living arrangements, patriotism, and work habits, in addition to the primary goal of literacy. These ideals gained traction in the textbooks by associating the literacy and productivity of good citizens with economic survival. The following examination of the content used in the teaching of English exposes the values embedded in these lessons. Often, they were responses to the suspicion surrounding immigrants; thus, the lessons directed behavior in a way that taught immigrants how to become integrated and productive members of American society.

Valuing Work as a Habit of Citizenship

Looking at this basic literacy instruction of the early twentieth century, which was intended predominantly for newcomers to American society, we can see the citizenship values that are conveyed, such as the practice of self-government and other rights and privileges associated with American citizenship. But interestingly, judging from the content of the instruction, the common civic activities of participation and voting were not the most important facet of citizenship that new and potential citizens needed to learn through these texts. Interspersed with lessons about Lincoln's birthday, Memorial Day, and the flag were other lessons to be learned about the habits of an American citizen, lessons focused on transformation of character and personality. There were lessons about going to the bank, being on time to school and to work, and the importance of going to school and the library, to name a few. In addition to teaching a kind of citizenship defined by patriotism and democratic participation, the textbooks also shaped new immigrants as economic entities by embedding messages about work and productivity in their literacy training. Many of the lessons focused on themes of making oneself worthy of citizenship through habits of productivity and literacy.

The continued production of training texts by the federal government and community groups after the 1921 quota act (which stipulated an effective and selective slowing of immigration to the United States) amplifies how cultural citizenship training was as crucial as restrictions were in preserving a particular conception of the American citizenry. The explicit training of citizens through federal Americanization programs demonstrated an ongoing concern about immigrants already residing in the country, regardless of the implementation of quotas and restrictions on undesirable populations. With Bolshevism looming in the background, these concerns could be characterized as not just cultural, but economic, whether over an individual's potential to be productive to the economy or his or her potential to be dissatisfied and promote radical labor views. Continuing cultural citizenship training through these classes and texts provided necessary instruction on behavior and habits of citizenship for those immigrants deemed potentially desirable. The texts encouraged particular habits of citizenship such as learning English, increasing literacy, and enhancing job productivity. Not only did immigrants learn English as a way to become American, but the learning of English became a marker and a means that directly affected their potential productivity and success as workers, and, in other words, their ability to attain full citizenship. While literacy was touted in conferences, deliberations, and textbook introductions as creating an *informed* citizenry, the lessons themselves demonstrated the importance of developing a *productive* citizenry. The focus on the singularity of an immigrant underscored the importance of both individual political participation and individual achievement in the economy; literacy served as a way to achieve both of these. The dual concern that immigrants both assimilate culturally and contribute economically worked itself into these training texts by repeating and emphasizing these traits as habits of good citizenship in the teaching of literacy.

The desire to create good workers through citizenship classes appeared in the texts most often in persuasive statements about citizenship, Americanization, and education, and in arguments about how becoming fully American would help in relationships with children and with more success at work. Knowledge of written and spoken English was positioned in these texts as contributing to the economic survival of immigrants' families and to the opportunities available to their children, including their ability to attain full citizenship in the United States. As previously discussed, learning English became a way for immigrants to provide a good faith gesture that they would become contributing members of American society, and the texts provided persuasive evidence—economic stability for themselves and for their families—to illustrate how this literacy training would produce good citizenship.

Connections between proficiency in English and success at work were generated from the circumstances surrounding the lives of immigrants, circumstances created by the government and workplaces. In discussions about the training programs themselves, employers and administrators talked about how they used literacy to promise employment to immigrants. For example, at the 1916 Citizenship Convention, Walton Schmidt, a member of the Chamber of Commerce from Detroit, reports how one auto factory, which is unnamed, "gave the men a threefold choice: 1. To attend factory class, 2. to attend public night schools, 3. to be laid off" (U.S., "Proceedings" 71). In fact, Schmidt relayed a Ford report that says accidents have decreased since they started their "English first" initiatives in the factories. Through the auto industry example, attendees at the Citizenship Convention were told that not only should immigrants learn English because they were now American, but the learning of English would directly affect their potential productivity, efficiency, and success as workers and, thus, allow them to realize their full citizenship. To the industrial field, teaching citizens English would help to guarantee that this process of making worker-citizens occurred.

Andrew Melville of the University of Wisconsin Extension even stated explicitly during the citizenship convention that the goal with this kind of citizenship education was not primarily "to make a civil engineer or an expert bookkeeper or an expert accountant of the student enrolled but essentially to make a more efficient workingman" (U.S., "Proceedings" 80–81). Melville's use of "efficient" in the era of scientific management feels deliberate, a way to convince those who doubted the power of literacy training and the resources needed for it that the investment in education would be returned by transforming immigrants into "efficient workingm[e]n," with no extraneous characteristics (e.g., radical political views or unhealthy lifestyles) that would come into conflict with the quality of work.

The lessons themselves conveyed similar messages to worker-students by showing how certain behavior would yield success and individual prosperity, as well as underscoring the importance of their potential contribution as new Americans. Explicit arguments about why immigrants should learn English connected it to economic success and stability. In the 1918 federal citizenship textbook, a lesson on school practices began by discussing time and neatness, but then also had lessons that stated: "I shall try to act as I have learned from this lesson. I come to the evening school to speak American English. It means a better opportunity and a better home for me in America. It means a better job for me. It means a better chance for my children. It means a better America. I shall do my part in making a better America" (U.S., *Student's Textbook* 11). Quite plainly, the lesson told students that learning English would provide better opportunities. Students learned about the importance of English language skills because it would bring with it these "better chance[s]." This call was not just about individual success; by taking advantage of these opportunities, the individual would also be taking responsibility for making a "better America" through a particular kind of economic contribution to the nation, which in turn would mean economic survival, or even prosperity. Enveloping these traits of worker identity into literacy training perpetuated a federally sponsored version of the American dream, in which both the individual and the country benefited from immigrant students learning English. Additionally, a "better America," an economically stable America with a trained immigrant population, ensured a certain national stability in a time of various immigration threats and anxieties.

Leading an industrious life was an essential element in becoming an American citizen. In the *Manual of the United States: For the Information of Immigrants and Foreigners*, produced by the Daughters of the American Revolution in 1924, the introduction discussed the purpose of their book: "It is one of the ways that we have of bidding you welcome, of telling you how to find homes and happiness in this great country of ours, which we promise shall be your country too, if you will lead industrious lives, walk in the fear of God and honor our laws and institutions" (Buel 10). Immigrants learned through this introduction that industriousness operated on the same level as godliness; presumably, those who followed this path would be able to "find homes and happiness" and be welcomed in the country. And learning English was the path to all of it. In the same book, a section entitled "Learn English" also explicitly connected proficiency in English with success at work: "English is the language spoken in the United States. It is very important that you learn it. You will need it to obtain work. You will need it in order to understand instructions given you by the men for whom you work. You must be able to read English to understand signs and warnings of danger. You can then do your work better, more easily and more safely. You may be able to obtain better positions and higher wages" (Buel 16–17). Again, the texts declared that learning English was a necessity for work. And the implication was that following this advice to understand instructions and be safe "may" not only bring job opportunities but also the possibility of advancement and higher wages.

These explicit messages about the necessity of English for success emerged not only in the books published by nongovernmental organizations. The federal books also provided lessons showing a direct relationship between the ability to speak and read English and opportunities for advancement and more money. In a lesson in the 1922 version of the federal student textbook called "Angelo's Promotion," the title character got promoted with better pay because the foreman liked his work. In the lesson, Angelo reported to his wife that the foreman told him why he got a promotion: "You keep at your work well. You follow my orders. You want to do your best. You obey the rules of the factory. You speak well of your bosses to other workmen. You can give directions well to the new help" (U.S., *Federal Citizenship Textbook* 145). So Angelo was obedient and followed the rules, but what was the ultimate sign for the foreman? He explains to Angelo, "I see you reading the bulletin board," and Angelo tells his wife, "I am glad I went to evening school." Angelo then says (humbly, of course) that "he just kept busy and did his best every day" (U.S., *Federal Citizenship Textbook* 145).[28] This lesson contained a number of essential traits for the productive worker-citizen. Not only did Angelo work hard and follow orders, he also learned to read, which demonstrated his engagement and commitment to the job. Through this lesson, immigrants saw the rewards available from practicing habits of citizenship such as learning how to read, following the rules, doing your best—a promotion at work. Additionally, the lesson's focus on individual achievement, that it was up to Angelo to act in this way, invoked the fundamental American belief in citizenship's achievability; it was achievable but dependent on the success or failure of the individual.

To that end, while there were many messages about the rewards of learning English and becoming a citizen and the promises of success and individual prosperity, lessons like "Angelo's Promotion" also embedded messages about the difficulty an individual may encounter while doing this work. *A Little Book for Immigrants in Boston*, published by the Committee for Americanism of the City of Boston, explicitly established the difficulties an immigrant might have had in finding work, learning the English language, and becoming a good citizen. The authors wrote, "It is hard to learn a new language well; hard for a tired working man to go to school in the evening; hard sometimes to renounce his old allegiance and become a citizen in a new land. But the hard things are often the best to do. They bring their reward. Labor is hard, but without labor we should all starve" (Committee 98). This lesson articulated the expectation that an immigrant should be a (tired) worker who must go through the hard labor of learning English because it would bring "reward," emphasizing hard labor as necessary, not just in the work environment, but also in the renunciation of old allegiances and shedding of old identities. Presumably learning a new language, along with the embrace of hard labor and the shedding of old identities, would bring some "reward" (and not doing so would bring starvation, all the fault of the individual's decision not to embrace these habits).

This teaching of tenacity, with the requisite rewards for both the individual (jobs) and the country (a stable immigrant population), was part of a larger effort to manage behavior through these lessons, as demonstrated in the texts. Even the choices of idioms to teach immigrants reflected the kinds of traits that were imagined to benefit them as good workers. For example, in the federal textbook *Teaching Our Language to Beginners* (1924), a lesson that involved a list of quotations and well-known sayings like "Honesty is the best policy" also included "A good name is better than great riches" (L. Clark 9). While "A good name is better than great riches" appears to contradict the assertion that economic interests drive much of this curriculum, the inclusion of this aphorism is actually consistent with the ways immigrants were to be shaped into worker-citizens. It taught that making an honest living should be more important than making a lot of money, thus creating a class of obedient workers who were taught to look beyond economic inequities in favor of having a "good name." A lesson in the 1918 book explained, "I can become a citizen of the United States. When I came to America I knew that I would have a better opportunity to care for myself. Since coming to America I have *learned* to love it" (U.S., *Student's Textbook* 22; emphasis added). This lesson hinged on the idea that immigrants might not be grateful immediately for being allowed entry to America with its economic and political opportunities, and, therefore, might not be willing to accept many of the conditions that came with immigrant status. Presumably, the immigrant needed to *learn* to love it after a certain amount of difficulty and hard work.

The desired behavior promoted in these texts ended up being those traits that helped the immigrant become a productive worker-citizen, and many opportunities are presented to help shape good worker behavior beyond simple industriousness. In a lesson called "Keeping Well" from the 1922 federal textbook, the reader was told, "We want to be well. Then we can keep at our work. We are not happy when we are sick. We should take care of our bodies. . . . Get plenty of sleep at night. We can work better the next day. . . . America needs strong, well people. There is much work to be done here" (U.S., *Federal Citizenship Textbook* 83). The active promotion of the idea that the United States needed hard-working and healthy people emphasized the link between work and citizenship; one did not get plenty of sleep because it made individuals healthier but because the country needed healthy workers. The emphasis on health had the residual benefit of promoting other acceptable habits of citizenship with a more puritanical motivation (e.g., workers at home sleeping would not be out carousing) and a political one (e.g., sleeping workers weren't at all-night meetings for unions or other political organizations).

Another lesson in the 1922 textbook used America's need for good workers when it showed women going to evening school and displaying some of their needlework. The women were praised by "English-speaking friends" and were told, "we bring much to America because we are able to do such fine work. America welcomes workers who are careful" (110). In these lessons, the primary identity of the immigrant was that of "worker," an identity that America welcomed, especially careful workers, while implying that the country may reject those who are not careful workers. With mentions of needing to be careful and healthy, these lessons delineated what habits and behaviors made a good worker-citizen.

The *Teacher's Manual* for the 1922 federal textbook included a lesson on the "-tion" construction with Thomas Edison as the subject and imbedded detailed instructions about work habits. The sentences progressed from "He worked in a telegraph station" to "For years he had a humble position" to "He seldom takes a vacation" (26). Edison provided a kind of model for being a citizen—strong and healthy, not taking vacations, willing to take humble positions, careful. With literacy training folded into further instructions about the habits of a good worker, these lessons taught the new immigrant that being a good citizen meant taking up all of these habits. Immigrants who took up Edison's work habits might not necessarily achieve Edison's success, but at least they would learn to understand that these "humble" traits were all part of what it meant to work in the United States.

At the 1916 Citizenship Convention, J. M. Berkey used testimonials from various European immigrants enrolled in citizenship classes to demonstrate the upshot of this training. These testimonials, while likely shaped by Berkey, served to show stakeholders, such as business owners, educators who would teach immigrants, or even Americans with anxiety over the growing immigrant presence, that making immigrants into good citizens had benefits for the broader population. The testimonials began with a general appreciation for access to education in the United States, quoting a Polish immigrant who said, "I have gratitude to those who rules [sic] this country, for workingmen can go to school and receive education." Other statements from immigrants made a more direct connection between learning English and the wide economic opportunities granted to them as a result. Berkey quoted a worker originally from Germany who attested, "I have been given a job as boss because I speak English much better than the rest," and a Greek immigrant who testified, "I came from Crete to this country to make a good living, but I can not get a job if I can not speak English. Now after a while I think I can ask for job any place. I like this country because if I speak good English I hope to learn any kind of industrial work forever" (U.S., "Proceedings" 39). With these testimonials, Berkey provided evidence that immigrants also believed learning English would provide them with the economic opportunities they sought when they emigrated. The imperative for literacy and the learning of English was not just enforced by the government or workplace but also, according to these arguments, something that immigrants desired as a way to gain economic opportunities.

Berkey's use of these testimonials, based in how English proficiency and work success came together, shows how the classes were designed to help solve many of the economic and cultural anxieties surrounding immigrants, while also having economic benefits. Thus, in literacy training sites such as these Americanization programs, which targeted mostly southern and eastern European immigrants, literacy explicitly became coupled with productivity, which in turn allowed literacy to represent good citizenship and attain its cultural value. The productive citizen was one who contributed to the American economy, rather than one who would drain it. This was an important concern, with many Americans at the time believing that hoards of immigrants were flooding the borders of the United States (Higham 301)—a perception that, in part, generated the production of these textbooks and other mechanisms of citizenship production in the first place. For these immigrants, citizenship meant not just voting and participating in self-government; the important message given to citizens and potential citizens was to make a better America and a better American through industry and work, with literacy marking the critical credential in gaining this status of good citizenship. Pursuits of literacy, productivity, and achievement as individualized activities channeled desires in a particular way, implying that personal economic successes and failures in the United States were the result of an individual's pursuit of them. The balance between individual and collective benefits was delicate because developers of the classes did not want the texts to emphasize collectivity too much and risk enforcing socialist, or even Bolshevik, values. While the classes were designed to help immigrants start to think of themselves as Americans, the goal was not to have workers think of themselves as a collective in other ways.

In sum, these literacy lessons and their implicit arguments for a particular construction of citizenship invoked a number of other narratives that circulated around American citizenship, aside from the ability to self-govern—pulling yourself up by your bootstraps, the cultivation of a worker/employee-oriented sensibility, openness of American society to all, and individual responsibility. These messages were carried through literacy training via lessons that addressed, explicitly and implicitly, work habits and ways that American citizens should act in a workplace context. And while immigrants benefited from these lessons in order to find jobs and gain economic stability in the United States, these same habits of citizenship also greatly helped industry by, ideally, producing obedient, industrious workers who were grateful for their opportunities. However, sometimes the lessons needed to be a little more direct in order to achieve this outcome, as illustrated by the number of direct critiques of radical and anti-business, pro-Marxist sentiments.

Fighting Radicalism through Literacy Training

Immigrants who were "too literate" were often seen as suspect, their literacy a sign that they might be bringing radical ideas to the United States. A Red Scare in the late 1910s (which extended into the 1920s) led to the passage of the previously mentioned 1918 amendment to the 1917 Immigration Act that allowed deportation of any individual thought to be in support of the "destruction of property, or anarchy, or overthrow of the United States Government" (cited in Recht 4) and encouraged the belief that the literacy of potential citizens needed to be shaped deliberately or else the country would be faced with large groups of immigrant radicals. These suspicions ultimately generated the explicit combination of literacy and productivity discourses in citizenship training texts, responding to fears that immigrants would import socialist or Marxist beliefs and incite unrest, as the Bolshevik revolution put many immigrants under suspicion of radicalism (Higham 222). The federal government and community groups worked to domesticate the immigrant labor force through literacy and other citizenship training programs, demonstrating how literacy's regulatory potential worked alongside its liberatory one. In exchange for economic opportunities, immigrants learned through literacy instruction how they must also work within these structures, practicing obedience and individual responsibility. By combining literacy instruction with messages of productivity and good work habits, Americanization proponents hoped the radical (and supposedly un-American) ideas associated with certain groups of immigrants could be counteracted.

While citizenship training texts do not overtly answer or reference these suspicions surrounding immigrants, the training seemed constructed to cultivate habits of citizenship, cooperation, and industriousness as a simple solution; workers who felt grateful for their positions would be less likely to feel the need to agitate. To that end, these textbooks not only projected a worker identity onto the immigrant along with seemingly benign traits such as industriousness and individual advancement, but they also contained fairly detailed instructions for how a good, productive worker should act, exposing the values and work habits that government officials hoped to instill in new immigrants through literacy training. Such habits ranged from punctuality to using banks, from making a household budget to handling a salary dispute. In the 1918 student textbook, a section on the Bureau of Naturalization even explicitly stated that that one of the goals of the citizenship classes was to help students negotiate the workplace:

> Through the public schools all over the United States, the Bureau of Naturalization is working so that the many hundreds of thousands of foreigners who

annually are candidates for citizenship may learn of their rights and responsibilities as American citizens. As 90 per cent of these applicants for naturalization are wage earners, this work of the public schools enables them to understand their rights as laboring people, enables them better to understand their surrounding conditions, so that they may wisely and fairly consider the problems which flow from the relations of employer and employee. (92)

"Fairness" in this context often meant the need for the employee to understand the employer's position. Particularly in the federal textbooks, the responsibility of the employee to be fair to the employer was an idea that cropped up repeatedly. The focus of these instructions indicates a desire to establish a harmonious relationship between employer and employee, one in which the employee, the new citizen, would easily fit into the structure of work in the United States. While there are no direct anti-union statements, issues of fairness, employer-employee relations, and potential grievances were often worked out when individuals simply communicated and understood each other, again illustrating how the literacy learned through these books attempted to enforce habits of citizenship that also enforced a worker identity.

Generally, the boss was portrayed as a friendly, genial, and knowledgeable father figure who simply looked out for his employees. In a lesson entitled "Taking Directions from the Overseer," a group of workers was scolded for talking while working and for "pushing and fooling near a machine in motion" (U.S., *Federal Citizenship Textbook* 105). The lesson provided a number of implicit messages about the paternalistic nature of the worker-boss relationship when the overseer told the workers, "You could be discharged. You may be hurt by your carelessness. I am really your friend. I am warning you. But you must obey the rules. You must take orders from me. Let's be fair with each other" (105). To reiterate the point, one of the workers remarked, "He is right, boys. We must follow the rules better. . . . We must respect those above us. It pays" (105). In another lesson called "The Foreman," George, a worker, decided to "not get cross" when the foreman showed him how to do a task correctly because "the foreman must send only good work." The lesson ended with the reminder, "Keep busy. It does not pay to get cross" (92). The messages in these lessons were overwhelmingly clear—workers must take orders from the boss, follow the rules, keep from getting angry, and value fairness. This kind of demeanor (rather than a socialist or union-oriented attitude) is what "pays" for new immigrants—in both economic and citizenship terms.

Issues pertinent to labor organizing—worker safety, work hours, disputes with employers—were also addressed within these lessons, with many messages about who was responsible for these issues. The 1922 *Federal Citizenship*

Textbook included a lesson on "Daywork-Piecework," in which two garment workers, Joe and Jim, discussed the benefits of both day work (being paid by the day) and piecework (being paid per completed piece). The comparison between the two kinds of labor ends with both workers feeling "satisfied" by their work arrangements (74). This lesson reflected the significance of the day work versus piecework issue for immigrants; historian David Montgomery explains how employers had a "widespread belief" that piecework was "the best pay system for immigrants" (37), but in fact, such a payment structure actually benefited employers because it "placed on the worker the full burden of any inefficiency," whether it was his or her own fault or the employer's (37). This intervention encouraged workers to overlook the inequities involved with piecework, chalking it up to a matter of individual choice, much like citizenship itself.

This same emphasis on individualism, this time on individual responsibility, was seen in later lessons in the 1922 textbook. In "Careless James," a worker who encountered a broken safeguard on a saw blade decided not to report it and consequently ended up getting hurt: "'I am glad my hand did not touch that saw,' he said. 'I am to blame for the accident. I did not report the broken guard. The rules say I should. The company was not to blame. I was careless'" (86). In this scenario, the worker was to blame, emphasizing his individual responsibility rather than the responsibility of the company. Workers learned that accidents such as these were the worker's own fault, not the factory's for having poorly maintained equipment. New workers learned through these lessons to shift culpability to themselves rather than learn to agitate for safe workplaces or other labor rights being touted by unions. Another lesson, "A Mistake in Pay," instructed immigrants on the employer's fair attitude toward workers with a story about Peter, who was shorted two dollars in his paycheck. At first, he was angry, but then he went to talk to the pay clerk, who gladly gave him the money. "'Here is the two dollars,' says the pay clerk. 'We made a mistake. We are glad to make it right. I am glad you reported it at once. I hope you did not think we would cheat you.' In response to this, Peter laughed. 'Of course the company is fair,' he said to himself'" (109). As in "Taking Directions from the Overseer," the lesson fostered trust in the employer by showing that the company would only make honest mistakes. Again, a lesson such as this reinforced the message about the general benevolence of the employer to immigrant workers, using citizenship and literacy training to create a cultural norm in which employees learn to be compliant and respectful of their bosses, no matter what the circumstances.

Lessons such as these encouraged immigrants to become obedient workers by teaching them to trust their employers. A generous reading of the lessons about employer/employee relations could be explained by a simple desire for harmonious workspaces, but the pervasive and overt anti-union messages belie that generous reading. The lessons even take a side on use of the common label of "worker" as opposed to being identified as a "laborer," which was the term preferred by unions because it implied the control of employers or those in control of capital. In the 1924 *Federal Textbook on Citizenship Training*, a lesson taught the grammatical construction of contractions with these examples: "Mr. Molnar is an experienced worker. He is not a laborer. He isn't a laborer" (79). The lesson made the distinction that Mr. Molnar is a machinist and an experienced worker, setting up a clear contrast between skilled workers and the supposedly unskilled workers who need to form unions and call themselves laborers. Through this status distinction, immigrants were taught the desirability of becoming an "experienced worker" rather than remaining a mere laborer.

The extensive attention paid in the lessons to the role of the employer could be read as a direct response to some basic Marxist concepts about the ownership of the means of production that were circulating among workers (or at least perceived to be, due to the Red Scare). Responding to socialist or Marxist ideals, the lessons tried to demonstrate how workers were, in fact, valued in the capitalist American system. In *Capital*, Marx warns that the productive labor process creates a divide between the labor of the hand and the labor of the head (516). A lesson in the 1922 *Federal Citizenship Textbook* on "Labor Day" seemed to naturalize that distinction between the labor of the hand and labor of the head, telling the reader: "We honor the man who works with his brain—the banker, the doctor, the lawyer, the engineer, and others. We also honor the man who works with his hands. We could not live without the help of this man" (159). This distinction sets up a division of labor and establishes two categories of workers, seeming to indicate that the man who works with his hands does not use his brain, or at least is not valued for it. But despite reinforcement of this divide, the lesson indicated that workers who worked with their hands were honored as much as those in high status professions.

However, just in case the worker got too confident about the contribution he or she made to the economy and started to see the work of the hands and the work of the brain as equal, the lesson continued: "It takes money to begin this work. It takes money to build factories, to buy machines, to buy tools. The employer furnishes this money, or capital. It takes wise planning to direct this work. The employer gives his business judgment. Both the workman and the employers are needed to make this a busy, growing country. America has been made by hard-working people. All have helped together—some with their hands, some with their brains, some with their money" (159). While the worker was positioned as an integral part of the economy, immigrants were reminded that capital was the foundation for business; without the owners and employers who have money, workers would not have the opportunity to work hard. The message was clear: the employer, the one who furnished the money, was in control of the work situation, and workers needed to recognize his importance in the system, rather than believing union arguments about the vitality and potential power of workers united. Americanizers hoped that immigrants would learn through the federal texts that what Marxists might term alienation was simply a necessary part of the process in which workers ceded to the direction of those who had the money and called it cooperation.

Another lesson, "Who Are the Workers in America?" established a similar emphasis on the valuing of all workers, undercut with the unwavering importance of capital. As in "Labor Day," its title captured the populist tone of worker solidarity, but the content also brought together those familiar themes of hard work and industry, combined with a valuing of the common worker. With simple sentences that remind the reader that the lesson was for the beginning language learner, it began, "America is a busy country. America believes in hard work. America honors all workers. There are many ways to work. Much work is done with their hands. Much work is done with the brain. We need trained minds. We need bright quick thinkers. It takes strong, skillful minds to plan and direct work" (U.S., *Federal Citizenship Textbook* 116). This part of the lesson maintained that all work, whether in a factory or at an office, involves "trained minds" and quick thinking, a message that praised all workers while simultaneously reinforcing the subjugated position of certain kinds of labor. Additionally, this kind of explicit instruction demonstrates how the federal texts were used to introduce new immigrants to the American work ethic and attitudes toward hard work, in addition to its stated goals of teaching citizenship and English. By reading about acceptable work habits and attitudes through these lessons, immigrants learned that if you happened to be enduring hard work, then that's just an expected part of America and being an American, rather than something they could protest against, as the unions argued.

To reinforce the power of those who owned the businesses with language that echoes some of the other lessons, "Who Are the Workers in America" also reminded workers that they cannot create work opportunities on their own, even with hard work and "strong, skillful minds":

> Money is needed to carry on work. It takes money to build factories and buy materials to start work. We need men who can furnish this money. They give work to the employees. They keep business running for the employee. The employee makes business for them. Together all workers make America a prosperous country. All these people are needed. All are workers. One group can not

do the work alone. We depend on each other. Each one should say: "I must do my work well. If I do not, I spoil the work for others." (U.S., *Federal Citizenship Textbook* 116)

Unlike union beliefs that workers could harness collective power to emphasize their role in the industrial process, this lesson emphasized the importance of the employer. Again, this lesson argued the importance of capital and the necessity of bosses and owners in response to Marxist beliefs against the accumulation of capital (Marx 635–42). "Who Are the Workers in America?" encouraged the idea that people must work together (obediently) but also sent the message that there would not be opportunities to work without the employer. While all people, from the factory owner to the person working the machines, were workers and were "needed," readers were told they must all work together and depend on one another. In other words, workers were being trained to see the importance of the people who "keep business running" or else they would "spoil" it for themselves and for others.

In the same lesson some "good rules for all workers" were also outlined, including: "1. Do not waste time. 2. Do not waste material. 3. Be honest. 4. Keep your word. 5. Be good natured. 6. Be loyal to your employers. 7. Don't be fooled by wrong talk. 8. Practice the square deal" (116). Contextualizing the logic of these rules within the atmosphere of union agitation during this period,[29] lessons such as these which would teach workers to be loyal to employers and practice the "square deal" could counteract "wrong talk" about organizing or participating in the labor movement to gain increased wages, an eight-hour day, or a weekend. Such practices were portrayed as wasteful and dishonest and did not fall under the habits of good workers or, rather, good citizens. The lesson that workers need employers, that they should respect and trust employers, that they should not see themselves as laborers, served as an attempt to counteract other narratives about the employer/employee relationship such as those forwarded by unions during this same period (discussed in more detail in chapter 3), all under the guise of helping to teach citizenship.

The explicit messages in these texts indicated a desire to deliberately shape all aspects of work habits down to the new immigrants' attitudes about work. Immigrant workers were taught that the work they did was important, but only within the structure established by employers and those in control of capital. The brains of the owners needed those who worked with their hands, but more importantly, those who worked with their hands were taught to appreciate the opportunities given to them by the people with the money. These texts offered a kind of literacy that attempted to close off radical possibilities, a particularly important goal to prevent people from using their newly formed literacy as a means for dissent or what contemporary readers might term critical literacy. By shaping work habits so finely, the literacy training of immigrants attempted to create an obedient worker who would remain productive; left alone, literacy might provide an avenue for a worker to develop into a radicalized laborer who was not as productive for business. With proper training, such a possibility was not left to chance.

The Literate Worker-Citizen

The immigrant training texts examined in this chapter represent part of a larger body of government, community-based, and general publications during this period that circulated citizenship concerns and provided some insight into literacy's role in the assessment of an immigrant's citizenship potential. Citizenship training reinforced the cultural narrative that learning English and becoming literate were essential to becoming good Americans. While these messages surely came from other sources as well, training programs clearly defined and emphasized their importance to immigrants who went through the legal naturalization process, a space for broad audiences to receive these repeated messages about literacy and citizenship. And when immigrants were learning English in these classes, they also learned much more. As in the example at the start of this chapter, with Mr. Brown reading about a school board issue and then understanding the importance of voting, the texts showed how literacy in English meant that immigrants would be able to participate in society. Likewise, while literacy certainly eased immigrants' acclimation to living in the United States, they were also made into "better" workers. As discussed here, the representation of literacy directed at potential citizens was infused with instruction on work habits, representing an ideal of the industrial citizen worker who was punctual, followed the company rules and did not agitate against the factory owner. Readers of these training texts learned that the economic opportunities available to them in the United States were privileges of being a citizen, of learning English, and of being literate.

Embedding these messages of productivity and the nature of work habits in the apparatus of literacy and citizenship training was a way to exert control over the kind of citizens that immigrants would become, responding to widespread anxieties about immigrants' ability and willingness to blend into, rather than corrupt, the American citizenry. The threat of the immigrant worker, however, was more than just a cultural fear; it was also an economic one in which immigrants were suspected of bringing values to the United States that would disrupt ways of doing business. This pervasive concern about citizenship for both immigrants and the native-born led to the use of education as one way to cultivate a productive and literate citizenship. In this gap between rhetoric and reality, literate skill (like work skills) was figured to constitute an economically productive subjectivity, one that promised to erase aspects of identity like race or national origin,[30] that has the potential to be incompatible with citizenship. In addition to teaching immigrants about the details of the naturalization process, citizenship training classes also taught speaking, reading, and writing in English, the language of the immigrant's new home. Immigrants were taught that they must learn the language in order to contribute to their new country, to become productive citizens and good workers. Their survival depended on it.

One result of this contribution-based citizenship was that a citizen's participation broadened to include much more than political participation. While participation through voting certainly was part of the vision of the citizen, participation in the economic apparatus of the nation played a significant role in government-sponsored citizenship instruction as demonstrated through these literacy programs. The training taught that being a good citizen meant being a good worker. Thus, literacy itself became wrapped up with work and individualized success and above all, the worker-citizen was just that—equally a worker and a citizen. These training books delivered the message that it was impossible to be one without also being the other; you were one because you were the other. An individual's work defined who he or she was as a citizen because work was what made a contribution to the country, a necessary habit of citizenship.

With the wave of mass manufacturing and the growing size and number of corporations in this era, industry in the United States needed workers that could fill these new positions.[31] In light of this, the complete stoppage of immigration through legislation like the 1917 Immigration Act or the 1921 Emergency Quota Act seemed unlikely. Put bluntly, literacy served to transform immigrants into workers who could be exploited, and literacy training enforced particular habits of work that kept workers from being too excitable or amenable to radicalization. This divide between exploitable worker and excitable laborer motivated the development of literacy classes, the desire to transform immigrants into worker-citizens. The imagined alternative, as demonstrated by the arguments in support of these classes and the materials used in the classes themselves, saw immigrants settled into enclaves and never truly becoming American, thus introducing a foreign element and threatening the fabric of the nation.

The explicit shaping of habits of citizenship reflected the anxiety surrounding immigrant populations, anxiety that also bore immigration legislation and restrictions during this same time period. While certain populations gained entry into the country, they nonetheless still needed to be "shaped," and literacy operated as one avenue to do such shaping through citizenship training. More broadly, literacy was being institutionally produced and regulated to a much greater extent than in previous immigration waves, particularly through the rise of public schooling and print media in the United States. Immigrants were sometimes literate in their own native languages before coming to the United States, but only a certain kind of literacy was deemed acceptable, as we've seen in this chapter, one that would engender a productive worker-citizen.

One longstanding consequence of this association of literacy and productivity is that literacy was (and is) seen as something attainable by the individual, echoes of which impact the view of literacy today. Literacy presents a rational and measurable path toward the achievement of citizenship, a path that appears to be accessible to anyone who makes the independent decision to pursue it. This appeal to individual attainment, achievement, and accessibility contrasts with a regime of immigration regulation (not to mention bureaucracy) that left—and still leaves—the pathway toward citizenship strewn with obstacles.[32] Unlike one's appearance or country of origin, literate ability, as learned through work practices, is changeable, and gaining literacy means being able to perform a particular construct of citizenship and be socially recognized. With literacy as a crucial aspect of their training for citizenship, immigrants learned a kind of individualism, making them solely accountable for whether or not they could gain full citizenship. Individual willingness to take up citizenship habits such as literacy determined immigrants' success at having full access to citizenship privileges and resources. Placing responsibility on individual actions and desires allowed for any poor treatment of new citizens to be concealed, making it the fault of the individual who did not fulfill citizenship's cultural requirements.

This shifted sense of responsibility subsequently conceals the "violence of literacy," as J. Elspeth Stuckey describes. Stuckey characterizes literacy as "a weapon, the knife that severs the society and slices the opportunities and rights of its poorest people" (118). When literacy acts as a marker in this way, it allows for these opportunities and rights to be distributed unequally but in a socially acceptable way, in a manner that conceals the violence. When these kinds of distributions are made according to who is literate and acceptable to the wide range of society, then the responsibility falls back on individuals. If they are unemployed, then perhaps they did not try hard enough to fit into the factory work. If they are sick, then perhaps they did not follow advice to eat well or sleep enough. All of these habits of citizenship become choices. Literacy, while slowly becoming a necessity in this period, was seen as a choice, one with benefits and consequences. The exclusion—the passed promotion, the shoddy work conditions, the poor pay—was a result of choice. In citizenship training, literacy was being used to regulate, but because of the way it became aligned with individual choice and good citizenship habits, it got concealed by a liberatory cover.

Citizenship training classes for immigrants in the late 1910s and 1920s served as a way to prepare workers and make them more efficient in order to fit into the new economic system that was developing. Literacy classes were used as a way to control beliefs about work and to enforce and reinforce how an American worker should act. This function of citizenship training classes was particularly important in light of the way literacy was being used by some immigrants. In fact, the lessons themselves kept immigrants from developing the "wrong" kind of literacy, such as the literacy practices promoted in union-sponsored worker education. The literacy taught here was bound up in obedience, good work habits, and voting rather than in agitation, protest, or identity. Literacy learning, the act of learning English, became permanently entangled with lessons about the habits of citizenship and more specifically, the work habits of an American citizen. Literacy is what brings hope but also rationalizes inequities; literacy is encouraged because it gives people hope that advancement is possible, while simultaneously putting responsibility for that advancement solely on the individual. By internalizing the messages taught by structures such as the citizenship and literacy training of immigrants, literacy has become valued in particular ways that make us feel as if we are liberated; yet while awareness and analysis can come with literacy, power does not necessarily accompany it, putting into question the liberatory hope of literacy.

In chapter 3, I examine the "wrong" kind of literacy, the threatening type that attempted to empower workers in the industrial economy rather than fit them into it, as did the literacy taught through the federal textbooks. The union education programs I explore in the next chapter injected hope into literacy learning with more of an emphasis on the collective over the individual. Along with the perceived power that literacy on its own supplied to people, these programs provided potent examples of how the structures that value literacy could also prevent literacy from being truly liberatory.

3

CLASS WORK
Labor Education and Literacy Hope

> It was in 1914 that a group of our members began to consider the ne-
> cessity of having our International [Ladies' Garment Workers' Union]
> initiate education—not the kind of education which was offered to
> adults with a view to making them more efficient and better workers,
> but rather the kind of education that would make them more intel-
> ligent workers and citizens of the community in which they reside.
> That group felt that since many of the workers leave school at an early
> age (before they have an opportunity to develop personality and gain
> character) and enter into the mills and factories and since under the
> strain of daily, continuous work they were apt to get out of touch with
> effective educational effort, that if our International would consider
> education as a part of its activities, they might bridge the gulf between
> childhood and manhood.
>
> —Fannia M. Cohn, "Our Workers' University," *Justice*, 23 April 1920

In the passage above from the labor newspaper *Justice*, Fannia M. Cohn, educational director of the International Ladies' Garment Workers' Union (ILG-
WU), explained the rationale behind the development of the workers' education movement in the United States during the 1910s and 1920s. To labor educators such as Cohn, workers' education was designed to help unionists become
"more intelligent workers and citizens of the community in which they reside"
as opposed to the "efficient and better workers," ones that would be obedient
enough to fit easily into the industrial economy, imagined to be produced by
other kinds of education, such as the federal citizenship programs discussed in
chapter 2. Cohn characterized labor education, which included the after-work
and weekend programs she helped to create, as education specific to the needs
of workers, designed to fill gaps in their education. And at the heart of this
characterization was a deeply held belief in the necessity of filling those gaps,
both literally (workers who did not have formal schooling) and figuratively
(workers were not well-served by the content of mainstream education), as a
way to harness the transformative power of education and literacy on behalf of
workers and their unions.

Cohn's articulation of how workers' education responded to these needs
more effectively than other kinds of education reflects the belief in education

and literacy learning as a labor strategy, one supported by the workers' education movement in the United States during the 1910s and 1920s. Analyzing discussions about the development, structures, and motivations of union-sponsored education from labor newspapers and other historical documents, this chapter explores why Cohn and other labor leaders promoted education as a strategy over other labor tactics and focused on the cultivation of educated worker-citizens over strikes, work slowdowns, and more overt tools for labor reform. Like the federal programs discussed in the previous chapter, some unions such as Cohn's ILGWU turned to education as a way to shape a specific kind of good citizen; in workers' education, these citizens were encouraged to develop habits (to return to Danielle Allen's term) that would help advance labor reform and other worker issues. In an effort to increase the efficacy of the labor movement, union education programs were imagined to meet the following goals: to supplement the public education union members did or did not have; to cultivate a working-class consciousness; to foster leadership for the union; to cultivate organizing skills among the rank and file; to create an educative space for workers where they could analyze the emerging economic structure, which would then illuminate the need for unions and the labor reform movement; and to allow workers to become as educated as the bosses, therefore leveling the playing field of negotiations between parties and within the public arena. By promoting habits and labeling such habits as "intelligent citizenship," the architects behind workers' education attempted to use the era's common discourse of citizen-making in order to cultivate citizens who would help strengthen the labor movement and introduce what were seen as more socialist ideals into definitions of U.S. citizenship.

Invocations of the citizen in these texts and the promotion of citizenship production are less explicit than in the federal programs, which were charged specifically with guiding immigrants down the legal and cultural paths to citizenship. Union education programs that promoted habits of citizenship focused less on political practices such as voting or cultural markers such as economic productivity of the individual and more on strategies, skills, and ways of thinking that would help guide workers to fight for recognition of their own contributions in industrial society. Organizers such as Cohn hoped to use education to cultivate "intelligent workers and citizens of the community" ("Our Workers' University") who were on equal footing with their employers, both in the workplace and the world, and would be able help the labor movement gain ground against what they saw as the growing power of industry. Workers' educational efforts were geared toward a unified labor-oriented education that would teach a "general education" curriculum (including English language

skills, reading, writing, argumentation, labor history, and economics) to laborers who were imagined to become more organized unionists as a result of this
education. In this chapter about how unions defined citizenship, I focus on how
leaders in the workers' education movement, specifically Fannia Cohn and her
associates from the ILGWU and the Workers' Education Bureau (WEB),[1] used
the teaching of literacy to publicly promote and circulate ideas about a worker-
oriented citizenship that focused on building collectivity and finding parity
with management, as opposed to a more individualized view of what such an
educational program could provide.

As in the federal documents discussed previously, literacy and proficiency
in English was seen as a gateway to other habits of citizenship. From newspaper
articles, planning documents, conference proceedings, and correspondence associated with the workers' education movement emerges a story about how labor leaders such as Cohn positioned literacy to help unions achieve the broader
goals of the labor reform movement, ultimately contributing to the valuing of
literate skill. Leaders of the workers' education movement hoped that the widespread literacy training they produced would help unions gain members and
strengthen their organizations, and additionally and perhaps more importantly, create a worker-oriented industrial citizenship that would encourage collectivity. Authors of these documents consistently imagined citizens who acted
intelligently, collectively, and on behalf of workers' conditions. The hope was
to inculcate habits of citizenship in the nascent industrial worker-citizen that
enacted civic responsibility to the union and its members.

In these conversations, literacy was imagined to play a central role in the
cultivation of what labor organizers saw as a full realization of a worker's citizenship. Labor reformers positioned literacy as a means for workers to acquire
and fully embrace the habits of citizenship defined not only in legal terms by
the naturalization laws of the United States, much like the Americanization
programs in the previous chapter, but more importantly, in the cultural terms
of the unions themselves. By encouraging the acquisition of literate skills, proponents of workers' education believed that the associated habits of citizenship,
like active participation in society and in the economy, would strengthen the
labor movement and act as a springboard to cultivate worker consciousness,
foster leadership and organizing skills among the rank and file, and alleviate
the hierarchy between management and workers by creating a more level playing field for negotiations. Labor reformers positioned literacy as a means to
accomplish these goals by helping workers gain control over their working situations, which I characterize as attempts to acquire full and equal citizenship.
By looking at the motives behind the literacy training for workers, I underscore

the unions' belief in a kind of literacy hope, in which literacy would work as a gateway to solutions for a multitude of issues for unions.

In a period fraught with anxiety over citizenship,[2] these programs represent an instance in which literacy was used to shape a labor-oriented citizen that was quite different from the compliant worker the federally funded literacy programs for immigrants were designed to construct. While development of workers' education emerged out of the same landscape of anxiety about citizenship that the federal programs did, their attempts to sort out the cultural and social meanings of American citizenship alongside labor struggles and the rise of corporations during this time indicates how important growing societal inequalities were to the American psyche. This growing inequality, especially between workers and employers, provided an opportunity to call into question the belief that Americans were all equal citizens; the discourse around workers' education leveraged that inequality to promote a labor-oriented version of citizenship. Additionally, the meaning of citizenship became even more important in the face of growing numbers of immigrant workers who joined unions such as the International Ladies' Garment Workers' Union, but were shunned from unions with more nativist tendencies (see Higham; Barrett). Unions attempted to mediate these tensions around citizenship and the question of whether workers could be equal citizens by developing literacy and citizenship programs as a means through which to distribute a discourse about citizenship that was rooted in collectivity and responsibility to fellow workers.

I use this example of the workers' education courses that took place after working hours or on weekends for full-time industrial workers as an opportunity to extend Anne Ruggles Gere's work on the extracurriculum of writing practices. With the publication of "Kitchen Tables and Rented Rooms: The Extracurriculum of Composition" in 1994, Gere brought attention to the "writing development [that] occurs regularly and successfully outside classroom walls" (78), which has launched an incredibly valuable tradition of research examining literacy education outside of formal school settings. Gere's recognition of the extracurricular has been influential on scholarship that investigates how literacy is learned in spaces beyond traditional school settings, underscoring the impact of the extracurricular when she describes how "the transformative quality of writing's performance speaks to the cultural work it accomplishes," as opposed to the "gatekeeping function" of writing that exists "within classroom walls" (89). Workers' education mimicked formal school with structures such as classroom-like settings and even the naming of its programs as "education" but, at the same time, was self-sponsored like the extracurriculum Gere describes. Yet while the concept of the extracurricular underscores the value of nonschool and informal avenues for the "cultural work" of literacy learning, it does not fully account for how extracurricular literacy can be hampered by external circumstances. In the case of workers' education, attempts to develop such programs were stymied in the face of fears of immigrants, socialism,[3] and self-preservation of a mainstream labor movement, all of which kept these programs from fulfilling what was imagined by its organizers. These resulting struggles to create credible programs in this atmosphere undercut the utility of the extracurriculum for individuals, who eventually found their programs faltering. While utility was far from the only value of literate skills, it was especially important when students had few resources or were trying to gain resources through education, such as in union-sponsored programs.

Workers' education, particularly the nonresidential part-time classes I study here, exemplifies the complexities behind making the extracurriculum meaningful outside the immediate context for its students. The dual work of union education programs—the cultivation of literate skill as well as external recognition of that skill—are crucial elements in understanding how nonschool literacy training can operate. Despite the belief that literacy skills would help improve the situation of workers and their unions, union efforts to legitimize their work (or recast the extracurricular into the curricular, to use Gere's terminology) also relied on the somewhat contradictory strategy of arguing that workers' education must have goals distinct from formal education in order to best benefit the union. This proved to be an ineffective strategy, as described in the last section of this chapter, in which labor education became marginalized even within the labor reform movement, ultimately undermining its hope of using literacy and education for worker equality.

In workers' education, literacy was used as a tool within a larger educational program to level the playing field in the face of growing social class divisions. The structures, motivations, development, and struggles of union-sponsored education programs were a response to the crisis surrounding the citizenship of workers who often struggled against their growing inequality within the burgeoning mass manufacturing economy in the United States. While liberatory in its goals, efforts to shape the citizen through literacy ended up being shut down through a variety of political and cultural circumstances such as fear of socialism and fear of immigrants. Motives behind literacy training for workers, such as the ones Cohn outlined, are reflected in how workers' education proponents constructed a belief in literacy as a solution, a "literacy hope." An examination of how the architects of these programs imagined literacy's goals and the resulting habits and obligations of a union-oriented citizen can help complicate how literacy is used as a tool in struggles for equality and the production of citizenship. By focusing on the motives behind literacy training for workers and the development of the unions' hope in literacy, I offer this union-oriented vision of literacy and citizenship in which the rank and file were potential citizens of both the nation and the union and were expected to use literacy for the benefit of fellow laborers.

The Rise of the Workers' Education Movement

The development of workers' education programs had its roots in the work-ingmen's colleges, clubs, and mechanics' institutes of the 1830s,[4] but the tradition waned over the next several decades until the early twentieth century. The resurgence of education for workers began in the 1910s as a response to a number of changing work conditions: the pressure of mass manufacturing as felt through technological advances and the advent of scientific management, the influx of immigrant workers who were perceived either as a strength or a threat to the labor movement, and decreasing worker autonomy. This period was marked by numerous labor struggles and attempts to gain fair working conditions particularly during an upsurge of strike activity in 1919 with threats of general strikes in cities like Seattle and a strike throughout the steel industry (in all, four million people in the United States were on strike at some point in 1919). Framing domestic labor conflicts were the Bolshevik revolution and the British Labor Party's plan for a New Order (Dubofsky, *The State* 76). To many, labor organizing was more than the conflicts between employees and employers but, depending on your perspective, a revolutionary threat or hope.[5] With both global and domestic attention to labor issues, unionists were increasingly active, but possibly suspicious, in the United States.

The rise of workers' education was one aspect of this increased union activity, part of growing union organizing and recruiting strategies in response to an ongoing shift from a craft-based to a mass manufacturing economy. Historian Richard Altenbaugh characterizes workers' education as a "modest but profound attempt by ordinary working people to conceive and support their own educational institutions" (3). Educational programs set themselves apart from the growing number of union organizing and recruiting strategies because workers' education provided an alternative that could cultivate union ideals like collectivity and class consciousness, but unlike other union activities such as strikes, slowdowns, and walkouts, do so in a seemingly less threatening or confrontational way.

Workers' education flourished, however briefly, because it was able to promote unionism while simultaneously tapping into Progressive era expectations of education and self-improvement, positioning itself as a way to supplement formal paths toward literacy with a labor-friendly alternative. Critiques about formal schooling were couched in proposals for such alternatives. As early as 1910, the American Federation of Labor (AFL) produced a pamphlet called "Labor and Education" that pointed out inadequacies of the public school system for workers and the need for workers to form their own educational venues. They argued, "Our school systems are giving only a one-sided education; the boy may go to school and prepare himself for professional or commercial life, or he may drop out of school and enter a trade with no particular preparation, and become a mediocre workman . . . while the public schools aim only at teaching professionals. . . . The greatest need of America, educationally, is the improvement of industrial intelligence and working efficiency in . . . the boy who will work with his hands" (13). This early discussion of workers' education made the point that workers needed to create programs more appropriate to their own needs than those provided by public schools. This AFL document provided a clear sense of the two different kinds of workers (the professional and the "boy who will work with his hands," much like the federal documents in the last chapter) and the necessity of two different kinds of education to meet their unique needs. While child labor laws and educational policy began to steer young people toward the public school system, unions such as the AFL and the ILGWU used this moment to organize their own classes because they felt public schools would not meet the needs of those who "work with his [sic] hands." Additionally, this passage invokes the popular idea of efficiency in their goals of the class-conscious worker. With public schools and colleges only serving to train "professionals" with their "one-sided education," union education offered a chance to cultivate worker-oriented skills like "industrial intelligence,"[6] setting the two modes of schooling against each other in order to argue the need for worker education.

As a result, these early beliefs about the inadequacies of mainstream education developed into a full-fledged movement by the end of the 1910s, culminating in the establishment of WEB in 1921 and the workers' education conferences they sponsored during the 1920s. Collectively, WEB and the ILGWU, and by association their leaders such as Fannia Cohn, had perhaps the greatest influence on workers' education because of their desire to actively promote it.[7] The pages of labor newspapers like *Justice* (published by the ILGWU) were filled with news of educational offerings, openings of residential labor colleges like Brookwood Labor College in Katonah, New York, and meetings about the development of worker education throughout much of the late 1910s and 1920s. *Justice*'s weekly page, "Educational Notes and Comment," made news of workers' education across the country, including notices and descriptions for classes, reviews of books, articles on worker education, and editorials.[8] As the educational director of the International Ladies' Garment Workers Union and a Workers' Education Bureau organizer, Cohn played an important role in workers' education during this period and emerges as a prominent figure in the ILGWU and WEB documents.[9] After an initial period of increased labor activity and disparate activities within individual unions, WEB formed as an umbrella organization in 1921 in an effort to coordinate multiple union education efforts. Serving as a resource for unions that wanted to begin educational programs for their members, WEB described their purposes in their constitution: "to collect and disseminate information relative to efforts at education on any part of organized labor; to coordinate and assist in every possible manner the educational work now carried on by organized workers; and to stimulate the creation of additional enterprises in labor education throughout North America" (*First National* 142). With the creation of WEB, workers' education seemed poised to make a bigger mark on workers and the landscape of unionism than it eventually did, and these goals, with their focus on consolidating, distributing, and supporting educational efforts, reflected a certain optimism about the scope and possibility surrounding workers' education at its inception.

The first objective in these efforts was to recruit as many union members to workers' education as possible to create a captive audience for the ideals presented and also to use workers' education to recruit potential members to the union. In order to appeal to the largest number of both current and potential members, union education programs took a variety of different forms—residential labor colleges designed for those on work slowdowns (an organized and purposeful slowing down of productivity), public lectures, plays, social activities, and more traditional classes that met during nonworking hours. Classes supported by WEB and the ILGWU were designed for full-time industrial workers and were held typically outside of work hours in the evening and on weekends, in contrast with the full-time residential labor colleges at places like Brookwood, summer programs at colleges like Bryn Mawr, and resorts like Unity House in the Poconos, which organized intensive sessions for workers over several weeks or even months.[10] Organizers also tried to increase accessibility for the largest number of workers by holding classes in multiple types of venues. For example, in New York the ILGWU established Unity Centers in spaces around the city where union members could easily attend free weekly classes in English, labor history, economics, and trade unionism, go to lectures on literature and art sponsored in conjunction with local universities and scholars, listen to musical concerts, and perform gymnasium work that could all fall under the umbrella of worker education, a union interpretation of the education that happened at universities. Courses were free to all dues-paying members of the union as an additional way to recruit new members.

The format of the more classroom-oriented educational activities was intended to set itself apart from mainstream education in its structure as well. Altenbaugh describes in his study of labor colleges how they "served liberating rather than adjustive outcomes," which was "in sharp contrast to the cultural and economic reproduction functions of the formal education system" (4). Part-time workers' education also strived for these same goals, reflected in the way the classes were taught. For example, the ILGWU program had "generally small classes [in which] teachers used a discussion format that emphasized problem-solving skills" (Altenbaugh 36).[11] With small classes and a focus on problem solving, workers' education deliberately distinguished itself from more mainstream educational venues, which were perceived to create a more industry-friendly student, like those channeled through the federal Americanization programs. Through this kind of structure, worker-students were taught they were gaining more control over what they learned and how they learned.

A 1921 editorial in the *New York Evening Post*, subsequently reprinted in *Justice*, speaks of the opportunity to let unionists, who were adult learners, have an influence on the curriculum, in contrast to how they imagined higher education. The author[12] writes: "These [labor] classes make use of special modes of teaching, special texts, and specially equipped teachers. Experience here and in England demonstrates that the classes cannot be autocratically controlled, as university classes usually are. They will not be satisfied with lectures, but demand full supplementary discussions. They insist upon open-minded attention to controversial economic and political issues" ("Colleges for Workers" 6). This passage illustrates the belief that not only was regular education inadequate to meet the workers' needs but also that workers would demand having a more participatory curriculum in order to satisfy and challenge their own educational needs and desires in the face of these inadequacies. In discussions like these that focused on workers' education, the word "education" was used to refer to a number of different educative goals, not just teacher-led lecture classes. Rather than simply pointing to the earning of a particular degree or being enrolled in a traditional school or university, "education" often referred to the special training process through which unionists would better understand their place in the economic structure and how their behavior should be shaped by that. This was an important distinction within the context of labor reform where literate skill was to be used actively, not simply as an accumulated credential.[13]

As a central part of this process, workers' education programs used small, interactive classes that emphasized participation over learning from an authority. In a speech titled, "What Can the Workers' Teacher Expect of His Students?" at the First National Conference on Workers' Education, Professor Broadus Mitchell of Johns Hopkins University told the audience, "In considering what effort the teacher of workers can expect of his students, it is hardly necessary to say that we have in mind not mass education, but instruction given to small groups made up of regular and earnest attendants, whether with the design of general cultural enrichment or of equipping union leaders and officials" (WEB 126). Mitchell differentiated the classes in workers' education programs as small and specialized, filled with dedicated students, as opposed to the mob of generic mass education. Mitchell, whose expertise and status as a university professor was noted, explained to potential students reading the article in *Justice* that the education found in unions would be dedicated to the needs of union members, underscoring that mass education would not do the same.

This kind of intimate and individualized classroom structure was made possible by the New York City Board of Education,[14] which provided public school space and instructors for many classes, an organizational system replicated in other cities like Boston, Philadelphia, and Cleveland. The ILGWU model of workers' education proliferated throughout other unions, with the support of WEB and the American Federation of Labor. In 1921, Evans Clark reported in the *Nation*, "Four years ago there were, in the entire United States, only four workers' educational groups. These were confined to two cities—New York and Chicago. Today there are twenty-six workers' colleges and schools located in twenty-two cities. . . . Workers' education, it thus appears, has definitely arrived" (670). The *New York Evening Post* reported on a number of colleges for workers, including the Boston Trade Union College, the Trade Union College of Washington, DC, the Workers' College of Seattle, the Rochester Labor College, the Baltimore Labor Class, the Philadelphia Trade Union College, the Pittsburgh Trade Union College, the Workers' University of Cleveland, the Workers' College of Minneapolis and the St. Paul Labor College, as well as ILGWU classes in a number of "small Pennsylvania cities, Amherst classes and schools with a social foundation, like the one for Finnish workers in Duluth. About 10,000 American workers are now regularly studying in their own higher institutions" ("Colleges for Workers" 6).

However, even when workers' education was growing, it was not a movement that unified labor reform organizations (although it strived to do so). Tensions within the labor reform movement around race and gender provided a telling backdrop for the development of workers' education. In particular, the debates within the labor movement about whether to organize as craft unions loosely aligned by an organization such as the AFL or as one large industrial union, which was favored by the more radical unionists in organizations like the International Workers of the World (IWW), can be mapped onto questions about who could be considered a citizen. Individual craft unions could use their narrow, industry-specific focus to close ranks and keep out certain groups of workers such as immigrants, women, and African Americans. In many respects, gaining the support of the AFL was both crucial in order for the workers' education movement to have a wide influence and impossible because of the associations of educational programs with immigrants and radicalism.

The AFL represented the most mainstream of labor organizations and had an enormous base that WEB wanted to reach—their membership rose from 1.7 million in 1904 to nearly 5 million in 1920. Samuel Gompers, the president of the American Federation of Labor, appeared convinced by the arguments of Cohn and other early workers' education supporters and gave significant support to the movement. An article on workers' education in the *American Federationist*, the AFL paper, included Gompers's views on the 1921 formation of the Workers' Education Bureau: "I regard the work of the Workers' Education Bureau as highly important. We must rely upon education in a very large measure for the advancement and development of our great movement. We must, through education, carry the message of organized labor to the members of organized labor" (Gompers 1080). But this support did not endure after the early years of the movement in the early 1920s.[15] Historian Melvyn Dubofsky describes the AFL craft unions as challenged by the "stable, semi-industrial, socialist organizations" (*Hard Work* 42) such as the ILGWU, which were often associated with workers' education. The threat the AFL craft unions felt had as much to do with the makeup of union membership as with suspicion about radical beliefs. These unions counted many Eastern and Southern European immigrants and women in their ranks, a demographic mix that was not as common in other AFL unions.

When the AFL membership numbers declined throughout the 1920s, its leaders worried that the labor movement was losing ground.[16] This prompted them to develop more accommodationist policies, with a belief that unions should work together with government and industry to create labor policy. The AFL feared appearing too radical to potential unionists and worked to make a clear distinction between themselves and the leftist unionists that embraced socialism and had ideological connections with international revolutionaries. These accommodationist sentiments led to the withdrawal of AFL support for workers' education because of its more radical undertones and its association with immigrant workers. In *False Promises*, Stanley Aronowitz describes how many leaders of the AFL saw Eastern and Southern European immigrants as "unorganizable, if not completely undesirable" (142), tapping into suspicions about the radical nature of immigrant labor in the United States. As opposed to native-born workers who were believed to be more loyal to the AFL brand of moderate unionism, immigrants were seen as both potential threats to gaining unity among workers because their cheap labor would weaken unions' bargaining power and also create barriers to garnering external support of the labor movement because of a fear of their "radical" beliefs. As a result, it was easy to undercut efforts that would help those populations become equal citizens and withdraw support in the face of accusations about radicalism that fed into the larger landscape of fear of immigrants. These attitudes against immigrants underscored a particular weakness in the workers' education movement in that it sought to bolster the labor movement through education; this strategy had limited appeal to more conservative or nativist constituencies because, by design, it sought to equalize the status of individuals and did not offer a way for the more established unions to sort out the desirables from the undesirables.

Workers' education strived to strengthen the citizenship of all laborers in the face of growing inequality, but its focus on those with tenuous citizenship status (or even citizenship potential) such as immigrants and women may have contributed to its eventual decline. While workers' education spread to unions in many industries, the prominence of immigrants eventually contributed to the belief that such programs were only for immigrant radicals and the cultivation of revolutionary beliefs. As will be discussed in more detail later, mainstream labor such as the AFL ended up discrediting workers' education in the face of the fear of foreigners and revolution, a widespread societal fear discussed in the previous chapter. Whereas citizenship cultivated through the federal Americanization programs were sponsored by the government, and by proxy the nation, workers' education was supported by the unions, a less stable sponsor with more tenuous backing. Even though the AFL monetarily supported WEB's work for a time, their support could not be sustained in conjunction with AFL's efforts to appear apolitical, especially when compared to the textile unions, which were the most active in the education movement, hoping to use education explicitly for political means and for the advancement of a union-oriented citizen.

The attempts of union educators to balance these different messages about what workers' education could yield for unionists, and determine what would be palatable to different constituencies, eventually proved to be a challenge, yet their efforts offer a useful example of the complexities behind using literacy and education for citizenship, especially when that citizenship was a departure from mainstream definitions such as those described in chapter 2. Union-sponsored programs, which included a curriculum of basic literacy classes, as well as classes on labor history, economics, literature, public speaking, physical education, and organizing, were used as a means to cultivate a labor-oriented citizenship that integrated traits like class-consciousness and worker identity.

Workers' education proponents forwarded the idea that literacy consisted of more than just the basic skills of reading and writing taught in spaces such as public schools and other mainstream venues of education. The goals for worker education stand in sharp contrast to the citizenship training programs that were run by the government and made explicit use of literacy toward Americanization and habits of citizenship intended to increase worker productivity. The contrast is not surprising, given the goals of each group. But these distinctions in how literacy has been deployed in the name of citizenship are critical for understanding how citizenship and literacy have become associated with one another for different purposes and goals.

Histories of worker education tend to focus on the ability of workers to gain control over their working situations through education. Richard J. Altenbaugh describes workers' education as serving a number of goals including the countering of "bourgeois hegemony—particularly that promulgated by the formal educational system" (32) and the training of union leadership. Following his characterization of workers' education programs, the next sections examine how architects of workers' education programs presented these issues in discussions about the programs and in recruitment materials and, despite waning support, remained committed to helping workers understand how education had the potential to transform their place in the industrial economy.

Worker Consciousness and Other Habits of Intelligent Citizenship

The belief that union education, namely the literacy and education of workers, could help unions create large-scale change in the labor market permeated discussions about the promotion of worker education. Labor educators believed that by educating members of the labor movement, they could advance their cause—in part by cultivating a shared workers' consciousness and a sense of collectivity, by strengthening leadership, and by helping workers gain intellectual and economic parity with employers.

"Intelligent citizenship," a common refrain in these documents, was used as shorthand for these different goals, and educational programs offered explicit training toward its cultivation.[17] At the 1921 workers' education convention in New York City, the first of a series of workers' education conventions that took place during the 1920s, Cohn described how

> those in charge of labor colleges must realize that the hope of the Labor movement lies in the increasing intelligence of the rank and file. Education and information must be the cornerstone of the society of the future. It is the intelligent citizenship in the unions—the rank and file—that will bring about an intelligent leadership. Hence, it must be understood that a workers' college

must organize activities for every group—for those who know very little as well as those who are advanced—for those who are the present leaders or will be the future leaders of the organization. (WEB, *First National* 42)

Proponents of workers' education like Cohn felt that union members would be better served if they were educated; the most talented of the rank and file could then become the future leaders of a now educated labor movement. Cohn's speech expressed how labor colleges were very invested in the idea that education could aid labor reform. The rationale was, as Cohn explained, that union members would be better served, both individually and collectively, if they were educated. Education was seen as the way to relay this message of labor reform, connecting the cultivation of a citizen with the cultivation of worker consciousness.

Workers' education was designed to transform unionists, not solely into productive workers like the federal programs, but rather into good citizens of the labor unions and eventually leaders of these unions. Labor educators and leaders did not simply envision the citizen as an individual member of a country, but also as a citizen of the union; the meanings of citizenship were changing along with developing industry and the developing labor movement, and unions sought to have some control over these meanings by educating their own members on what it meant to be a citizen. Historian Joyce Kornbluh provides some helpful orientation for how workers' education connected to "restoring or inculcating patriotism (of one sort or another) and promoting citizenship activities" (8). She argues that education worked as a primary mechanism to produce community through loyalty to the union. She writes, "The ideal bond of loyalty was construed in different ways—to God, nation, trade, employer, or class. The prevailing notion was that continuing change in an industrial society required continuing education to reorient and invigorate the dislocated worker" (8). Unions developed extracurricular literacy programs designed particularly for their members in order to cultivate community in a quickly changing industrial landscape and as an opportunity to create a sense of empowerment in the face of an evolving industrial economy as it shifted from craft production to mass production.

To the federal government, being a worker-citizen, for the most part, meant contributing to the economy as an obedient worker; to those in the workers' education movement, however, worker-citizen meant taking on a citizenship identity that had as much to do with being a laborer as it did with national identity. As a result, labor educators used arguments that linked citizenship habits and civic identity with a labor identity, thus connecting the enactment of citizenship with how people made their living. To labor leaders, the quality of a worker's citizenship was determined by qualities like worker consciousness that could be cultivated in the programs. In turn, union education programs tended to emphasize group and collective benefits with having a more literate and educated group of workers. Education was intended as a way to make gains in both of these areas: the individual and the collective.

The good citizen that workers' education proponents hoped to cultivate was one that enacted individual and collective habits of citizenship. Unlike in the federal training, the good of the individual and the group are positioned as equally important in union efforts. Often, a worker's position within an industry and his or her position as a citizen were placed together in recruitment articles that attempted to convince more readers to attend educational classes. A notice of events in *Justice*'s "In Our Educational Department" told readers that "as men and women and as citizens of a community, we are interested in all things that affect us, and especially as workers we are very much concerned with the main points of our industrial system" (Friedland 6). In "Classes Begin at International Unity Centers," Cohn touts education as a way to confront the social and economic problems they have as "members of a labor organization and as citizens of a community" (1). And in "Our Workers' University," Cohn described the difficulties and hardships that workers must "overcome while studying: the exhaustion of mechanical labor; the demand upon [their] leisure made by unregulated overtime . . . the irregular hours of employment," reminding readers that despite these hardships they must be overcome to perform "the many duties of [their] own class as a member of the Trade Union, as a citizen of a community" (3). The encouragement to become a citizen of a community acts as a refrain or talking point, its prominence pointing toward the importance of a model of citizenship that emphasizes membership in a community of workers and the contribution individuals might make to this group.

While workers were encouraged to participate in educational activities for individual benefits, they were always reminded of the greater social and economic system, how individuals fit into this system, and their potential to change it collectively. Union leaders publicly discussed the goals of workers' education classes both in print through newspapers and at conferences. These discussions demonstrate how these two threads within educational programs—the individual and collective—shaped a citizenship that appealed to both those who desired that individualized brand of American citizenship alongside the collectivity of the union. In this way, workers and education leaders tried to bring these two seemingly contradictory strands of habits of citizenship together.

Labor historian Susan Stone Wong describes this as "social unionism," which focused not just on the negotiations with employers but also encompassed "the workers' wishes for a general and wide-ranging education, for individual self-improvement, and for social and intellectual respectability, and for recreation" (44). A 1920 announcement for the beginning of classes in the labor newspaper *Justice* (Cohn, "Classes Begin") tried to show how individual gains would lead to group benefits by explaining that the classes would give "an opportunity for self-expression," but one that contributed to the "fuller understanding of the great social and economic problems with which they are confronted" by educating them "as members of a labor organization and as citizens of a community" (1). In the article "Our Workers' University," Cohn explained that the object of educational activities was "two-fold: individual and social. It is our aim that the individual be given an opportunity for self-expression and a chance to develop character and gain personality, and to get a fuller understanding of the great social, economic and philosophic problems with which is he confronted" (3). The use of "self-expression" in these instances reflects well-worn tropes of individualism within American citizenship, but it is an individualism defined by an understanding of the "social, economic and philosophic," using self-expression in relation to understanding society at large and the role of workers within it, as opposed to self-expression only for individual gains.

To Cohn in particular, self-expression was not solely an individualized activity, but one that allowed workers to develop their character in the context of understanding the social and economic context of workers in order to participate fully as citizens in American society and in the labor union. The common pairing of citizens' identities as self-actualized, to use a contemporary term, and as part of the trade union community signifies the connection labor leaders like Cohn made between the two identities and the belief that education could help improve the status of both. Labor and citizenship identities were juxtaposed with the individual's self-expression, implying a belief that citizenship was collectively and intimately linked to identity as a worker.

Beyond beliefs about collectivity, workers' education also used language that veered away from the creation of democratically defined citizens, instead positioning workers' education as creating citizens that understood and perhaps even indicted their place in the industrial economy. Much like Bryan Turner's characterization of citizenship as a structure to allocate resources, as described in chapter 1, the citizenship cultivated by workers' education used the inequality of these allocations as a way to argue that workers' education was a first step in a larger fight against the industrial economy. Workers' education could help to cultivate citizenship, not just for access to voting rights, but also to other citizenship practices in the form of resources like education or power over working conditions. At the First National Conference on Workers' Education in 1921, Bertha Mailley of the Rand School of Social Science named three primary goals of workers' education, illustrating how the citizens developed by workers' education could achieve economic parity by way of their training: "1. To make workers articulate. For thousands of years the majority of the members of society have [been] dumbly slaved. . . . 2. To train the workers as the directors of the class struggle. . . . and 3. To prepare definitely trained technicians and administrators in order to insure proper efficiency in the coming change of society" (WEB, *First National* 25). Mailley's discussion about the purposes of workers' education highlights many of the driving motivations for developing these programs. To workers' education proponents, education was necessary to make workers articulate, which would in turn allow them to free themselves from being "dumbly slaved" and to gain the power to change their status. The use of "slaved" suggests a comparison of workers' conditions to slavery, emphasizing the poor working conditions for unionists and the necessity for workers to use education as a way to unchain themselves from this reality. She also asserted that workers must be in charge of their own struggle and that education is the way to help prepare workers to negotiate changing industry. Arguments like these on the purpose of worker education demonstrate how workers' educational programs responded to specific tensions about the growing inequality between workers and their employers.[18] The organizers of workers' education often expressed a desire and need to use wide-reaching (and therefore, wide-influencing) education to help create a stronger sense of worker consciousness among laborers, attempting to persuade people that education was a necessary element to further class struggle and labor reform.

Sometimes, as in the Mailley excerpt above, the use of the language of efficiency seemed to reflect the culture of scientific management, but instead, educational leaders appropriated and used that language to talk about the need for educated workers to help strengthen the labor movement. An article in *Justice* titled "The Function of Labor Education" describes how this juxtaposition was presented in a 1922 appeal to union members: "It is our sacred duty to find these men and women, and give them the knowledge and vision which will enable them to serve their fellow workers efficiently. This can be accomplished best by further development of labor education. . . . Their doors must be flung wide open to attract as many of the rank and file as are sufficiently interested to enter. All of those who enter must be given proper training for they will be the great labor army of tomorrow" (10). Here, labor education was viewed as a means to reach a broad number of people, but it also expressed the obligation, the "duty," to extend knowledge to workers. The literacy that workers were imagined to gain through labor education would help cultivate in them the habits of citizenship that included a collective identity. Interestingly, the "proper training" of such large numbers of the rank and file were to be used in the service of "the great labor army," which could be read either as an invocation of a global Marxist movement,[19] or at least a reflection of the "one big union," an organizing strategy favored by radical laborers like those in the IWW who believed that workers could only make gains through unity across industries. Regardless of the degree to which the use of a "great labor army" was meant as radical or revolutionary, the reference to labor struggles as a battle speaks to the integration of power struggles into workers' education.

And as Cohn made clear, education was a weapon in the battle to gain equal citizenship. In "Labor Day Thoughts," Cohn developed this connection between workers' education and struggles over economic power even further when she wrote, "It is well for us to remember that while organization gives us power, education gives us the ability to use our power wisely and effectively, and that ignorance is essential to Industrial slavery; while knowledge is essential to industrial democracy, and the group which accumulates knowledge is the one which predominates in our economic and social life" (6). Here, Cohn asserted the value of education to labor organization; by associating ignorance with "industrial slavery" and knowledge with industrial democracy, Cohn presented industrial democracy as within reach for workers, imagining that knowledge, combined with union organization, would give workers the power to usurp economic inequities "wisely and effectively" as opposed to doing so through brute force.

Again, like Mailley, Cohn's use of "industrial slavery" is quite powerful in its comparison of workers' position to slavery in the United States. The stance that manufacturing work was establishing a system of "wage slavery" was somewhat common among leftist unionists during this period but not a comparison that was widely accepted.[20] She tempers what might be seen as an extreme position by presenting workers with a way out of this slavery: by overthrowing their own ignorance, they will be able to overcome. To workers' education advocates like Cohn, workers could use literacy and knowledge as a way to free themselves from wage slavery. These views, while overtly inflected with Marxism,[21] were also folded into American citizenship ideals about individualism, freedom, and control over one's life. The Workers' Education Bureau itself was formed in an attempt to mainstream these ideas and bring them to a wide range of workers; a critical step was to prove to the workers themselves that the education of workers was both crucial and unique to their livelihoods.

In order to make the idea of worker consciousness and worker identity appealing, program designers like Cohn employed many familiar themes about citizenship, education, and literacy with a sense of urgency that, at least in the beginning of the movement, would have interested the less radical laborer and those outside of the labor movement. An editorial in *Justice* titled "The Educational Work of the International" articulates many of the different ways the ILGWU and the workers' education movement developed exigency for the task of education:

> The activities of our Organization are conducted in an intelligent, democratic manner, where every enterprise, every new plan must find the support of the large membership. Such a system of course can only function to the best interest of the workers when the large majority of our members can think for themselves. And the more our rank and file think independently the safer will be the very life of our Organization. Education is the only means toward this end. The prime purpose of the Union must be in offering educational facilities whereby our members can develop their thinking capacities and be able to cope with the daily problems which life presents to them. That is why the educational work of the International is not a secondary matter. It has not a decorative value. It is a prime necessity. (4)

This editorial, which explained the urgency and necessity of workers' education,[22] also revealed some of the rationales employed by the architects of the movement who actively imagined what workers' education could do. Arguments about the transformative aspects of education relied on the expression of some familiar themes about the importance of education to a democracy and the fulfillment of democratic citizenship. By using phrases like "intelligent, democratic," the editorial invoked some core values of American citizenship in relation to workers' education. The democratic and intelligent practices in workers' education were intended to produce workers with the ability to be independent thinkers, who could "think for themselves" and "develop their thinking capacities." On the surface, these key goals sound quite similar to those of any democratic citizen, whether formed by the federal Americanization programs or contemporary literacy instruction. Yet the ability to think in the context of the labor movement, what contemporary instructors might call "critical thinking," relied on a worker-oriented citizenship.

Proponents of workers' education often used the idea of self-sufficiency and independent thinking as part of the workers' way of thinking in connection with discussions about the value of their programs. In a three-part series in *Justice* on "The Education of Class Conscious Workers," J. M. Mactavish wrote: "Because the aim of working class education must be the development and enrichment of working class consciousness it is imperative that the workers should build up, organize and control their own educational movement, while welcoming the co-operation of the finest minds willing to serve it. Such a movement must aim at equipping the workers to evolve their own social valuations, their own moral standard, judgments, codes of honor and fit them to give effect to their own conceptions of how industry and society ought to be run" (10). In this article, the organization of the union and the control over what is taught remain key strengths in the eyes of worker education proponents. While the article nods to sympathetic academics by mentioning the "co-operation of the finest minds," education, as designed by unions, remained squarely in the hands of workers and aimed to serve the needs of the working class, what they determined was useful for themselves.

In this way, workers' education could be characterized as taking on the mantle of Gere's "extracurriculum" because it established itself as teaching something beyond the normal curriculum. At the same time organizers wanted their programs to be equally worthwhile. And in doing so, they also expressed the *necessity* of validation when it came to the extracurriculum in this context. In their attempts to express the different and distinct educative goals that produced worker-oriented citizens, the authors of these pro-worker education documents established clear differences between the education needed by laborers and that offered by the public school system and other established venues of higher education. By arguing that workers' education was more appropriate for workers than that offered in other venues, they demonstrated the need for a labor-specific education to readers and for legitimacy of the extracurricular education being offered.

Workers' education proponents made the argument that union members made a particular kind of exceptional student, one who would benefit from a self-sponsored education program as opposed to mass education at any level. To these organizers, presenting the attitudes and intelligence of worker-students as being just as good as, if not better than, those at universities was a way to establish the seriousness and rigor of union-directed education. Louis Friedland, the educational director of the ILGWU and a former college educator, told readers "that we have a quality of students in our classes which beats anything that a former college professor has known in many years of experience goes without saying, and yet to the educational producer, quantity is a quality which is also desirable" ("In Our Educational Department" 4). By initially referring to himself as former professor, Friedland positions himself as having the authority to make comparisons between union students and college students. In another article, he speaks to the strength of the Workers' University in that those who enroll are not just "eager, earnest and responsive students," but also will benefit and take advantage of the opportunities afforded through education. L. M. Cosgrove, a professor at the University of Pittsburgh and the Pittsburgh Trade Union College, told conference attendees of the First National Conference on Worker Education that workers are easier to educate because "they realize more fully their need for an education" (WEB, *First National* 100), characterizing the worker as eager to learn, particularly in comparison to typical college students. He believed workers could understand the "serious nature of the social, political and economic problems that confront the world at the present time, and they are willing in consequence to work hard in classes, dealing with history, economics, sociology, law or government" (100). He talked about how "more care will in most cases be needed in this direction by the teacher in the workers' classes than by one in the ordinary college because the students in the former will be less 'standardized'—they will not have had any uniform previous training as have regular college students" (101). Their portrayal of standardization in traditional colleges evokes the language of standard mechanization and Fordism as was being used in industry. This admittance of workers not fitting in to traditional educational structures was embraced in order to create spaces for worker education as designed by workers.

These characterizations of union students produce a portrait of students in union education programs that are superior to college students in their eagerness, presence, and contribution to the greater "aim and purpose" of workers' education. Workers' education proponents attempted to demonstrate how their education was superior and more appropriate than mainstream education at every turn—from the exceptional quality of the students to the importance of a relevant curriculum to the necessity of a self-sponsored institutional structure. In doing so, organizers of workers' education often used language that paralleled those of their formal education counterparts but made their distinctions clear.

For example, workers' educators hoped that the union-designed education would make accessible to workers habits of citizenship such as democratic expression and participation as a result of its emphasis on workers' consciousness and habits of thinking. Sarah Shapiro, a student and member of the ILGWU, testified at the First National Conference on Workers' Education about how "When we begin to know the reasons why and ask questions, I believe we will begin to solve problems. If we know why we have to work, why the doors of the colleges are closed to us, why we are limited to a certain time for our education and for our pleasure, and begin to ask those questions, I believe that this will do a great deal to bring about real social progress" (WEB, *First National* 88). Shapiro made explicit the connection between the ability to ask questions and solve problems, or in union terms, to question the status of workers in the industrial economy and then figure out ways to fight against employers using the means available to workers as citizens. She also connected these industrial inequalities to inequalities in education, asking her fellow workers to confront the closed doors of colleges and other limitations,[23] to consider how union education would be able to achieve the goals of union work because they did not just teach rote skills to individuals as colleges did, but also because those skills could be meaningful in making "real social progress." Workers' education programs provided a space for workers to not only ask these questions, but also to *learn* to ask these questions as a way to strengthen a more class-conscious citizenship.

A number of arguments in favor of workers' education utilized critiques about the structure of higher education and how its curriculum was influenced by business and other external factors. By showing how traditional colleges were hampered by their institutional affiliations, organizations such as WEB hoped to prove how it would be impossible for colleges and universities to educate workers in a way that would help to bolster their citizenship and increase their status. In his speech to the First National Conference on Workers' Education, Cosgrove described how "the workers' college is, so far as America is concerned, a new institution and has not collected about it those traditions that sometimes interfere with the efficiency of instruction in our institutions of higher learning" (WEB, *First National* 100). To Cosgrove, the traditions of a college or university, such as grades, examinations, and diplomas "as an incentive to study" (100), interfered with learning, unlike the more genuine learning that he trusted took place in workers' education. It is interesting that he uses the phrase "efficiency of instruction" to describe the educational work being performed at labor colleges, which seems to underscore the lack of effectiveness of the rote education they imagined was being offered at institutions of higher education, places that would simply produce the most efficient workers for industry as opposed to the fully conscious students in workers' education. A profile of "Prof. Egbert of Columbia and Labor Education" maintains a similar critique about the structure of higher education in that "university professors are controlled and supervised by university authorities, who are in practically all cases controlled and supervised by trustees, whose economic interests are diametrically opposed to those of workers. The university professors cannot and will not give workers information, which might be utilized by them to weaken the power of these trustees" ("Prof. Egbert" 10). By positioning university trustees and professors as guarding the economic interests of the wealthy, of those who were already economically powerful, worker education programs established a space in which the working class could protect their own interests as workers.

With the cultivation of worker consciousness a primary goal of workers' education, an educated rank and file would help workers not only understand their place in the industrial economy, but also would provide them with the tools to organize and make gains against employers. As Frank Fenton from the Boston Trade Union Colleges told the First National Conference on Workers' Education, "This ignorance amongst ourselves must be fought before we can successfully combat the active ignorance of unscrupulous employers. For ignorance is a disease that is death and darkness to the mind. Education is the timely stimulant that will effect a cure" (WEB, *First National* 89–90). Supporters of workers' education such as Fenton and Cohn held up education as a means to fight a larger labor battle, one that usually took place on the picket line. They crafted these arguments about the need for a general education, one with a wide range of subjects that went beyond strike rules, to cultivate worker consciousness by talking about traits like collectivity while integrating American ideals like individualism. Within this general education for social unionism, literacy was held as one of the primary tools available to workers to accomplish these goals and to unions to transform the labor movement. The organizers behind these programs positioned literacy as a vital, foundational skill for the success of individuals but also for the labor reform movement because it would help foster loyalty to the sponsoring organization.

Using Literacy as a Gateway to Intelligent Citizenship

The training of workers I discuss here explicitly sought transformation, not just of an individual's skills but also his or her consciousness. Within these discussions about education for workers, the most overt imperative was for workers to learn English as a way to access this transformation. As we saw in the Americanization texts discussed in chapter 2, mastering English became associated with a number of other desirable habits as defined by the federal government. Similarly, literacy through workers' education helped shape habits of citizenship that would help support the labor movement. Workers were also told of the importance of gaining proficiency in reading, writing, and speaking, but their version of literacy was intimately and explicitly intertwined with the cultivation of union-oriented citizenship values, the "intelligent citizenship" discussed earlier. Literacy programs were "sold" to workers by touting these different transformations, cultivating ideals about literate skill as not only an individual action but also a collective one, or at least having collective benefits. Through rationales about how programs operated, organizers of workers' education used the promise of literacy as a way to promote class-conscious citizenship.

While literacy was not always explicitly named in union materials about workers' education (in fact, its opposite, "illiteracy," was used more often in the context of something that must be eradicated among workers, much like ignorance), the common presence of language learning classes indicates its importance to the larger curriculum. English classes were the only ones offered as a sequence, progressing from Beginner to Advanced to High School levels. The largest number of classes taught in ILGWU and WEB education programs was in reading and writing.[24] On one level, the expressed goals of English classes sound familiar and echo assumptions about attention to correctness and form that one might have about a writing classroom in the 1920s (see Connors, "Mechanical Correctness"). One course description for a public speaking class focuses on the correction of "defects," while several levels of English classes are described as being "organized under competent teachers where every member of the International will have an opportunity to know how to speak, read and write the English language" (Friedland, "In Our Educational Department" 6). The notice also tells students that this almost daily class (it met four evenings a week) "gives students a large amount of training in public speaking, composition, and literature" ("Educational Comment and Notes," 29 Jan. 1921, 6). A notice about a high-school–level class, the highest of the sequence, tells readers, "It is urged that more members of the International take advantage of the opportunity offered by this class to perfect themselves in the use of the English language." With these kinds of reports on workers' English classes in union publications like *Justice*, workers were informed about the importance of having good, even perfect, English skills.

But union educators intended for literacy to be more than a quotidian skill, not just for the individual worker, but also for what the skill provided to the organization—a means to enact wider labor reform practices and increase the efficacy and support of union activity. While perfection and correctness were important, they were not the only goals. Cohn described how in ILGWU courses "our students express their opinions and exchange views" ("Our Workers' University" 3). Within the context of labor reform, literate skill was to be used actively, not simply as an accumulated credential, but in the context of public speaking for the good of union organizing, becoming adept at writing persuasively about the condition of workers, and becoming culturally literate through the study of literature as a way to demonstrate that workers could be as learned as those with more formal education.

Considering the immigrant status of many workers in the programs, messages about learning English followed the general efforts toward Americanization during this early-twentieth-century period. On one level, unions were yet another party invested in making over immigrants into good citizens and suspicious foreigners into becoming acceptable Americans because unions were invested in getting American society to view all of their members as citizens.

But their more explicit efforts to use literacy as a tool to strengthen the labor movement, which did not fall in line with, for example, the way literacy was being used by the federal Americanization programs, indicate a specific hope in connection with making their members literate. Like the Americanization programs discussed in the previous chapter, there were elements of these educational programs that specifically targeted immigrant and illiterate workers. An article in *Justice* called "Our English Classes" told readers that "it is needless to say that those of our members who intend to join the classes realize very well that without a good knowledge of the ENGLISH LANGUAGE they cannot be useful to themselves, to their Union and to the Labor Movement. They must know the language of the country in which they live and work. Otherwise they cannot express themselves effectively and they cannot voice their ideas for the advantage of their fellow workers" (10). Like Angelo from the federal citizenship texts who gained a promotion after being seen reading the company bulletin board, immigrants were told here that their literacy skills would provide them with tools for individual economic success. But while this passage did tell readers that the English language was useful to "themselves," the emphasis was much more on the "union," the "Labor Movement," and "their fellow workers." In contrast to the federal Americanization texts that forwarded a much more self-interested idea of literacy, articles like this one associated knowledge of the English language with the ability to "express themselves effectively" and "voice their ideas." While the federal textbooks connected literacy with a promise of promotions and raises and being able to provide for family, these union classes wanted to instill a literacy associated with benefits to the labor movement instead of solely to the individual, which could help workers help the union, by being more persuasive advocates and organizers.

Many calls from workers' education supporters promoted the belief that basic literacy alone could not serve workers by incorporating references to the developing industrial democracy; becoming literate also meant learning labor history and economics, which would help to promote a sense of worker consciousness among students. The belief that literacy served as a gateway to this kind of transformation emerged in force at the First National Conference on Workers' Education in 1921. George Snyder, from the Musicians' Union in Reading, Pennsylvania, discussed the meaning of worker education and how it should push beyond traditional expectations of basic skills. He told this audience of union leaders and workers, "The workers are creating a new education. The aim of this new education is to prepare the worker for complete living . . . too many of us think of workers' education as if it meant only to read, write, and use a few figures" (WEB, *First National* 92). As he talks about the hope that workers' education would help to cultivate "complete living" for workers,

Snyder's sentiments highlight the belief in literacy's impact on lives beyond the ability to "read, write, and use a few figures." In workers' education, the "complete living" represents the full citizenship, which is more than just one single practice or status, but rather a number of habits of citizenship. A realization of full citizenship for workers cannot be achieved without the critical literacy that they are creating for themselves, particularly in the context of the inequality of the growing industrial economy.

This all-encompassing approach to education made literacy a crucial component, indicating that the hope in literacy was a way to help workers realize their full citizenship. Workers' education programs went beyond a basic skills orientation and taught the fundamentals of "economics, labor history and problems, and English" in connection with "a broad education" ("Educational Comment and Notes," 22 July 1921, 6). Such a broad education that "encompassed the workers' wishes for a general and wide-ranging education, for individual self-improvement, and for social and intellectual respectability, and for recreation" (Wong 44) could help unions shape the full citizenship of its members. These classes operated as a space to instill workers with functional to advanced literacy, depending on their proficiency, but also provided an English language arts education in conjunction with other subjects. Through the use of the term "broad education," organizers hoped to convey that the programs would not just instill a discrete body of knowledge, but also have a "broad" influence on how students in the classes would interact with the world around them. Basic literacy classes acted as a gateway to both other educational offerings like economics and labor history and to union membership; together, these would help to transform worker consciousness. To be sure, the schools taught basic language skills, and these classes were popular, but more crucially, workers who were already considered literate and those who became proficient in English were encouraged to develop something that today we might call "critical literacy," connecting the activity of reading and writing to understanding their position in the industrial economy, which is why many of these skills-oriented classes were taught in conjunction with economics or labor history. Doing so was designed to help cultivate what Cohn called "social unionism," which saw unions as not only negotiating for work terms, but also attending to the "the building of a union to the creation of a new and better social order" (Wong 43).

With social unionism as a goal of this wide-ranging curriculum, the promotion of literacy among workers was a necessary preliminary goal. Algernon Lee from the Rand School of Social Science believed that the goal of literacy training was necessary in order to prepare workers for the broader and transformative curriculum of history, economics, and political science. He observed,

"The teaching of English spelling, grammar, and composition must necessarily occupy much of our time. This leads on to public speaking and debating and to parliamentary law" (WEB, *First National* 114). These more advanced skills, the benefit of more basic literacy, were important because it was expected that unionists wanted to run their own meetings democratically, but also wanted to understand the government better, to participate more effectively as citizens, as well as be more successful in their negotiations with bosses. Lee implored people to understand how literate activities are related to other subjects: "But the public speaker must not only know how to say something; first of all he must know just what he wants to say. This involves training in the art of research, and also straight thinking and getting one's thoughts into the minds of others" (114). If workers could hone their skills of argumentation through public speaking and debate, then it was hoped that they could more effectively transform not only their own thinking but also the thinking of others like employers, political leaders, the public, as well as other workers, about the value of labor reform. Lee and others often expressed this clearly articulated sense of the power that advanced literacy could have for the labor movement through promoting a more educated stance in the public sphere; the skill of literacy was not just important on its own but indeed, there was the sense that one must do something with it to make it truly valuable. The emphasis of union leaders on literacy learning beyond basic skills and as a gateway to other topics underscores how union programs differed from other educational programs because students were expected to do something to support the union with the skills they were taught, and in turn the skills would ultimately benefit other workers too. The end goal of the education of workers was, then, to strengthen the labor movement.

With the broader goals of workers' education in mind, the arguments of union leaders about why workers should learn English also expressed a desire to draw the individual and collective ideals of citizenship together. The repeated theme of education's promise to give workers more control over their work conditions and equality with their supervisors melded with literacy as a personal skill with its broader consequences for the labor movement and for working people who were struggling in the workplace and battling over labor reform. In his "Topics of the Week" column in *Justice*, Max M. Danish drew on this dual promise of literacy as he tried to recruit new students from his readership by arguing, "Not only is a knowledge of English an advantage in the industrial world; for the advancement of the trade-union movement in America as well as for personal benefit it is advisable that each one should have as much English in his control as possible" (2). These common refrains about literacy, the need to learn English, and the possession of control spoke to the tension between being a subordinate at one's job and viewing education and literacy as a way to make gains, whether personal or collective; English was necessary to gain an advantage on the new battlefield of the industrial world. Danish's remarks position literacy as a powerful resource that workers needed to acquire and distribute in order to alleviate this tension and gain both personal benefit and collective power.

Because one of the goals of literacy and literacy training was to shape the identity of workers with little formal education or immigrants who were not literate in English while simultaneously providing them with English skills, rationales for English classes for workers relied on the necessity of English skills in order to be a good union citizen—one who would not be taken advantage of by unscrupulous bosses and as a result put other workers at risk for the same type of exploitation. These documents repeatedly employed themes of ignorance and of being duped by manipulative bosses as a way to convince readers that knowledge of English for workers and the teaching of English for unions were vital activities to the broader movement, making appeals for solidarity and group identity. An article in *Justice* from 1921 called "Learn English" emphasized this point by telling potential students that without a worker-oriented literacy they were setting themselves up for exploitation. It discussed the importance of why "the American worker must know the English language. He lives in an English speaking country; he is placed in an English-speaking environment. He deals with English-speaking industry" (6). But in addition to the imperative to know English because of living in an English-speaking country, the author warned that "without an adequate knowledge of the language in this country, the worker is at the mercy of unscrupulous persons who take advantage of his ignorance, and exploit him easier than those who speak it" (6). The standard and typical arguments about needing to know the language of the country where one lives develop into more union-oriented discussions of fear of employers' exploitative attitudes, which would affect both English and non-English-speaking workers. When discussing the learning of English, writers mounted arguments to convince unionists that the workers who did not know English might be easily manipulated by bosses; these arguments demonstrated how worker education would be beneficial to individuals but also for all workers as a group. Union educators argued that workers who knew English would not want to establish a situation where non-English speakers unknowingly underbid them in the labor market, convinced by duplicitous bosses to work more and earn less than their English-speaking counterparts.[25]

A letter to the editor published in *Justice* from a student, M. Roll, Local

25, expressed these sentiments: "If the workers were educated things would be very much different from what they are today. In other words, every worker would feel competent and capable of being his own supervisor. An illiterate worker cannot take advantage of the many opportunities that are offered in this great world" (Roll 6). The writer[26] believed in the benefits a worker could gain from literacy, gains with political and material consequences in the job situation, which echoes common arguments for worker education and the transformative effect it would have collectively, not just individually. Through the letter-to-the-editor genre, Roll contributed an authentic voice as "a student" to the discussions,[27] rather than those of educational leaders, who presumably penned the remainder of the educational news. When Roll said literate workers would "feel" competent and capable, the implication is that they would not be so willing to be in the subordinate positions in the industrial economy because they would more fully perceive injustice, that "things would be very much different," specifically, that workers would be more in control of their economic situations. To that end, the value of literacy for workers did not just lie in attaining the skill of literacy, but rather emerged from a desire to be equal to their supervisors, as democracy promised, and more importantly, to keep from being taken advantage of by their superiors and eventually gain the power to supervise themselves.

Underlying this argument for the learning of English was the pervasive belief promulgated in *Justice* and other pro-workers' education outlets that if workers just had knowledge, whether through language fluency or through advanced literacy or by understanding industrial history, they would be able to overcome industrial and economic inequity. Union educators saw literacy as having the power to do this. Recurring themes in discussions and promotion of union education include, not surprisingly, which course content and means of dissemination would strengthen labor reform the most. This goal to develop a worker consciousness and identity through educational programs predates what present-day readers might characterize as a Freirean approach of liberatory education, or even an enactment of a kind of "literacy myth," to use Harvey Graff's term, because union educators made the connection between the learning of literacy and a specific kind of empowerment in workers' lives.

While lack of English skills defined illiteracy for some (like the federal government), union discussions sometimes avoided and even contested the labeling of non-English speakers as illiterate.[28] In his address to the ILGWU convention on 12 January 1920, Louis S. Friedland, the educational director of the ILGWU, described what workers could achieve with their literate skills and the consequences of illiteracy to the labor movement. In a discussion about the complications involved with educational work, he compared the U.S. workers' education movement with that in England: "Thousands and thousands of them cannot read or write the language, so that these folks are really illiterate; and others cannot read and write the language, so that all are in need of some sort of education, but they have the advantage of knowing the spoken language. In America the situation is entirely different. Ours is a cosmopolitan country" ("The Bases" 5). Because many of the men and women educated by the unions in the United States did not speak English as a second language but were literate in their native language, he portrayed American workers as more educated and literate than their British counterparts. In this, he implied the ease with which American workers could be educated because they already were educated, even if they did not already know English, but also pointed to the challenges to workers' education because of the language difference that the movement in England did not have. By labeling immigrant workers in the United States as already literate, Friedland put them (his audience) in a position distinct from the "really illiterate" workers of England who created a successful and effective education movement, despite their illiteracy. These distinctions blurred the lines among American workers who were considered literate, illiterate, or proficient in English; sometimes these labels could be used to describe a single person's abilities. Yet despite the labels put onto workers, union education supporters targeted all members, regardless of their literate ability, wanting to tap into the potential to be empowered that was perceived to exist among American workers.

Union students were portrayed as distinct from more traditional students because they had more potential to use their literacy beyond mere mechanical skill. Broadus Mitchell of Johns Hopkins University, an ally of workers' education, believed workers were at an advantage compared to those with more traditional school education because they had something at stake in developing their writing and communication skills. At the 1921 conference on worker education, he sums up many of the pertinent issues and characteristics surrounding workers as students:

> Writing is hard for the majority of the most advanced students; for the worker who lacks in primary training it may never become a simple matter. The chief obstacle in the way of the ordinary written exercise is that the student, with however excellent knowledge of form, has insufficient equipment in fact. He knows perhaps how to say it, but has nothing to say. Here the worker is better off. His maturity and industrial experience, even without a complement of book information, gives him a foundation to build upon. And it has been found that the mechanics of writing are soon mastered under these conditions.

> Grammar and rhetoric and spelling are subservient to the insistence on ideas. Requirement of certain reading and preparation of papers, sympathetically assigned by the teacher, will not discourage a class of workers, but will add to the zest of the undertaking. (WEB, *First National* 127)

With the emphasis on the experience and maturity the worker brings to writing and on the "insistence on ideas" over grammar, Mitchell places workers at an advantage vis-à-vis more typical college students, encouraging workers to see their strengths as they enter the classrooms from which they might feel alienated. Here, literacy is also used to engender a labor reform movement that was trying to change specific work conditions. When Mitchell uses the phrase "class of workers" and emphasizes workers' ideas, he also reflects a transformative movement that was attempting to foment a widespread ideological shift in workers as a group, seeing education as a way to cultivate a working-class consciousness.

But more importantly, unions also believed that if workers acquired the habit of thinking by becoming literate, the newly literate rank and file would understand the need for the solidarity of workers in labor reform efforts. They often demonstrated this through testimonials from workers who had benefited from worker education programs. Mollie Friedman, a needle worker, made this sentiment clear in a 1918 address to the AFL convention.

> I am a product of that education. . . . Working at the machine or sticking pins in dresses does not do much for the education of the members, but after my work was done, I was offered an opportunity by my organization to study in a school and learn in classes where I was taught the philosophy of trade unionism, taught the history of the Knights of Labor, the American Federation of Labor, the history of the trade union movement of England, France, and Germany and other countries. . . . Our International found that teaching girls how to picket a shop was not sufficient, and they taught us how to read books. (ILGWU, *Garment Workers Speak*)

Later in her speech, Friedman tells her audience of the value of education, not just for the individual, but for the labor movement: "When I was asked to join the union, I felt I had to join it, but now I feel that I would give my life for an organization that will educate its members." Friedman offers an authentic voice of the worker, an enthusiastic "product of that education," telling other workers of the value in what she has learned. Rather than just viewing workers' education as merely instrumental, Friedman describes how unions did more than teach her how to "picket a shop." Rather than just a venue for agitation, the union portrayed itself as a place to learn how to read books, for education, for literacy, which would help to transform a worker's way of thinking as opposed to just thinking of him or her as a body on a picket line.

Friedman characterized these classes as an "opportunity" which, in addition to being a space for workers to learn how to fulfill the responsibility of citizenship, also served to recruit workers to the unions themselves. When Friedman described gaining access to books like labor histories, literacy was positioned as acting as a gateway to other union ideals. The use of English proficiency served as a kind of gateway, to not only other union-oriented habits of citizenship, but also as a gateway through which to bring new members to unions like the ILGWU, who had many immigrants in their ranks; presumably immigrants would start taking English classes and then become interested in engaging in even more union activities as a result. Union leaders wanted to foster spaces for immigrant workers to learn English and become literate, and they provided education as a way to recruit them to the unions. Literacy was positioned as a way to access opportunities, allow workers the opportunity to lead themselves, have control over working conditions and gain agency, and keep other from taking advantage of them.

But Friedman also provides an interesting example about the balance between consciousness raising and indoctrination, and this line is often straddled in efforts to convince others about the value of workers' education. Workers' education organizers touted the transformative power of literacy, implying that literacy had a great deal of currency among certain union members. But the constant persuasive element in these materials also indicates that people needed to be reminded of literacy's importance, both those who did not yet believe educational activities would help to facilitate labor reform as well as those who suspected such goals were too radical.

Marginalizing Labor Education

By looking only at program growth as a measure, the efforts of the worker education movement seemed to be effective. The numbers of students and programs grew with the inception of WEB and the organized strategies of individual unions like the ILGWU and the Amalgamated Clothing Workers' Union. Yet the pronouncement of the success of workers' education and the rise in numbers obscured many of the tensions between the radical and conservative factions of the labor movement.

Despite hopes about what literacy and workers' education could do to transform the labor movement, workers' education as a significant program weakened and definitively departed from its more liberatory roots less than a decade after the formation of the Workers' Education Bureau in 1921, a high point that represented the widespread support of the labor unions. Richard Altenbaugh blames the decline on "internal political disputes throughout the 1920s." He explains that these internal disputes among unions about how radical or political an organization should be were much more detrimental than external ones they might have with business interests, and "ultimately altered the fundamental aims of union education, particularly among garment workers. Fierce political conflicts, initiated by Communist members, undermined financial stability and sapped union strength. The ILGWU, as a result, had little energy to divert to long-term schemes for educating workers; it was too distracted by the very struggle for existence" (40). The converging influences of internal and external politics, views about the women and immigrants connected to the movement, and the influence of a politically charged atmosphere all contributed to the process of marginalizing workers' education, a situation that might illuminate some of the enduring roadblocks for groups who hoped to cultivate spaces for extracurricular literacy, particularly in the context of using literacy for power and liberation.

As discussed earlier, workers' education proponents attempted to position their programs as a means to transform and empower workers, and thus the greater labor movement. But the essential tension that undermined this main tenet of workers' education was whether such a transformation should emphasize illuminating and edifying the individual citizen or strengthening the power of a group of workers. If workers' education followed the lead of international labor organization movements, they might choose collective action, but the U.S. context and widely held beliefs about citizens emphasized the importance of the individual. This question exemplifies the primary friction that developed within unions and labor education specifically by the mid-1920s, ones that influenced the work of the labor movement at large. Radical factions saw union education as a way to acculturate worker consciousness and dedication to the movement, as described here. More conservative or accommodationist members of the labor movement became suspicious of how education was being deployed, marking the beginning of a shift in what unions wanted education to do for their ranks, the kind of citizen they wanted workers' education to produce. These tensions developed around negotiations of how a worker-citizen was being defined by the labor movement at large. The definition moved between whether the worker-citizen was more than just a citizen who worked or rather a citizen who embodied a worker consciousness. With its citizen-building and citizen-producing mechanisms, workers' education programs simultaneously offered a threat and a solution for a mainstream labor movement. Depending on what kind of citizen being imagined, workers' education could have widely disparate goals, ranging from a tool for self-improvement or recruitment to a radical, strife-inducing mark of social disruption.

The process of marginalizing workers' education by labeling it as radical eventually led to a less vibrant, less assertive education for workers. Significant cracks in the workers' education movement began to show when the AFL and WEB was forced to publicly deny any radical goals under increasing pressure and accusations from other union leaders. Matthew Woll, vice president of the AFL, responded to accusations in publications like *The Railway Review* that WEB was spreading revolutionary propaganda on a "large scale" and was "under the control of labor leaders, ex-college professors and college Bolsheviki" (Woll 9). Such accusations and the resulting defenses stoked anxieties about the growing influence of eastern and southern European immigrants who populated the unions most involved in worker education.

Spencer Miller Jr., the secretary of WEB, also denied such accusations and any formal associations with the Socialist Party of America, the Rand School, the New School, or the League for Industrial Democracy, among other organizations that were seen as revolutionary and many of which were early supporters of labor education. In response to these allegations, Miller told the *New York Times*,

> It is concerned primarily with the promotion of adult education among working men and women in its country. It will not nor has it given its support to any form of propaganda. It is not interested in teaching people *what to think, but how to think*. It asserts that education is a continuous process and should parallel human life. It believes that in our modern industrial world, knowledge increases more rapidly than our understanding and that one of the functions of the workers' education movement is restatement briefly and simply for working people some of the fundamental social and economic problems of the day. ("Says Workers' Bureau" 23)

Miller's denial underscored what became a common belief about labor education by the early 1920s—that these programs were clearly aligned with a radical doctrine, in turn producing an education that told people what they should think. Given Miller's insistence that this was not the case, that these programs wanted to teach "how to think," his response indicated an explicit departure from the initial, more radical hopes attached to union education. And more so, his response reflects the fear of radical implications in the face of the ever-present Red Scare pervading the 1920s United States. Labor historian Wong writes that "the link between workers' education and social action that had so vitalized the [ILGWU educational] department during its early days was strained by the general conservatism of the 1920s" (51). The association of unions as part of the threat of communism marked the beginning of a split among supporters of education for workers—those who felt that worker consciousness should remain a goal of worker education and those who thought that the radical undertones of education were a liability for the labor movement at large.

As the controversy about the radical goals of workers' education developed, the AFL threatened to withdraw support for WEB at its 1923 convention, a move that was averted ultimately because of statements like Miller's, distancing WEB from any kind of cultivation of worker identity and shifting the construction of the worker-citizen closer to that desired by business, that of the citizen who works. Of the public defenses by the AFL and WEB, the *New York Times* reported that WEB did not endorse Soviet recognition and that it "went out of its way to prove it would have nothing to do with radicalism" ("Workers Twice"). This movement away from overtly political education and developing worker consciousness can be partially attributed to pressures from the AFL. The Workers' Education Bureau had used its association with the AFL in order to reach the organization's numerous members, but in practice, the AFL's influence ended up contributing to the deterioration of the movement. Aronowitz notes that during this time period, "the AFL leadership were caught in the interstices of the big-business offensive and their own desire for institutional survival" (233). While education was a possible avenue to preserve the number of members because such a service would be a means for recruitment, the AFL also dedicated itself to eradicating any radical associations for the same self-preservation reasons. Because the AFL had to fight off any radical associations for the sake of its own survival, the result was a workers' education movement that needed to decide whether it was going to continue to pursue its more radical agenda or support the mainstream labor movement.

Discussions in support of workers' education began positioning educational programs as a means to battle radicalism and socialism internally, in contrast to externally fighting new industrialism, mass manufacturing, and unscrupulous employers—the initial goals of worker education. A 1925 *New York Times* article on the increase of labor education activities reported that "the future of such a movement has vast potentialities. Socialism bulks large on the horizon. That is inevitable, panaceas having irresistible attraction for inexperienced minds" ("Labor Seeks Education" 16). So while the number of activities remained on the rise, the nature of the education itself had shifted, driven by the need to separate the work of education with socialism. Rather than incorporate socialist ideals like collectivity with markers of American citizenship, workers' education was positioned as helping to rescue "the darkness of inexperienced minds" from socialism rather than from unscrupulous employers.

By the end of the decade, only eight years after the formation of WEB, this turn away from socialism to more mainstream and individualized ideals about citizenship was the norm, rather than the exception. The 1929 Report of the Committee on Curricula at the Workers Education Bureau Convention gives some more compelling details about this shift in focus of workers' education over the course of the decade. In a discussion about the distinction between adult education and workers' education, WEB reports that adult education "tends to neglect the distinct place of workers in society." They write, "Workers' education, on the other hand, should give expression to the conviction that the mission of workers is to establish individual democracy and to reconstruct society on a basis of cooperation and for the happiness of the man" (WEB, *Sixth National* 1). The emphasis on the individual here—individual democracy, the happiness of the person, and cooperation (meaning cooperation with management to try to work out agreements as opposed to strike or take other kinds of disruptive action)—lies in stark contrast to the arguments surrounding workers' education at its formation with discussions of class struggle against employers and industry. While these themes about individualism were present in earlier years of the organization, they took a backseat to ideals like transforming worker consciousness. This moment marks a significant shift as the leadership of the educational movement made a definitive move toward emphasizing habits of citizenship that affected the individual most directly, rather than laborers as a group.

Even one of the main founders of the workers' education movement, Fannia Cohn, publicly supported the move to make workers' education a more individualized and less collective endeavor in an effort to sustain support for the workers' education movement. This meant moving the curriculum away from "thinking" and toward the more practical. By 1929, she was urging "that the material taught should be of practical assistance to their industrial and trade union experience when they are on the job, and to this end recommend that plans be devised to make a study to enable us to know where and how the workers translate their educational experiences back into practical situations, quite as we seek to have their practical experiences expressed in educational work" (*Sixth National* 5).

Cohn's own attempts to keep workers' education out of the fray and above the political battles between socialists and communists, between the ILGWU and more mainstream unions, and by diminishing any associations with radicals resulted in a less potent program.[29] Wong describes how courses on the political economy were replaced with less highly charged activities and writes, "The belief that workers' education would train workers to create a new world became increasingly tenuous as classes in the social sciences were replaced with trips to museums and Broadway shows. Whereas Cohn had once designed programs to help unionists deal with the world in which they lived, she now increasingly offered entertainments to help them escape it" (Wong 51). At this later date, Cohn emphasized the practical in addition to the cultivation of a working-class consciousness, perhaps an indication of the reception of audiences to established arguments for workers' education and the difficulties with making social unionism come to fruition.

The original emphasis on worker consciousness unwittingly created a target, particularly in light of the fear of socialism and communism in the 1920s. As a result, mainstream labor organizations like the AFL, and pioneers like WEB, seized on fortifying this weak spot by trying to recast how the worker-citizen was being constructed through education. Supporting workers' education through the consciousness model became more of a liability than an asset, as demonstrated by the AFL's subsequent influence on workers' education programs and public rejection of Brookwood College in 1928.[30] As the AFL continued to associate education, communism, and propaganda, there was an implicit separation of mainstream labor unions from socialists. Interestingly, the AFL positioned the literacy and educative work of WEB as products of immigrant radicals as a way to force worker education programs in the 1920s to take on a less radical stance.

This trend of alienating socialists reflected the persistent marginalizing of women, African Americans, and immigrants in the larger labor movement, one that ended up replicating itself in workers' education. At the heart of these tensions were racial suspicions and distrust, the belief that nonwhite, nonmale workers were the ones who were underbidding "real" workers, those who made up the majority of union members, particularly within the AFL.[31] Wong describes how the change in goals from worker consciousness to more "individual enrichment" meant that "No longer were garment workers foreigners spouting radical political doctrines in strange tongues" (55), which served to integrate and assimilate those foreign-born workers who were not completely excluded from unions. While these exclusions of immigrant or politically radical members cannot wholly explain the decline of the workers' education movement, these factors certainly contributed to the decline of its efficacy and growth, particularly with the proliferation of less political part-time classes, which workers could attend after the work day was over. In contrast, the initial workers' education documents and programs imagined the possibility of a literacy training integrated with an overt and progressive political position, a belief that such programs could shape conceptions of citizenship and consciousness.

Workers' education and its originally conceived curriculum, of course, lived on beyond the activities of WEB described here, such as full-time labor colleges like Brookwood, but for the immediate time after the decline of WEB, they often were focused more on parliamentary procedure and collective bargaining elements rather than on literacy and the teaching and learning of English such as in the after-work programs.[32] Labor colleges were full-time endeavors for fully committed unionists who would become leaders[33] and targeted many fewer workers than programs like the ILGWU's. And weekly and local programs, which could reach a larger number of workers, became more vocational and had less ambition to transform the way workers thought. But in neither the after-work programs, now focused on the idea of practical education, nor in labor colleges, which carried on the mantle of a broad education, English speaking and literacy was no longer used as a gateway to the transformation of the mind, but rather took on more utilitarian purposes.

So while workers' education still exists in many forms today, by the end of the 1920s, a more fully articulated workers' education movement that cultivated a worker-defined citizenship had drifted away from its original purposes and structures that Cohn and her colleagues established for workers and for the labor movement at large toward a more general and vocationally oriented education program. The hope originally put into these programs and the teaching of literacy as a key component of that larger vision fell victim to these discriminations, allowing this venue of transformative education to become closed to workers.

Literacy Hope for Worker-Citizens

The construction of the worker-citizen through education began with the belief that organized labor could use literacy and education to counter the effects of a mass manufacturing economy, namely a highly stratified society in a country that exalted the equality of all citizens as an ideal. But the dispute over workers' education is ultimately about the kinds of worker-citizens that different factions of the labor movement wanted to cultivate—whether it's a matter of strength in numbers or strength in worker consciousness—which ended up thwarting labor's attempt to reconcile republican ideals in the face of growing economic stratification.

The citizenship promoted through union education is that of the industrial democratic citizen. While voting rights and other legal obligations were important, so was the imperative to find additional ways to influence industrial society for the benefit of workers collectively. The kind of comprehensive worker education I have been discussing connected basic skills like reading, writing and public speaking to other topics like economics and history as a means to further the everyday living conditions of union members, both as workers and as individual citizens. In addition to cultivating individual citizen voices through the development of literate skills, union education programs called for an understanding of the union member's place in the industrial democracy and provided a structure—the union—under which these opinions and ideas could be enacted. As seen in their writing in *Justice* and other venues, proponents of workers' education consistently imagined citizens who acted intelligently, collectively, and on behalf of workers' condition. The hope was to develop habits of citizenship for the nascent industrial worker-citizen that enacted civic responsibility to one another, as demonstrated through the numerous connections between literacy and the raising of a collective consciousness made in the pages of labor newspapers, at conferences, and other venues. These habits contrast with those developed by the Americanization programs discussed in chapter 2, which constructed citizens as highly individualized political and economic entities instead of members of a community with shared goals and aspirations.

Unions constructed meaning around literacy, connecting it intimately with the success of the movement for a number of reasons including the cultivation of leadership in the ranks, the recruitment of more educated workers leading to a stronger and larger labor movement, and the acquisition of intellectual equality with those in power such as bosses and politicians. Yet while the workers' education movement appears to present a historical precedent of training for critical literacy, one which takes up notions of the public and citizenship in explicit ways, I hesitate to hold them up as a model for contemporary writing classrooms. One cannot take practices out of context; rather, the importance of these programs lies in the opportunity they provide for understanding the complexities behind nonschool and politically oriented educative sites and why they never thrived in the way their organizers had hoped.

Union education provides insight into how different constituencies used literacy to imagine citizens and the terms of their citizenship. Labor education gives the modern day reader more than the opportunity to reflect on how to encourage civic participation through literacy training, but also a lens through which to understand the underlying struggles over literacy training to begin with. To return to Bryan Turner's view of citizenship as a practice that determines the flow of society's resources, the union literacy training programs were an attempt to gain ground on the everyday citizenship of workers, citizenship that union leaders saw being threatened by mass production and factory work.

Labor unions hoped that the widespread literacy training they offered would help them gain members and strengthen their organizations, and additionally and perhaps more importantly, create a worker-oriented industrial citizenship that would encourage collectivity and thus a more equitable society.

The emergence of the worker education movement complicated common beliefs surrounding literacy and the learning of English as skills that were somehow enforced by the powerful toward a particular model of citizenship, one that accepted political parity without economic parity, and ignored how legally conferred citizenship status masked other inequalities and imbalances in the opportunities for full citizenship as access to society's resources. Workers' education attempted to unmask these assumptions about the equality of citizenship. By becoming more educated, workers felt they could gain the practical and intellectual tools to negotiate for labor reform; these tools were intended to complement (and sometimes even compete against) other labor reform strategies like strikes, walkouts, slowdowns, and legislation. But also, in an abstract sense, workers invested valuable time and energy in literacy training, often after exhausting workdays, because they hoped to make employers view them as equals. This more intangible goal was not new to union workers, of course, and is, indeed, foundational to the idea of American citizenship itself.

Questions about the equality of citizenship permeate various kinds of literacy training, even in its most elite forms. In contrast to the literacy training within Americanization programs and union education programs, higher education offered literacy training to those who appeared to have less tenuous citizenship status, but the curriculum was still rooted in developing a class of workers and easing broader societal anxieties.

ENGLISH AND USEFUL CITIZENSHIP IN A CULTURE OF ASPIRATION

n his 1916 *English Journal* article "The Outside of the Cup," Louis Rapeer from Pennsylvania State College (now University) asked English educators, "What are you contributing in the way of knowledge, habits, ideals, and appreciations to one or more of these dominant aims of education? . . . What about citizenship?" (382).[1] He questioned whether the focus of English courses should be obtaining knowledge of a particular body of work or the form of language, or as he put it, studying the vessel itself or what lies "outside the cup." He believed that teachers "have the greatest opportunity . . . to mold the character of the American people; their chief fault, which we attempt here to dissect and diagnose in order to cure and prevent, is that of not discovering and realizing their peculiar function" (379). Rapeer's belief that the English curriculum had a particularly powerful influence in creating Americans in the late Progressive era reflects broadly asked questions about education and its influences during this period. Although Rapeer focused on high school teachers, he also articulated a set of concerns that animated curriculum shifts in the discipline of English at the college level; namely, an indictment of composition for addressing issues outside of the classroom and the boundaries of literature and language—for being too "engrossed in the contemplation of the outside of the cup" (379).

Contemporary scholars and teachers in English studies may certainly recognize this tension between the study of literature and the teaching of writing, between what is validated as knowledge and what is seen as a form of correctness. For Rapeer and his contemporaries, these questions about the goals of an English curriculum and the content of that curriculum reverberated against larger questions about the expansion of higher education and the simultaneous role of education in certifying a certain population of young people as middle class (at the very least). Educational historian John R. Thelin explains how at this time "college-going was rising in popularity, for several reasons. It was a means of socioeconomic mobility and hence an experience coveted by an increasing number of adolescents. In addition to increasing earning power, a bachelor's degree was perceived as a way for a nouveau riche family to gain social standing" (155). This flux, in which institutions were moving away from exclusively being spaces for the elite to perpetuate themselves, shaped a new role for higher education.

Educational historian David O. Levine characterizes this attitude toward education around the First World War as being steeped in the "culture of aspiration," which guided the expansion of higher education and changes in curriculum and structure to help facilitate education's new role as a social engine. Levine claims that this culture of aspiration "stimulated an unprecedented demand for higher education of any kind as a symbol of economic and social mobility" (21). While enrollments did not increase in the same way they did during the post–World War II years (the era most commonly associated with the realization of mass and public higher education),[2] Levine contends that in this early-twentieth-century period, higher education shifted from a space that reinforced social and economic status to becoming a space intertwined with increasing one's social and economic standing.[3]

In terms of how this culture of aspiration influenced curriculum, Levine describes how, "after World War I, institutions of higher learning were no longer content to educate; they now set out to train, accredit, and impart social status to their students. The curriculum became inextricably tied to the nation's economic structure, particularly its burgeoning white-collar, middle-class sector" (19). This did not mean that vast numbers of young people from a variety of backgrounds flocked to universities and colleges, but there was some expansion in terms of numbers. Thelin reports that, "whereas fewer than 5 percent of Americans between the ages of eighteen and twenty attended college in 1917, over the next two decades that figure increased to 15 percent" (205). So while not every young person was attending college as a way to enter the middle class, particularly in light of race and gender restrictions at many institutions, that number was growing. The culture of aspiration developed around college attendance such that education was establishing itself as a more common way U.S. citizens attempted to gain class and social status. With the development of an increasing number of private and public institutions and a corresponding number of students wanting to attend and benefit from higher education, institutions distinguished themselves with their curricula and their admission standards in order to establish themselves in this newly evolving role as social engines, producing a broader group of citizens as opposed to a reproduction of status for the elite.

In the two previous chapters, literacy training programs designed for immigrants and for workers as sites of citizen production illustrated how citizenship was often defined in terms of productivity, economics, and advancement. Architects of these programs positioned literacy as a crucial component of the newly styled American citizen and cultivated a kind of citizenship that incorporated literacy as an essential tool in the fulfillment of equality and democracy by way of also shaping work habits and attitudes. In these Americanization programs and union education programs, students were imagined as worker-citizens who, respectively, could either be conciliatory toward employers or stand up and fight for workers' rights. Literacy teaching and literacy classes provided ways to distribute messages and, depending on the course of study, offered a means for advancement at work or to negotiate for fairer working conditions. These programs encouraged citizens and potential citizens to take up literacy in order to fulfill a promise of equality and democracy; regardless of whether this promise was realized, architects of these programs positioned literacy as a crucial component of the newly styled American citizen, one with carefully cultivated work habits and attitudes.

In contrast to the productive citizenry of new immigrants discussed in chapter 2 or the transformative citizenry of union members that was the goal of the training examined in chapter 3, the university-oriented literacy studied in this chapter illustrates how the concept of citizenship was used to construct a burgeoning middle class.[4] This definition of citizenship focused on lessons of productivity for individual social mobility and stability with a particular emphasis on a more middle- to upper-class population alongside those aspiring to use education to reach those class statuses. The making of middle-class or upper-middle class citizens at universities and colleges was not entirely divorced from the citizenship production in other more contested spaces. But the citizen-making work of the writing classroom and the increasingly public university, coupled with the economic and political landscape of the United States helps us to better understand how literacy for economic advancement or stability, and the belief the citizenship could be defined as such, was perpetuated through institutions of higher education.

Discussions about curriculum and writing instruction played out in the pages of *English Journal*, and organizational reports from the National Council of Teachers of English (NCTE) provide a picture of how the professional organization saw the discipline of English fitting into higher education more broadly. Kelly Ritter pronounces these early publications as serving "a valuable archival function" because they give a way to "look into various programs and program attitudes and philosophies from a range of institutions and institutional types" (51). The formation in 1911 and the early publication years of the *English Journal* coincided with the anxiety-ridden period discussed in previous chapters during which federal Americanization programs and workers' education programs were flourishing. The publications by the NCTE offer a way to examine teacher practices and get a glimpse into how they saw themselves responding to the needs of students and the role of the English classroom, as shaped by the external circumstances of the time.

In particular, their deliberations on the usefulness of the writing classroom provide valuable insight into the motivations of teachers and subsequent associations of the writing classroom with the citizenship-producing enterprise, an association that has continued in its current twenty-first-century incarnation. As with the sites discussed in chapters 2 and 3, this connection of literacy to the production of citizenship relies on the imagining of the student subject as a useful citizen, with literacy serving as the means to cultivate a kind of assurance for future productivity. This argument was most often made in relation to work, namely how English classes would or should help prepare students for life outside the classroom. In this, we can see the pressure being exerted, both in high school classes and in college classes—education not just for education's sake, but also with a certain specific and practical utility.

Through its publications, the NCTE reflected a desire to understand how the discipline of English could serve the public. In particular, the *English Journal* and its discussions about the usefulness of the discipline reflect an anxiety about the status and responsibility of English departments, as well as how English teachers were proposing to carry out these more public goals. The NCTE's connections and shared dialogue between high school and college educators in the early years leads me to characterize their concerns as consistent with a more broad-based approach to English teaching, one that married what was happening in the college classroom with what was going on in the secondary classroom. The NCTE itself was formed out of concern that high school curricula were being unduly influenced by the required readings lists of colleges, but even so, the establishment of credentialed high schools during the early twentieth century set themselves up to prepare a wide and aspiring population for college, even though only a limited population was actually attending at the time.[5] The NCTE addressed the role of English in a college education, but because its main membership was secondary teachers, what was happening in higher education became inextricably linked to public high schools, thus giving an underlying sense that philosophical discussions about usefulness, access, and education for all applied to the discipline of English in both the high school and college context. The boundary between the two, particularly in discussions about the purpose of the discipline of English, was fluid.

As with the literacy learning of immigrants and workers, the attainment of literate skill in institutions of higher education, particularly with those public affiliations, emerged out of institutional expansion and an increasing demand for higher education. In this period, the ideas of mobility and aspiration became embedded in the ethos of academic writing courses, bolstering the literacy myth itself, as described by Harvey Graff. School-based literacy is not just about developing literate skills, but attaining the credential that would help you advance or at least maintain your social and economic status, particularly in the face of political or economic instability.

The architects behind first-year composition addressed such goals by taking up issues of citizenship and work and highlighting the circumstances that would support this kind of literacy training and the importance of the accumulating value of advanced education. Language skills made visible the effects of a college education, particularly in the workplace. Facility with language showed that one was worthy of the label of being literate, of being college educated. Instructors demonstrated clear concern for cultivating these everyday practices of citizenship through various teaching approaches and conversations. The ability to analyze and communicate was seen as an integral goal of the writing classroom to help students succeed as both citizens and workers. Teachers' discussions about pedagogy during the NCTE's early years demonstrate how societal concerns about citizenship manifested themselves in classroom practices that were intended to shape students into a certain model of citizen, and teachers imagined literacy skills as a means to accomplish this goal.

A Public Turn in Higher Education

As a result of the shifting terrain of higher education at the beginning of the twentieth century, writing teachers tried to fit into and respond to both populist and economic influences on their classrooms and produce citizens through a more useful curriculum. Much like the Americanization programs described in chapter 2, institutions of higher education worked to address the growing number of students—and the growing number of different kinds of students—who wanted to go to college.[6] While histories of higher education often note its expansion in terms of numbers of institutions, numbers of students, and curriculum shifts (see Levine, Rudolph, and Thelin), they also track the influence of restrictions on institutions; in particular, they document the attempts of institutions to specialize in more specific ways (liberal arts, research institutions, public institutions, and so on) and their subsequent restrictions on policies like admissions. These rising higher enrollment numbers and the expansion of higher education led to the need for institutions and the disciplines within them to stake a claim on their purpose, which Levine describes as a "steady process of internal differentiation" (162). Some institutions became more elite, such as the Ivy League, and others developed specialized reputations like normal schools to train teachers, liberal arts colleges, or even major state schools that sometimes emulated the more elite institutions (Levine 162). Their specializations often developed in response to efforts to make institutions more efficient and to respond to vocational demands, such as in the growth of normal schools. The specialization and expansion of institutions grew simultaneously alongside restrictions, particularly in admissions, to presumably help preserve the reputations of schools. Simultaneously, anxiety emerged about who was going to be college educated, who was going to gain the status of citizen through what was once an elite institution, the gates of which were opening, leading to various restrictions.[7] Levine describes how "in the 1920s, once collegiate training had come to be viewed as a critical avenue of economic and social mobility, it became important to exclude from elite schools those individuals and social groups deemed to be of inappropriate background and character to take advantage of the opportunities and privileges afforded by a college degree" (148), citing the rise of College Board examinations as a specific strategy to keep Jewish students out. These restrictions directed educators to be more explicit about what kinds of students they wanted to produce. In this way, institutions of higher education were influenced by the same changes in the world, such as immigration shifts and changes in work that existed outside the walls of the academy.

While specialization and reputation-building led many institutions to make their admission standards more strict, Levine writes how "urban and public institutions offered new courses and new hope to those who clamored for an opportunity to move up the economic social ladder," in contrast to selective liberal arts colleges that saw themselves as a check against the "undesired democratization" that these more public institutions provided (21). One such exception to the restrictive admission standards of institutions during this period was City College in New York City, an example of an explicitly public approach to higher education. While City College was something of a rare breed during its time in that many other institutions were excluding the immigrant populations, particularly Jewish students,[8] that City College accepted, it nonetheless provides an important example of nascent efforts toward establishing a more equitable public education. They (and institutions like them) demonstrate how populist values were infiltrating higher education and, in turn, the writing classroom.

In a broader sense, what came out of this moment was a growing belief about the role of higher education as a critical part of the social engine as well as the idea that higher education needed to be not a space to perpetuate privilege, but rather a space to increase social status or at least maintain it. Levine describes how higher education became possible for more young people, but still maintained its role ensuring "class status" for those who wanted a "step up" the economic ladder or an "insurance against a step downward" (219). The aspirational ethos of public institutions began to emerge in the period around World War I as they fulfilled this role of class and status supporter. In addition to the influence of vocational and population shifts, part of this can also be explained by Progressive era thinking that made an impact on general attitudes toward education. In *Progressive Politics and the Training of America's Persuaders*, Katherine Adams describes how Progressives targeted school reform at the elementary school level and sometimes high school, but not at the college level (37). However, attitudes about college writing instruction were also influenced by late Progressive era ideals, although often combined with attention to economic mobility and achievement (Berlin, *Rhetoric and Reality* 58).

The belief that educational institutions could be spaces to create citizens within this more public view of higher education went beyond the Jeffersonian ideal of citizens as leaders and tapped into more populist views about citizenship. The presence of citizen-making as an explicit goal of higher education is not nearly as present in the World War I and Progressive era as it was in the years after World War II[9] but what is particularly interesting about the earlier period is that in addition to the restrictive influence of citizenship controversies such as those over the status and access of immigrants, some institutions of higher education shifted to a discourse of public responsibility and increased student populations beyond the elite, particularly publicly funded institutions. In the early twentieth century, the institution of higher education was not seen as the means to gain democracy and equality in the same way that twenty-first-century students and teachers might see it. But during this period, institutions began to lay the groundwork for a belief in public education for a mass number of the population, a way of thinking that developed substantially in the middle of the century. For the most part, higher education was still reinforcing an upper-class version of the citizen, but there begins to emerge some elements of general citizenship production, not just reproduction of status to its role as an enforcer of status.

Thinking about who higher education should serve and how it should do so affected not only individual institutions but also stakeholders with interests in the broader impacts on institutions, people, and the profession. Educational historian Lawrence A. Cremin writes, "As education came increasingly to be seen as the principal engine of an 'intentionally progressive' society—the phrase was Dewey's—interest groups with divergent views of what society ought to look like staked their claims upon education and in the process politicized education" (154). Founded in 1911, the newly formed NCTE was one of these groups, representing English educators and publicizing how their concerns intersected with the production of citizens in an "intentionally progressive" society. Groups such as the NCTE formed as a way to ascertain what the study of English was supposed to be, whether a cultural foundation, a basis for good citizenship and communication, or a stamp of preparedness for education and the workplace.[10] During the early twentieth century, when English departments were still establishing themselves and higher education itself was expanding, members of the NCTE made arguments for why the study of English should be a critical component of advanced education and what that study should look like. At their core, these discussions parsed the desires for what an English class should be, but also offered a sense of the rationale for the teaching of English, the values that were supposed to be imparted through such a class, and the external demands put upon the course. As an organization, the NCTE articulated how to teach English and distribute literacy, which were inflected with these larger debates about the contributions—productive, cultural, or otherwise—that citizens should make.

Robert Connors characterizes the period between 1890 and 1930 as a "consolidation period" in which "lessons/exercise format [was] perfected on the secondary level, and then feeding the resulting product into an increasingly centralized mass textbook market" (*Composition-Rhetoric* 84). And while Berlin describes other "schools" like the rhetoric of liberal culture and transactional rhetoric between 1910 and 1920 (*Rhetoric and Reality* 43), he also tends to consolidate the teaching of writing into the current-traditional approaches. Because this period overlaps with a time of citizenship anxiety discussed in the previous chapters, I contend that this period, rather than one of consolidation, actually reflects the flux and turmoil found outside the college classroom; this turmoil is evident in the NCTE's sustained introspection about what the profession should be doing. For example, in November 1917, Esse Hathaway discussed the necessity of ongoing revision for the ever-present English course at an NCTE meeting in Chicago: "The nature of the subject determines that this must be so, as ever-shifting demands of our American public and the varying cosmopolitan make-up of our student body cannot be satisfied with a fixed course in English. . . . Flexibility combined with steadfastness in scholarly ideals appears as the exceedingly difficult achievement of an English course of study in an American school of today" (526). Hathaway demonstrated the complexity of "ever-shifting demands" of the course; teachers had to fit the needs of different kinds of students and the demands of the public and had to contend with the difficulty of "flexibility" while upholding a scholarly ideal. Yet Hathaway believed this was "the nature of the subject." He not only acknowledged the variety of burdens put upon the discipline, but also expressed a desire and a sense of responsibility to meet these burdens through revising and assessing how English was taught in the context of a changing world and a changing educational system.

Rather than the insularity one might expect in the conversations of a "shrunken in-group of mostly Midwestern teachers" (*Composition-Rhetoric* 101), as Robert Connors describes the NCTE until 1930, cooperation and dialogue among a variety of instructors, particularly those high schools and public colleges with goals more explicitly connected to public concerns, characterized these discussions. In the early growth years of the organization, its broad-based influence must be acknowledged. The organization performed national work with the Bureau of Education in studies like Hosic's *Reorganization of English in Secondary Schools*, Edwin Hopkins's *The Labor and Cost of the Teaching of English in Colleges and Secondary Schools with Special Reference to English Composition*, and John Mantle Clapp's *The Place of English in American Life*. The working committees that issued such reports were composed of a mix of high school and college faculty. Additionally, the pages of *English Journal* reflect a body of teachers who were not just midwestern but from a variety of institutions, both public and private, secondary and college. The 1913 *English Journal* published an editorial entitled "The Constituency of the *English Journal*," which described subscribers ranging from high school teachers to college professors, heads of departments, and libraries around the country. While the *Journal* obviously had a vested interest in making something out of the NCTE community, I do think that the variety of subscribers, many of them in positions of power, reflects a perhaps small but diverse group of interested parties, many from public institutions. It is also worth considering that many of the articles in the *English Journal* are reprints of talks given at larger meetings, both national and regional, held several times during the course of the year, which widened the audience even further.

The intersection between high school and college goals—debates about what an English department was supposed to be doing and the decisions made over how teachers should accomplish these goals—illustrates the multiple paths that English departments could have taken at this moment, whether an emphasis on college preparation, work training, cultural improvement, or citizenship training (and I would argue that citizenship training would encompass the rest). The growing connections between high school and college, as well as subsequent efforts to disconnect the two, indicate a further expansion of the idea of higher education for all. While one of the reasons the NCTE was formed was to mitigate the influence of college on high school curricula, such connections were already being forged, most prominently demonstrated by these efforts to keep them separate. In 2011, Erika Lindemann describes how the "NCTE was able to establish itself and grow because the personal and professional relationships among its founders and the representative structure they built for the new organization encouraged college and school teachers to collaborate" (514).

Such collaboration was necessary because the shape of English studies and writing instruction in both high school and college were profoundly affected by the establishment of uniform requirements and entrance exams such as the one at Harvard. Schools developed different kinds of exams in the last two decades of the nineteenth century that eventually consolidated into the Uniform Entrance Requirements (Applebee 31).[11] From these discussions about the influence of entrance requirements and exams emerge two main issues: the content of the requirement and the influence the requirement would have on high school teaching. The Uniform Entrance Requirements were a result of other colleges and universities following Harvard's lead to codify the kind of preparation high school students needed for entrance. The separation and then dominance of literature over other aspects of English studies, including composition, in these requirements established a hierarchy of knowledge with composition as the gateway to the more important work of literary study. In the years that followed, the establishment of the universal writing requirement for college students, English studies, and the development of composition at the universities evolved to fit into the needs of the twentieth-century university and its efforts to be relevant to a wider population of high school graduates.[12]

As a result, the English class no longer had the simple undertaking of "teaching English," if that belief in simplicity ever meant anything in the first place. In "A New Task for the English Teacher," published in the *English Journal*, Emma J. Breck, a teacher from Oakland High School in California, wrote:

> Education is no longer the comparatively simple process of a few generations ago, when the same kind of training sufficed for all. With the realization that different classes of society have different needs, and that we must meet those needs or perish from our own hospitality, has come the development of varying types of schools, and in place of the old academic college-preparatory school,

or side by side with it, has sprung up the agricultural school of the country districts, the various vocational schools of the city, each trying to meet directly and quickly the most crying needs of the students to whom they minister. . . . For instance, in English work, boys and girls this country over are forced to plod their too often weary way through fields marked out by the universities and colleges, regardless of whether they ever intend to go to college and of whether the work fits their immediate needs or desires or has in it any permanent vitality for the future. (66–67)

Breck's article articulates the pressure high schools felt from elite colleges who were putting too much influence on what should be taught. In particular, educators and policy makers were debating about what would ultimately be useful for the majority of students, and teachers recognized that not all students were going to go on to the same kinds of colleges, or even college at all. Of course, this is why the requirement was implemented in the first place, to establish a standard of student allowed into the college gates, all in the face of larger shifts in the American population. But because of the growing attitudes toward higher education as a public good that everyone should be able to access, the English classroom, often the universal class, became a space where these tensions came to bear on the institution.

The English Classroom as a Citizen-Making Space

In chapters 2 and 3, I mapped out how literacy was used as a way to respond to anxieties about immigrant populations and as a means of guiding Americanization efforts and encouraging particular habits of citizenship. The English classroom was no exception in taking on this mantle of creating American citizens. As the goals of higher education articulated by teachers, administrators, and policy makers became more focused on shaping a larger part of the citizenry, the curriculum followed along with it, developing more vocational training with majors such as engineering and business to meet the preparatory desires of a growing student body in addition to the more classical arts and letters curriculum. By the 1910s and 1920s, most college curricula were based around the elective system with a major and some general education requirements to provide flexibility to a broader student population (Rudolph 192; Veysey 10). The elective system expanded during this period, which increasingly included literature courses, yet what remained was the required writing class and the location of English composition (and sometimes speech) at the core of a liberal arts curriculum (Wozniak 147).

Even though the composition course was not a wildly popular teaching assignment within English departments,[13] the universality of the first-year writing requirement made English departments a logical conduit for the mission of citizenship production that was taken on by the entire institution, much like we might see it today. Foundational beliefs about English departments as citizen-making spaces, a belief that often still permeates the rhetoric of our scholarly mission statements, has strong roots in the period around the First World War with its anxieties about the growing numbers of immigrants and shifting work expectations. Particularly in the face of these anxieties, the ubiquity of the writing requirement allowed departments to demonstrate how educational institutions were responding to demands and critiques about students' literate skills, while simultaneously positioning the discipline of English as a means to respond to societal concerns about citizenship.

The growth and specialization of the discipline itself also encouraged English teachers to think about the value and goals of what was being taught in English classrooms. In his 1977 book on *Curriculum*, Frederick Rudolph includes English literature as one of a group of disciplines, which also included American history, fine arts, and music, that developed specialized knowledge of the discipline during this period because it was formerly considered extra-curricular knowledge and available to all (12–13). Sharon Crowley describes this process as a way to "define English as a language from which its native speakers were alienated" (60); by making English strange to native speakers, the need for its academic study was justified. The next step was to link new ways of teaching and thinking about English as a discipline with goals for what students would gain from these courses, goals that indicate how citizenship was imagined through the discipline itself.

Because of the growing importance of the discipline of English in the wider curriculum, debates about the goals of the universal English class among English teachers filled the pages of *English Journal*. Some focused on the connection between the discipline and what students could contribute to society as a result of learning it. Helen Louise Cohen, an English teacher at Washington Irving High School in New York,[14] wrote in *English Journal* about the influence the English classroom could have on the shaping of the citizenship of young students, emphasizing the "community motive" behind the teaching of English. She wrote explicitly about the responsibility of English as a discipline:

> English instruction, to express the idea directly, should be organized so as to keep constantly in the foreground the needs of society in which the pupil is playing his part at the present moment, and in which his role will, with the years, become more and more important. As a matter of fact, all of the curriculum should be taught with a view to preparing young people to be socially valuable, but English, to my mind, offers to the teacher more oppor-

tunities for training human beings to live well than any other of the high-school studies. (623)

Cohen, who undoubtedly taught immigrants in her New York City public school classroom, saw the writing classroom as an opportunity to make students understand their part in a larger society or community. For Cohen, the teaching of English was uniquely positioned to address the citizenship-building elements of the classroom, like the message to students that they should see themselves as socially valuable and contribute to society. Cohen believed that this goal for the English class needed to be "in the foreground" over other course objectives. Rather than thinking about English instruction as imparting a body of knowledge about literature or even composition, she imagined that students would integrate into their lives the way of thinking learned in English classrooms so that they would be "socially valuable" and "live well," perhaps as a means to empowerment or as a way to think about how English could help prevent students from becoming social burdens.

D. Davis Farrington, a professor of English at Hunter College in New York City, brought these conversations to the college classroom, believing that the skills learned in an English class would not only help students become socially valuable, but would produce more effective citizens that would benefit the national democracy. To Farrington, composition classes, particularly oral composition classes, would help students develop "clear thinking" so they could participate in a "democracy—the very atmosphere of our country" (479). She argued for the importance of making students understand the obligation they should feel to the democracy as recipients of education. She asserted, "What they freely accept in the interest of good citizenship, they must freely return in the interest of good citizenship" (43), making the vital connection between students' access to education within a democracy, which in turn made their active participation in that democracy as citizens an obligation. To teachers like Farrington, the English classroom, with its focus on language skills, was positioned as vital to students' potential to become good citizens. As a result of their experience in English classes, students would be able to think "clearly," as a good citizen should.

Charles S. Pendleton, a professor from the University of Wisconsin, positioned the new composition curriculum as appropriate for helping students take on this citizenly obligation, particularly in the context of changes within higher education. English as a discipline could play a central role in the shift toward expanding public education from the previous, more elite version and the growth of education in both specialization and student population, as described by Thelin (205). Pendleton argued, "The old ideal of education tended to set him who received it apart from the workaday world, to create an 'educated' caste; it filled the mind full of learning not directly useful in itself, although it was supposed in a vague general way to strengthen mental powers. But the new kind of education is based directly and deliberately upon social needs. Underlying it is a careful study of citizenship" (575). Here, citizenship provides the theoretical foundation for the importance of composition; through composition classes, students learn how to fulfill the promise of citizenship offered to them by their public schooling. English was seen as a vital part of the "infinitely larger thing, a new fundamental thought about education which has taken the world by storm. In our own day there has come into being a brand-new conception of the function of school, that is not to store up ponderous, unworldly wisdom in the mental warehouses of children, but to develop directly a self-active thoughtful citizenship" (Pendleton 575). By thinking of the English classroom as playing a part in citizen production, proponents saw the goals of the course shifting from teaching the content of literature and other cultural texts to teaching the communicative, intellectual, and ethical skills needed to be a self-governed citizen. Through the English classroom, young people would learn how to fulfill the role of the citizen in a democracy, moving away from old functions of education that established an elite class through education and toward the production of a citizen more broadly conceived.

Both Farrington and Pendleton articulate vital associations between English departments and the work of democratic citizen production. This impulse toward the cultivation of citizenship did not just affect the abstract purpose of the English course, but the content as well. One of the assignments that Helen Louise Cohen, the high school teacher at Washington Irving High School in New York, proposed in order to reach this goal in her high school class of immigrant students was the use of magazines as texts in the classroom, but not simply to bring "to their attention the contemporary achievements of the arts of poetry, prose, music, painting and sculpture" (Cohen 623). She described how efforts to "elevate the taste of future readers" were "fatuous and trifling" and instead "[defended] the regular use of the magazine in English classes because I consider this practice a conspicuously effective way of relating the study of English to community life" (623). By analyzing magazines, mass market publications as opposed to the high culture of literature, teachers such as Cohen established assignments in English classes that were relevant to students' lives in a wider context and encouraged students to think about their place in society. According to another English teacher, Cornelia Carhart Ward, this engagement with the outside world was vital to making students into citizens. She outlined several courses on the war and on patriotism as a way to "center [students'] thoughts on their part in these stirring times" (Ward 368). As a result, "the work of the English teacher assumes even greater importance. His is the greatest opportunity for service in the making of loyal American citizens for the future" (364). Both Cohen and Ward impressed upon readers—their audience of other teachers—the importance of providing opportunities for students to engage in issues outside of the classroom as a way to teach writing and citizenship (and perhaps simultaneously boost the importance of the profession).

In light of more civic goals, some teachers positioned the classroom as a microcosm of the public, a space where students would learn to exercise the duties and responsibilities of citizenship, much like the scholarship discussed in chapter 1. School newspapers and assignments that revolved around public issues attempted to address this desire for seeing the writing classroom in this way. For example, R. R. Smith's pedagogical approaches were very much tied to preparation for life outside of the classroom, as well as action to influence the community. In the article, "Increasing Satisfactory Production in Composition," Smith, a Chicago high school teacher, discussed how methods such as debate made the high school classroom a "little republic" (467) with the objective of "getting the best possible development of oral and written composition through activities of students in their government" (467). Smith encouraged making students "do things" (468) with their literacy, including getting a new school building commissioned. In doing these kinds of tasks, students "developed ability in leadership, in co-operative work, in speaking and writing for a purpose, which they could not have gained in ordinary class work" (468). When analyzing the results of this kind of teaching, Smith believed classes were more effective when students were given actual responsibility and at the end of course evaluated it by asking the following questions:

> (1) Have students been more interested as a result of this treatment? (2) Have they shown greater initiative and resourcefulness, and have they worked harder? (3) Have they shown more freedom in oral expression, and have they written with greater ease? (4) Have they produced greater volume than classes usually do, and have they shown greater care in mechanics? (6) [sic] Have they taken the work right into the home, and have they made their families a part of the class? (7) Have they gained in ability to gather material and in ability to think through this material? (470)

These questions indicate how far Smith imagined the composition classroom reaching. Not only would this approach solve many problems with students' compositions by making them more engaged learners, it would also make them better thinkers and more involved and effective citizens, even penetrating the home and involving family members in the learning process.

Charles Dawson, a high school teacher from Syracuse, New York, wrote about "Two Experiments in Experience," which also articulated the importance of recognizing and even mimicking the world outside the classroom walls. In his article, he argued that experience should "furnish material for composition" (438). He proposed, "The English class is made to form a little 'world outside the classroom,' a little 'public,' demanding, as does the larger world, that one who would speak to it must adapt himself and his words to the given conditions" (441). Dawson saw the English classroom as a way for students to cultivate the skills needed to be responsible citizens who would be able to interact with the world by "speaking to it." The content he discussed reflected his desire for students to think of the classroom as a "little world" with reading topics that include immigration, wood-carving, and oratory. Dawson researched other classes that operated in this way and shared testimonials from other teachers. One teacher reported to him that "the students enjoyed the work, entered into it with enthusiasm, and seemed to appreciate the fact that they were to have some freedom of choice, and that they were to have a chance to interest someone else in subjects that they enjoyed. A certain independent pride was created in the pupils, whose opinions and taste were to be respected in these matters. . . . It encouraged a spirit of confidence and careful expression" (444). Dawson offered a view of a class in which the content was the lives of students, and he testified that this made for more effective teaching with a cultivation of the habits of the "little public," like freedom, independent pride, and careful expression among students, echoing the ideal behavior of the larger public. Through such positioning of the English classroom as a citizenship-producing space, teachers connected course content to the outside world, attempting to cultivate habits and skills that would help students participate in democratic society as engaged and knowledgeable self-governing citizens.

While these attitudes also carried into the college classroom, as Pendleton described, it is important to remember the numbers and realities of the college student population and that these attitudes about citizenship applied only to a certain section of the population at the college level, particularly in the face of growing beliefs about access to education, and in turn what I have earlier called full citizenship. As previously discussed, most students in college writing classes were most likely born in the United States; in *American Education and the European Immigrant*, Bernard Weiss cites an Immigration Commission study in 1909 that reported that "the off-spring of the old immigrants from the British Isles and Germany made up the great majority of those students with foreign-born parents, constituting about 25 percent of the student body in the seventy-seven colleges and universities surveyed. The foreign-born students comprised about 10 percent of the total, with Jews being the single largest group in this category and Italians and Slavs barely represented" (xxiv). Thelin emphasizes the importance of the cultural dimension of the college experience, writing that "college enrollments represented less than 5 percent of the American population of eighteen- to twenty-two-year-olds" and that even within that elite group, "not every undergraduate enjoyed first-class citizenship in the campus community" (169). Despite the sense that higher education was expanding, as measured by institutions and enrollment numbers, this did not mean it was also becoming more democratic in terms of equality and accessibility. Levine describes how "even so-called liberals of the day . . . more often than not doubted whether the immigrants were capable of becoming full participants in American democratic life," citing the confluence of the restrictive immigration laws of 1921 and 1924 and the actions of "college administrators [who] were looking for ways to limit, if not eliminate, unwanted Jewish and other ethnic students" (147). While the rhetoric around the expansion of education and resulting curricula was connected to democracy and citizenship, access to education continued to be determined by privilege, with the rate of expansion actually moving quite slowly.

Such tensions between beliefs about education as a way to increase citizenship and democracy and anxieties about citizenship and class status influenced curricula and the citizenship it created.[15] As a response to the changing populations of students and potential students as seen through the filter of high schools, some in higher education argued for the necessity of patriotism and citizenship building as part of the classroom because of the possibility of immigrants in the classroom. Sometimes this motivation was as explicit as arguing for a more patriotic curriculum inflected with rhetoric about the influx of immigrants. In "On Teaching American" (1914), Rose Alden wrote about the populations of English classes being mostly the "third, fourth, perhaps even tenth generation of Americanized immigrants" with college English courses "held still more firmly in the clutches of the cultured native" (182). Because, in some sense, all students are immigrants, Alden was a proponent of integrating "American" into the discipline of English, characterizing immigrants as benevolent and willing citizens-in-training who would rightly choose "Lincoln over Milton" in their U.S. classes. Tapping into students' desires to learn about citizenship and how to be American, Alden argued that teachers should feel an obligation to teach American language and literature in English classes because of the growing numbers of immigrants in the course who would have varying levels of citizenship potential. She wrote that "sometimes to us come flashlights from the off-shore liners with their steerage hordes. We set our jaw squarely and prepare to teach the coming millions English" (182). In response to English teachers who must confront these "hordes," she asks, "Why not teach them American?" (182). There is a subtext of anxiety with the gritty determination implied by setting "our jaw squarely" and the mention of "coming millions." In light of these invading hordes, she seems to suggest that the English class-room can be space to not just teach the language but the culture of the society through the content of the course as a bulwark against such an onslaught.

The writing curriculum at an urban public institution like City College, and other institutions with a disproportionately high number of immigrant students, reflected its student body in that it aspired to look like that of more elite institutions in an effort to put their students on equal footing with more privileged students. City College saw itself on par with local counterparts like Yale and Columbia, and their writing classes tracked with the national trends at the time. The college bulletin from 1910–11 describes a first-year rhet-oric course based on argumentation using Lamont's *English Composition* and Genung's *Handbook of Rhetorical Analysis*, two texts that were widely used in many composition classes. In 1918, their classes shift from rhetoric to compos-ing. The first-year writing course is still called "Rhetoric," but the emphasis is on "paragraph and essay writing." Even in 1919, when the college offered a two-course sequence of rhetoric, paragraph and essay writing was the emphasis in the first class and in the second "more stress [was placed] upon the larger forms of composition, and practical methods of self-expression" (91). Rhetoric drops out, much as it did in first-year writing classes across the country.

Wozniak traces this trend across more elite institutions in his *English Composition in Eastern Colleges, 1850–1940*. While to Wozniak, "eastern col-leges" meant the elite colleges along the East Coast (Pittsburgh, Rutgers, and Vermont are the only schools out of the 38 examined with public affiliation), City College's first-year writing curriculum reflects his characterization of a writing class that did not take up rhetoric in favor of either "literary" composi-tion (Yale, Princeton) or "logical" composition (Harvard, Columbia) (139). This change in the curriculum that moved away from rhetoric *and* from the curric-ular trends of more elite institutions is consistent with the characterization of Irving Norman Feinstein, a City College student who wrote his thesis on the history of the City College English department in 1934. He describes the shift in population, when "the typical City college undergraduate was no longer the son of a family with an American background, but the son of an immigrant from an environment where accurate expression had not been practiced" (5), as a moment when the English department "ceased teaching 'eloquence' and 'rhetoric,' and took upon itself the humble task of helping the thinking mind to find words and a form of expression as quickly and as easily as possible" (5).

Particularly at municipal institutions like City College, which had a more (for the times) diverse student population, these two purposes, the elite and the populist, dovetailed in these resulting curricular decisions.

While City College did proclaim itself the Harvard of the proletariat, the institution also responded to the responsibility of citizen-making more directly in ways that also acknowledged the different station and origins of its students. At the same time that curricular decisions were being made within the English department, the larger institution was responding to anxieties around foreigners, attempting to shape and even ensure the quality of the citizens produced by the school. With many more immigrants enrolled, in 1920 the school unanimously decided to offer a special English course for students from "foreign universities and high schools" (City College, CLAS Faculty Council). This mandate became a two-course sequence on the mechanics of composition. The 1922 course register describes the "A" version of this course as being for those "otherwise qualified to pursue college studies" who are "handicapped by weakness in English composition. This applies especially to those of foreign birth, those who have not gone through High School, and those who have long been out of school" (249). Such a course indicated a desire to provide classes for those students who may not be traditional college students but also reveals shades of remediation in the task of incorporating the foreign-born into the general student population. So while the institution welcomed these students because of its public mission, it also took measures to make sure those foreign students were produced in a particular way.[16]

With the growth of anxiety about immigrants in U.S. society, the college wanted to ensure the kind of student citizen they produced. In 1918, near the end of the First World War, City College implemented a "Pledge of Loyalty." All entering students needed to sign an oath that stated:

> As some small recognition of the large gift of education which, in the American spirit of freedom and self-government, is now offered me by the College of the City of New York, I hereby pledge myself as follows: 1. I will be actively loyal in support of constitutional government in the United States and in the State and City of New York and in this College. 2. I will seek to preserve and even to enhance the value of all public property now or hereafter entrusted to my care. 3. As a student, I will uphold the discipline and order of the College. (City College, *1918 College Bulletin*, 94)

With this pledge, the school acted as an institutional guarantor in its citizenship production beyond the ways of thinking that were taught in classes like English. Here, citizenship moved beyond a way of thinking and engaging with society, a democratic version of citizenship, toward a citizenship that privileged loyalty. The self-government and freedom conferred by an education at City College was imagined to produce loyalty, discipline, and order, in contrast to the social unrest and disruption that lay outside the college gates.

This more utilitarian approach to citizenship was not limited to City College alone. In particular, the writing classroom as a citizen-producing space took hold in the face of these questions about relevancy of the discipline. Discussions like these about what should be taught directly reflected anxieties about the usefulness of education and what role schools were playing in shaping and certifying the country's young citizens.

Useful English for Useful Citizens

Citizenship as styled by an English classroom was not just instruction inflected with patriotism or concerned with the creation of little publics. In fact, the English classroom's cultivation of citizenship also had in it traces of the importance of productivity and work, much like those literacy learning spaces in Americanization programs and union education programs. Not surprisingly, the discipline of English attended to these tensions between the growing vocational and more traditional courses of study, often in conversations about the purpose of English classes. In numerous discussions about what was "useful" about the English course for students, up for debate was not just what to teach—literature, business English, composition, speech—but also how to teach it and what students were expected to gain from it. Because the classroom served as a citizenship-producing space, classroom practices and goals indicated the desired habits of citizenship meant to be cultivated there. These courses telegraphed appropriate habits for citizens who were not just considered "literate," but seen among the most highly literate of citizens because they were attaining a college education.

Here, we see the cultural associations of advanced literacy beyond having more sophisticated reading and writing skills. In particular, the habits that these courses encouraged—literary appreciation, error-free prose, effective communication skills, the ability to think—were positioned as useful for students. Arguments made by members of the NCTE about the usefulness of English as a vital part of the curriculum had multiple motivations. For one, arguments in favor of the usefulness of English were responses to the larger societal anxiety about the quality of American citizenship and the college student as part of the citizenry. Institutions increased and revised their writing instruction to reflect how the new generation of college graduates could suit the needs of a new economy, as well as the role of institutions of higher education within the new economy. At the same time, the NCTE was making a case for itself; by proving English as useful to students, by establishing it as the necessary and universal discipline, English studies could confirm its essential role in advanced schooling at the high school and college level.

The members of the NCTE debated about what the English course should accomplish, whether the course should be focused on vocational preparation or connected to a broader sense of self, debates that also permeated higher education at large. Levine describes how "with the rise of business and other professional programs and with the influx of vocational-oriented students, educational institutions were pushed and pulled between the values of expansion and consolidation, utility and liberal culture, democracy and elitism" (89). On the table in these debates was the question of "whether practical subjects ought to be included in the curriculum; no question seemed more basic as educators struggled to develop a role for higher education in a modern society" (89). These goals reflected different perspectives on how citizens should be reacting to the changing culture—through cultivating skills that would make an individual valuable and employable, by encouraging the independent thinking and a greater sense of self outside of industry definitions, as a means to help students gain greater communication skills, or in trying to find ways to do it all. T. W. Gosling, from Hughes High School in Cincinnati, told *English Journal* readers in 1913 that one of the chief aims of the high school composition course was to "enable every pupil to discover and to develop his latent possibilities" (513) as well as to perpetuate the "growth of altruism" (515). He understood that not every student in these courses would go on to have careers that involved writing but that the "great aim" was to "establish a consciousness of selfhood" (517). From articles like Gosling's emerged a sense of the power of an English course, that it was responsible not just for a student's literate ability but also a specific sense of self and being in the world that cultivated an individual's citizenship.

Of course, Gosling's views of English classes as a means to cultivate character traits like altruism represented the way teachers extended the goals of the writing classroom beyond learning specific course content. The composition course was in a position to be seen as useful because its teachers made explicit assertions that skills learned in it would serve students in future situations. Sometimes these future situations were other classes, promoting the idea that the freshman writing class would prepare students for academic writing. But more often, there was a desire to make the course useful for students once they left the educational setting, namely the ways that the literacy learned in the classroom would aid students in future work and civic engagement. Criticisms of illiteracy and the ineffectiveness of English instruction were found outside

educational circles, as evidenced by numerous articles in general interest publications that discussed whether composition instruction and English studies
prepared students for future situations in the workplace and in the community.[17] These concerns about students' illiteracy mirrored questions about the recently expanded presence of institutionalized schooling in people's lives, which
English classes represented. As a result, English classes became the target of
these public discussions because, unlike those disciplines with a clear vocational purpose—for instance, math—English became the discipline that was associated with personal development, as Gosling argued. Additionally, a person's
literacy and facility with the English language was one that an outsider could
seemingly assess. Because of that ease of assessment, English classes became
the object of critique and needed to prove themselves as useful, a sentiment expressed often in *English Journal*. By demonstrating that a citizen produced by
the English classroom was a *useful* citizen, the role and goals of English courses
attempted to make themselves legible to a more critical public.

English instructors attempted to come to terms with the various goals of
the courses they taught, either by staking a claim in one or by trying to reconcile the different goals and demands with one another. In his history of the
discipline of English, Arthur N. Applebee describes how changes in outlook,
like shifts in psychology that focus on child development and the influence of
John Dewey, produced an education that "must adjust to the student, meeting
his personal and social needs" (46), creating a space for the needs of the student, whether personal, social, or even vocational, to influence the goals of the
discipline. Herbert Wynford Hill from the University of Nevada exemplified
this tension when he spoke at an NCTE meeting in 1913 about the necessity of
"harmonizing . . . aesthetic interests with the commercial and industrial trends
of our times" (609). For Hill, English class was a space to process and respond
to industrialism. Hill saw the work of English instructors, particularly literary
and aesthetic aims, as essential for the industrialized American citizen: "In
America today we are in the midst of tremendous industrial and commercial
activity. Factories are springing up, railroads and canals are lacing the cities
and country, agricultural enterprises are taking the place of farming, the professions are commercialized, even teachers are demanding higher wages. But
close upon the heels of this activity comes another. Art treasures are filling
our museums, libraries have multiplied, universities have increased in number
and wealth, music and drama are liberally supported" (610). Hill's commentary
illustrates how English and other arts were seen, in some camps, as a necessary
antidote to the rapidly industrializing society in which citizens found themselves. The occupational, civic, and aesthetic goals of advanced literacy training

in educational institutions seem at odds with one another, yet their intercon-
nectedness speaks to the complicated demands put upon teachers of literacy.
Others, like Hill, believed that a course in English could be useful to students
in their negotiations of this mass-manufacturing world. Those students who
learned to think more expansively about their industrial lives could "enter
broader and higher fields of interests whereas the individual not so trained can
only run a bit faster on his tiny treadmill" (612). In the face of vocational demands, English not only could prepare students for economic success, but also
aid their intellectual survival in this industrial and commercial realm.

In light of the new demands placed on English as a discipline, NCTE member John M. Clapp from Lake Forest College characterized the development
of English from "formal class instruction" to "the principal culture study of
our time" (18), making a distinction between two views of English—as "culture study or a utility study" (18). Samuel Chandler Earle, a professor at Tufts,
helpfully illustrated how writing classes contributed to English's new role, explaining: "As for composition, it is of two sorts, utilitarian and literary; these
differ in essential ways, and each in turn may be studied either as an art or as a
science" (478). These two branches of composition teaching, the literary-based
instruction and the more utilitarian, represented beliefs about what would
characterize good citizens. Proponents of nonliterary composition and business English believed growing communication skills were important for young
citizens. What teachers labeled as "useful" for students about English classes
reflected their interpretations of what habits of citizenship should be produced
through the course. In previous chapters, literacy was considered useful because it was seen to encourage particular habits of citizenship appropriate for
a particular group of students, whether Americanization, productivity, or solidarity. In the college classroom, the same can be seen. English classes, as spaces
where literacy was distributed, did not have inherent value simply for content,
but made themselves relevant to the citizenship-building concerns of the time.

Yet the utility of composition was not limited to a wholly vocational definition, but also forwarded its cultural benefits to students. Pendleton parsed
this tension as a rift between the old and new ways of teaching. He made the
distinction that "the old was interested mainly in subject-matter; the new
thinks primarily of the pupil, and the subject is chiefly a means for effecting
the child's development. The old thought of knowledge as an end in itself; the
new thinks of it as a tool, a means to an end; and the end—in a large, inclusive
sense, not mere utilitarianism—is civic betterment" (576). By engaging with the
utilitarian role of composition courses within English studies, writing teachers
could attempt to unite the explicitly practical with the ability to think. May

McKitrick, a teacher at the East Technical High School in Cleveland, wrote an article entitled "The Adaptation of the Work in English to the Actual Needs and Interests of the Pupils" as a response to the ways teachers of composition felt obligated to students' needs. McKitrick wrote:

> The situation then is this: the public demanding results in the way of definite, tangible efficiency; the colleges requiring of our pupils power and appreciation; the teachers asking, "How can we unify these divergent demands?" We must show that the results of our training are intellectual power and spiritual growth—on the intellectual side particularly the power to think clearly. I believe that we are all agreed that if we can get our pupils to think clearly it is a comparatively easy task to teach them to write good English. The question is: "Does our course in English tend to clear thinking? Have we helped or retarded?" (407)

J. M. Thomas from the University of Minnesota also connected utilitarian goals with a need for teachers to "guide" thinking. In "Training for Teaching Composition in Colleges," he described in detail how "the fact that the aim of composition is so practical, so utilitarian, means that its subject-matter must be drawn from whatever students are, or may be, interested in and thinking about. This necessitates that the teacher who is to guide her thinking and the expression of their thoughts must have not only a wide range of interests but also a correspondingly wide range of information" (455). Both McKitrick and Thomas indicated a desire for teachers to figure out students' needs in order to make the course useful for students and the belief that, as McKitrick wrote with regards to the course, "it is our business to create an interest" (414). These teachers purported that part of a teacher's training is learning how to fulfill this responsibility and obligation.

A desire to cultivate an ability to think is consistent with the concept of the "habit of thinking" preferred by unionists as a key characteristic of the good citizen, as discussed in chapter 3. Literacy became an indication of a citizen who could think and could take up the responsibilities of citizenship. In "The Reign of Red Ink," Walter Barnes from the Glenville State Normal School in West Virginia wrote, "the most important educative value of composition work is not the mere training in writing. It is the training in thinking and talking. And that teacher whose eyes are focused on the writing value is almost invariably a weak teacher of composition work and a short-sighted critic of themes" (159). In the context of training English teachers, Barnes argued that a strong teacher knows that the teaching of "thinking and talking" is more important than a myopic focus on the conventions of writing. While such a focus might produce error-free prose, Barnes believed that writing instruction should be measured by a student's ability to use writing to communicate thinking.

Dudley Miles, a high school teacher at DeWitt Clinton High School in New York, extended the idea of composition classes providing "training in thought" to the need for writing teachers to clarify the utility of writing classes to students. He notes, "If English composition does not foster in the student, besides care for grammatical correctness in expression, a habit of following up and testing the ideas that are suggested by the topics on which he writes, then English composition is falling short of what it should accomplish" (363). Miles saw these courses as helping students for "habits of thought for life" (363). Interestingly, he also made a connection between the literacy training of the classroom and the student's citizenship outside of the classroom through the incorporation of job-oriented content into the writing classroom. He proposed a "What I Should Consider besides Pay in Accepting a Position" as a topic for exploration in class and in writing, hoping that it served as an example of deliberation and careful thought, as well as an opportunity to write. Miles believed that

> these illustrations should make clear what is meant by saying that composition may be used to train thought. And when it is used to train thought it affords a more general preparation for later living than is provided by exclusive attention to matters of spelling and other points of usage. . . . In short, he will not only dictate a clearer business letter or draw up a more orderly report, but he will display a more intelligent attitude toward all matters of discussion. He should be more successful in his vocation and more helpful as a citizen. (365)

To teachers like Miles, having an explicit use for the skills learned in class provided a way for students to see the class as relevant. Miles linked the different goals of the writing classroom together—training for thought, being successful at a job, acting like a good citizen. If the writing classroom could be seen as an essential part of preparing students to accomplish all of these goals, then the course itself became an essential part of citizenship-building and as a result, an essential part of society.

While some members of the NCTE thought about goals and arguments with regard to how English studies would be useful for students, others addressed methods—the strategies for how to improve employment opportunities, personal enlightenment, and civic identity in the classroom. Articles in *English Journal* often proposed new projects and assignments for the writing classroom, attempting to bring to fruition some of the goals of the writing classroom such as preparation for life outside of the university through work and civic identities. Often termed "experiments" by authors, these assignments reflected a wide array of activities that responded to current events, changes in employment, and other anxieties in American society. Authors provided a clear sense of ideal outcomes for these assignments, the hopes and goals put into their proposed pedagogical practices.

Many teachers advocated assignments that drew from students' everyday lives. Teachers thought of content as a way to make the work of the composition class relevant to students. For example, W. D. Lewis, a teacher from the William Penn High School in Philadelphia, compared the need for students to write on relevant topics as a kind of antidote for the pervasiveness of teaching literature. He asked, "Have we aimed at the wrong thing? Whatever may be our theory as to the reason for teaching literature, we have, consciously or unconsciously, taught for knowledge rather than for power" (11).[18] He did not seem to denigrate the teaching of literature but, rather, critiqued the way it (and writing) had been taught in the classroom. With both literature and writing, learning had become a rote task, rather than a pursuit of dynamic topics with relevance to the daily lives of students. He described his ideal classroom:

> Let's make our theme assignments as short as possible, teach one thing at a time, hammer on that, have a great deal of work in class, go around while the work is being done as the teacher of science does in the laboratory, on stated days have the class time used as a study period while we can give conferences, see as many pupils for conference as we can at off hours and before and after school, have other days for pupils to read their themes in class for criticism and comment by pupils and teacher, hold up the best as a model and send the rest home to endeavor to do as well; then use the time we formerly spent in red-inking themes for anything from vaudeville to a Browning club. (14)

Teachers like Lewis proposed that composition should be thought of less like a literature class and more like a laboratory course, akin to chemistry or biology. Not only did these teachers hope for the increased funding per student like those in laboratory classes, they believed that writing could be taught better through hands-on laboratory methods. In a laboratory setting, students would closely link participation and engagement with the learning of writing and the practice of literacy. Samuel Chandler Earle from Tufts provided a detailed look at what a composition laboratory would look like with workshops, conferences, modeling, and less error correction. He saw a laboratory method that attended to both the artistic and scientific aspects of composition teaching and hoped that the work of the composition classroom could be combined to create more of a laboratory class. To its advocates, his method would allow for attention to both form and substance.[19] Both Lewis and Earle proposed methods in the class that called for students' engagement and cultivated spaces where habits of citizenship could be practiced.

Charles Pendleton from the University of Wisconsin saw value in varying activities and having students do more than just write rote exercises. He established this practice as a characteristic of a new kind of teacher. He complained, "The modern teacher keeps his pupils busy, in school and in their home study-hour, and he devises procedures to insure that the one activity shall not merely duplicate the other" (581). Pendleton advocated that students be responsible to one another, proposing the use of "one or two of the excellent pupils" to become assistant teachers. Pendleton saw students and teachers working together "in the spirit of democracy and co-operation" (581). He glimpsed potential in taking up the characteristics of a democracy to make an effective classroom and used democracy as a rationale for his classroom practices. To this end, Pendleton made a call for "co-operation" that did not involve solely teachers and members of the writing class, but also required the cooperation of those across campus. The NCTE advocated cooperation, which asked that teachers from all disciplines participate in writing instruction. Like Pendleton's view of students and teachers working together in "the spirit of democracy," teachers across campus who worked together could also invoke the democratic spirit through the teaching of writing. Such a broad, cross-campus view of writing instruction as part of a democratic project injected the college education with a sense of relevancy and usefulness.

My intention here is not to map contemporary methods onto these practices from a previous era. While one cannot deny that the similarities (writing across the curriculum as a kind of latter-day cooperation, the cultivation of student-centered classrooms, the desire for relevant, student-driven research, the importance of class discussion), I do not see them as strict parallels, somehow endorsing or enlightening our current practices. Instead, I draw from these conversations the long history of teachers wanting to integrate citizenship and relevancy into the teaching of literacy, namely composition. During this period of time when English departments were arguing for their own usefulness, they used citizenship as a way to demonstrate connections between the work they did and more general societal concerns about the health of citizens.

The Responsibility of Citizenship Production

Not every teacher agreed with the ever-expanding goals of the composition course, particularly because some felt that these implicit, public goals were inextricably connected to the task of literacy training, while others supported a more focused course that simply dealt with language and how to use it. But those who supported the move to enfold citizenship concerns into the English classroom often saw it as a consequence of the changing role of schooling in contemporary life. For example, a 1913 meeting of teachers in New York reports, "The modern city high school has become a center of social endeavor. The burden of this enlarged scope falls most heavily upon the teacher of English. School papers, school annuals, debating clubs, dramatic societies, short-story clubs, and the new cult of vocational guidance fill our free periods, occupy our afternoons, and encroach upon our evenings" ("News and Notes" 531). While some teachers saw the incorporation of citizenship as crucial to making the curriculum relevant, others resisted, believing that the additional burden of citizenship teaching and attention to civic issues put undue responsibilities on the writing classroom. Citizenship was just one of many responsibilities the English teacher needed to take on; but for some, they were put upon.

Dora V. Smith warned teachers of this danger in a paper at a 1925 NCTE meeting in Indianapolis, telling her audience that "there is nothing, apparently, which cannot be taught through the medium of English composition. Moral training, school spirit, patriotism, safety first, worthy home membership, vocational guidance, thrift, public health, community problems—all these and more are thrust upon the teacher of composition and must be fitted somewhere into her program" (416). Composition thus becomes the channel for writing instruction, but also life instruction. And I contend that this life instruction, as with the Americanization programs discussed in chapter 2, was part of citizenship training. By talking about being moral, patriotic, and thrifty, Smith delineated the characteristics that make a good citizen. Smith, along with others, resisted this responsibility in favor of what she saw as the primary goals of the writing classroom, cautioning her fellow teachers, "Too frequently in the press of disseminating information upon a large variety of topics, the teacher of composition loses her chief function in the school, and the world wonders why our children, many of them, have a slip-shod manner of expression, irrational ideas, and undeveloped powers of reflection and analysis" (416). Smith reminded her audience of their responsibility for teaching writing skills over teaching the other traits that are "thrust upon the teacher of composition" (416) and argued that by taking on all of these other responsibilities, the course would be set up to fail.

Like Smith, other teachers and administrators attempted to figure out how they could meet the ever-growing demands on the writing classroom. In a 1923 issue of *English Journal*, J. R. Rutland from the Alabama Polytechnic Institute reported on a national study of "freshman English," namely teacher and institutional opinions on the "gradually changing aims and methods" of the course

(1). The study offers an enlightening picture of how teachers and programs were responding to the growing responsibilities and development of the first-year English course. Rutland discussed the troubling aspects of the course as it had become more entrenched in the college curriculum, including the secondary status of the course and, as a result, the secondary status of its teachers. To Rutland, the content of the course caused this decline in status. He described a "disturbing tendency" toward "simply a course in writing," articulating his belief that writing instruction was best taught through "an introduction to intellectual culture" (4). Rutland's worry about the cultural aim of writing instruction being slowly eliminated was particularly high with regard to technical schools: "But this age of business and invention is somewhat skeptical of the value of culture. Technical and business leaders who see nothing practical in literary study often prefer readiness of speech to good taste or even correctness. Even educational theorists, finding that English teachers are more successful in teaching sentence structure than in widening mental horizons, have decided that they had better attempt only what they know they can do" (4–5). Rutland associated this loss of culture with a shift away from literature in composition classes. He commended attempts to teach writing in conjunction with other courses, whether literature or political science or history, singling out a course, Problems of Citizenship including English Composition, which was taught at the University of Missouri. And he praised these attempts to have a "more comprehensive aim of enlarging the student's world of interests, of helping him toward culture" (4). Rutland expressed an anxiety about the encroachment of writing instruction on the more intellectual and cultural aims of English as a discipline, with citizenship as one way to keep the writing classroom from becoming what we would now call a service course. But he suggested that if the English classroom was going to move away from literature, it could at least keep its intellectual bent through the incorporation of topics like citizenship.

As previously discussed, English teachers often found themselves justifying what they were doing in the classroom to outsiders from business and politics who felt like they had a stake in the products of the educational system; interested parties wanted productive and literate worker-citizens. Teacher's College faculty member Franklin T. Baker's course, The Teacher of English, depicted some of the pressure felt from public evaluations of the work being done in the writing classroom. He described the pervasive feelings of critique that affected the discipline, noting, "Even the business man, who used to be distrustful of his judgment in things scholastic, has picked up the cat-o'-nine-tails and laid it on with a will" (335). And from these numerous critiques arises the common (and somewhat contradictory) conception "that anyone can teach English, if he can talk it and read it; aspirants in the field often cherish this delusion" (336). As a result of this public perception, he recognized the need for English teachers to show themselves as holding specialized qualifications—in particular, their abilities to successfully teach language, social temperament, and memory. He extolled the value of these characteristics as a way to demonstrate the difficulties of being an effective English teacher: "The same gifts—with zealous self-interest substituted for modesty—would beg worth in business five or even ten times that sum. And yet there are business men, on boards of education, who wonder why they cannot get teachers who can bring their sons and daughters to love literature and to use good English" (338). Baker emphasized the worth of these teacher skills by arguing that these same skills would be highly valuable and even rare in the business world. In situating his response about the effectiveness of English teachers in the business world, I see the impulse to make the work of the discipline visible, measurable, and significant, impulses that became reflected in the multiple identities of the discipline—teacher of cultural education through literary appreciation versus provider of vocational education through communication skills with composition and business English.

C. S. Duncan from the Ohio State painted a picture of the discipline concerned with how those in English were responding to public critiques of the effectiveness of English classes in a 1914 article entitled, "A Rebellious Word on English Composition": "In colleges, though the attitude is different, the same dissatisfaction exists, Harvard is just now investigating the subject of poor English among its students, and so are Vassar and many engineering and technical schools. Every time it is the Department of English that feels the brunt of the criticism. In defense, the teachers of English may contend that students enter poorly prepared, often without any appreciable basis of knowledge upon which to build, and yet it is expected that all deficiencies will be corrected by one course of a few hours per week" (155). Duncan expressed a common frustration over the expectation of what was supposed to happen in an English classroom. He attempted to answer why students came to college poorly prepared, indicating that there were nationwide "lamentations over the 'illiteracy' of pupils in high schools and colleges" (154). By citing influences outside of the classroom like home language, Duncan indicated one way that teachers responded to the realities of an English classroom. In some ways, teachers wanted to investigate how the English classroom could react to this crisis, making themselves clearly relevant within formal education. But at the same time, English classes could not be held entirely culpable for the illiteracy of young people, as demonstrated by references to external influences such as the "deteriorating effects of the abuse of English on the street, in the home, in the newspapers, in 'trashy literature'" (155) or the waning of knowledge of Latin and Greek. These attempts to respond to the culminating citizenship and literacy crises of the time through innovative assignments and methods speak to how elusive this task was. And often, English teachers found themselves in the crossfire of other societal anxieties over the quality of citizenship, as visible through a young person's literate abilities.

The Writing Classroom as a Site of Citizenship Training

Discussions among teachers of English offer a view of a discipline in a moment of fluctuation, one concerned about its status in the public eye and within the university. The pages of the *English Journal* were filled with anxiety about the status and responsibility of English departments, and by extension, the status and responsibility of members of English departments. Whether through business English, composition, or literary study, all English classes saw themselves making their students literate; they just had different definitions and approaches for how they accomplished this task. Teachers' varied means to gaining this advanced literacy signaled a complex time in the history of teaching writing, one that fundamentally responded to citizenship concerns. The high school and college literacy training discussed in this chapter contrasts with the more explicitly productive and worker-oriented goals and approaches of the literacy training of immigrants and unionists, yet in all of these instances, the teachers are asked to imagine how literacy will serve their students in their future situations.

As in previous discussions of immigrant and worker literacy training, this chapter draws on themes of citizenship production and work that circulated through and are reflected by professional publications like *English Journal* as an organizing scheme to examine literacy training. These narratives about teaching writing in traditional classroom settings describe how writing is supposed to respond to larger concerns about citizenship and work (and the changing definitions of each), situating literacy training in higher education as part of a larger process of citizen-making. Teachers attempted to position the teaching of writing as a response to the larger societal anxieties about citizenship and to manage expectations for what the discipline of English was expected to accomplish. This instance of advanced literacy training imposed upon an educated, already literate population worked to create a segment of the citizenry that fit into the economies of literacy.

A focus on higher education as a public good, which Berlin describes as "social rhetoric" in *Rhetoric and Reality*, perpetuated the belief that education should be designed to benefit and enrich a broader citizenry. Citizenship in connection with higher education has often allowed educational institutions to take on the rhetoric of democracy, a space where students become more engaged citizens as a result of their educations. This belief gains support not just because society wants to produce more highly engaged citizens, but also because these desires for better citizens stand in for other anxieties about the tenuous state of citizenship, such as when City College used curriculum and policy to make citizens out of its students. Anxieties about citizenship during this period were not solely because of new immigrant populations or the First World War, but also changing economic conditions. In response to this societal flux, we see English curricula being discussed in two distinct ways—one as a space to reinforce or produce citizens in a direct way and the other as a space to perpetuate the ideals of useful citizenship or the citizen as a useful member of society.

Supporters and administrators of public institutions positioned university-styled literacy as a crucial component in a college education and thus in social mobility. The way universities articulated the goals of literacy, particularly as schools were developing into comprehensive and specialized institutions, offers a glimpse into citizenship as defined by institutions of higher education and literacy's role in shaping that definition. Viewing first-year composition as one of many sites of literacy training and as part of a larger citizenship-producing endeavor, we cannot so easily re-inscribe an enlightenment narrative in which college classrooms develop the power to change student subjectivity through the power of thought without consideration of other factors like students' vocational desires and needs.

This formative moment in the evolution of the first-year writing class was not simply a consequence of the entry of new student populations and the expanding research university (Berlin, Crowley, Paine). Developments in English studies and composition, such as with literacy training more broadly during this period, also served as a response to demographic shifts in the country more generally, the coinciding shifts of the U.S. economy into a mass manufacturing posture, and the shaping of the citizen-as-worker, whose primary responsibility was economic. The early twentieth century saw the rise of factory and office work along with scientific management and the development of technology, which influenced the division of labor in both of these arenas.[20] Whether manual or office laborer, the worker was increasingly employed by another person, marking a shift from the craft orientation that characterized work in the previous century.[21] To fit into this kind of employment system, individuals needed to demonstrate their credentials for particular occupations. Schooling attempted to prepare students for these new jobs, as evidenced by attention to communication skills like writing and speech. Students were taught advanced literacy skills in preparation for work, which in a way was similar to certain groups of immigrants in the federal Americanization programs; however, students were training for a different kind of work. An understanding of the teaching of writing in tandem with a work-inflected idea of citizenship in the early part of the twentieth century helps to contextualize contemporary tensions between fortifying citizenship and building vocational identities in the writing classroom.

As discussed here, the university-styled literacy that resulted should be understood both in terms of preparation for citizenship and for work, just as with other instantiations of literacy. Additionally, it is particularly important to think about this kind of university-styled literacy in terms of use, or perceived usefulness. Teachers, despite what they are teaching, are always arguing for why the course is useful and relevant to students, whether implicitly or explicitly. The writing courses described in the early years of the *English Journal* were responding to changes in work and anxieties about citizenship, similar to that of worker education and immigrant literacy programs. In teachers' discussions about their classes and the discipline of English, we begin to see how citizens produced by colleges and high schools indicated an imagined future for these particular students and how the kind of literacy training being forwarded invited college-educated students to consider their place in it. By identifying students as both citizens- and workers-in-training, these institutions contributed to the increased valuing of literacy for economic survival over the course of the twentieth century and into the twenty-first.

5

TEACHING LITERACY AND CITIZENSHIP IN THE TWENTY-FIRST CENTURY

I n the context of citizenship training in the United States, literacy has been used as a means to ease anxieties about citizenship by cultivating assimilation, empowerment, and employability. The imperative for literacy in each of the three training sites examined in the previous chapters has been influenced by the imagined ways that literacy will prepare students for future identities in the face of anxiety about changes to work, to the demographics of the country, to the economy, and even to the legal boundaries of citizenship. These anxieties, especially those rooted in concerns about economic survival and creating a culture of productivity among a certain segment of Americans, shaped citizenship training—what it taught, where it happened, and who it targeted. In the immigrant citizenship programs, students learned lessons of punctuality and obedience through literacy learning. For the union education supporters, literacy represented a means to gain power in the workplace by increasing union membership and empowering unionists. And for students gaining the credential of formal higher education, teachers of advanced literacy showed themselves to be immensely concerned with the usefulness of writing classes for students' futures as both workers and engaged citizens. From all of these disparate ideas of how literacy would shape citizenship and the quality of that citizenship for students emerges a narrative of equality that is essential to defining the American citizen. The importance of these different locations and manifestations of literacy supports an ever-present American equality narrative, positioning literacy as a crucial component in the achievement of equal citizenship.

Such anxieties about citizenship persist in the United States, a nation that prides itself on being a country of immigrants.[1] And literacy, in its various forms and definitions, continues to play a role. The early twentieth century's development of the "culture of aspiration," as David O. Levine characterizes it, marked the beginning of a period of profound growth in higher education, thus allowing literacy to be increasingly defined by formal education. Throughout the twentieth century, higher education operated on a mode of expansion as governmental guidance toward providing equal opportunity in higher education, such as the 1944 G.I. Bill (Thelin 262), the 1947 President's Commission on Higher Education (Hutcheson 364), and the development of regional public institutions (Thelin 206). Additionally, the expansion of higher education was generated by fights over access to institutions by those who have been traditionally shut out, such as during the civil rights movement and with the open admissions of the 1970s (Otte and Mlynarczyk 5), and by the culture of higher education, which saw the rise of the "multiversity" with its "varied, even conflicting" interests over how to provide mass education (Kerr 15). As Kerr describes, this expansion often relied on a combination of government, political, and cultural interests, such as with the Defense Education Act of 1958, which channeled federal funds into university research as a response to Cold War anxieties and thus expanded the reach of higher education (Kerr 53; Thelin 278).[2] This expansion has continued into the twenty-first century. With the White House statement, "Building American Skills through Community Colleges," in 2010, the Obama administration made another national effort to expand higher education, establishing two national goals for higher education to be met by 2020: graduating the highest proportion of college students than any other country and creating resources for community colleges to graduate an additional 5 million students.

As a result of this expansion and the increasing ubiquity of higher education, university-styled advanced literacy has become even more influential in the production of citizenship. This chapter looks to the present day and the continuing uses of education and employability as measures of an individual's potential for citizenship through concerns about reforming immigration policy, growing questions about the relevance of a college degree, the expansion of higher education, and the belief that higher education can help a person's chances for employment. All are rooted in the same faith in what literacy can do to help produce good citizens, versions of the literacy hope found in union education programs and the productivity and usefulness underscored by Americanization programs and in college classrooms. It is imperative to recognize the cultural management of citizenship that occurred through different kinds of literacy training and to understand what kind of cultural management we as teachers are conducting today. The values that we impress upon our students when we make calls for citizenship are not neutral, and this should be acknowledged and carefully considered.

With its numerous questions about immigration laws, growth in higher education, and changing economic and labor conditions, this description of the period around the First World War could also apply today. Almost a century later, these same tensions over definitions of citizenship, what citizenship means, who has access to which resources, and how literacy cultivates certain values of citizenship are all present in current battles over higher education curriculum and immigration reform. The values and ideals about citizenship and literacy from this previous time of mass manufacturing ascendancy are still relevant and have an impact on how literacy and citizenship distribution respond to present-day anxieties during the decline of mass manufacturing and the rise of the service and knowledge economies in the United States.

Educational and legal responses to current citizenship anxieties illuminate how literacy continues to be implicated in the production of habits of citizenship and often obscure the economic dimensions of how literacy operates as a tool of citizenship production. Because concerns about perpetual economic inequity and survival infiltrate the process of citizenship production, anxieties about citizenship can only be shifted onto, or are even amplified in, other spaces like those where literacy is acquired, as exemplified by the push for more education even in the face of growing student debt or by immigration reform that relies on potential productivity as a measure of citizenship potential. The rhetoric around policy trends, such as in institutions of higher education and their desire to produce globalized citizens or in different proposals for temporary work policies, help to shape the production of habits of citizenship. Trends in higher education and legal policy around immigrant populations construct a sense of citizenship that is highly individualized and based on productive potential, which in turn shapes an individual's experience of what can be gained through a college education.

Contemporary citizenship production in higher education offers a compelling window through which to understand current anxieties about citizenship, particularly in light of the vocational turn in higher education, which W. Norton Grubb and Martin Lazerson call "the most substantial transformation in American schooling over the past century" (4). They describe how "our most vocationalized institutions—the high school, the second-tier comprehensive university, the professionalized research university, the community college" will provide to a broad section of the population "the earlier ideals of political and moral education . . . though they now have to share space with vocational goals" (247). University documents such as strategic plans and learning goals reflect the vocational, political, and moral goals of an institution with-in a global marketplace. These documents reinforce definitions of the ideal citizen as "global" while situating that status within economic and cultural, rather than legal, frameworks. These legal frameworks are impossible to ig-nore in proposed immigration reform such as the DREAM Act (Development, Relief, and Education for Alien Minors) in which the tight bind of literacy as proof of citizenship is used to define citizens both culturally and legally or in temporary work programs in which transnational migration is legitimized but also limited and impermanent. By understanding how contemporary anxieties about citizenship and the use of literacy in the measurement and production of citizenship echoes previous moments, we can understand the implications of changing economic opportunities on our present expectations for citizenship and subsequently, how educators are managing those expectations in the writ-ing classroom in efforts to create literate citizens.

Higher Education and the Production of Citizenship

Citizenship is a state of being with real and urgent consequences. All that in-fluences citizenship—how we define it as a term, the consequences of seeing citizenship as a status anyone can achieve, the way citizenship can help to mask certain inequalities—are not merely theoretical issues that get worked out in scholarship and teaching philosophies. In the space of a classroom, the uses of citizenship can be personalized to a particular teacher's goals or to the stu-dents who are present. Citizenship as a classroom practice can be addressed on this smaller scale, but the use of citizenship as a broader curricular goal has a cumulative effect on an institution's citizenship production, as seen in general education guidelines or strategic plans. And what's at stake is wheth-er—or, rather, which—students are able to effectively marshal that citizenship into material, intellectual, and political citizenship once they have earned their degrees.

At a moment when the call for the production of "global citizens" seems pervasive in the rhetoric of higher education, and while there are simultaneous attacks on the legitimacy of the citizenship of certain individuals, particularly students of color, educators need to answer *how* we are defining citizenship in this context of education and literacy learning. How do we know when a person has become a better citizen as a result of a class or an education? Higher education, and in particular the writing classroom, has built up a strong con-nection to the practice of citizen-making over the last century, and the ever-increasing diversity of student populations, particularly at public institutions, calls for critical attention to that commonplace association. However, does this goal of citizenship production work when certain student populations are not and might not ever be citizens? When do certain students have increased access to full citizenship as compared to others? To that end, it is important to examine the range of implicit and explicit definitions of citizenship that institutions of higher education invoke. When it comes to education's influence on citizenship, the most obvious impact is not necessarily on legal status and its explicit citizenship boundaries, but rather the cultural and social citizenship habits such as informed deliberation, participation, patriotism, and productivity.

Reflecting on schooling, particularly in higher education, in the twentieth century and moving into the twenty-first, educational theorists like Henry Giroux, Claudia Goldin and Lawrence F. Katz, and W. Norton Grubb and Marvin Lazerson, have described its trajectory as moving away from the teaching of moral and civic values to a more vocational effort in which education is associated with preparation for employment of all kinds. In *The Education Gospel*, Grubb and Lazerson argue that the emphasis on vocational goals has been extremely influential, "opening the door to enormous growth in enrollments as well as to many other changes in the purposes of education, the curricular, the meaning schooling has in our society, the mechanisms of upward mobility, the patterns of inequality, conceptions of equity, and a new version of the American dream" (4). Yet this movement toward the vocational also needs to be reconciled with more traditional liberal educational goals of civic and moral values with newer vocational ones, creating a tension indicative of those found across higher education. The ideas discussed in chapter 1 and throughout this book—common beliefs about citizenship and the enactment of equality, achievability, and participation—take on a greater urgency for a growing body of students who may have economic reasons to support a more instrumental version of general education and perhaps a necessary vocational turn in higher education. Citizenship, then, seems to offer this reconciliatory path between liberal arts and vocational goals, yet must be carefully considered.

Academic gadfly Stanley Fish has articulated some concerns about citizenship in the academy by arguing that citizenship issues have no place there. In a widely discussed *New York Times* opinion piece entitled "Why We Built the Ivory Tower," Fish chides colleagues who try to include citizenship in the curriculum by integrating political concerns: "Do your job; don't try to do someone else's job, as you are unlikely to be qualified." The work of academics, he says, is not to produce citizenship, but rather to pursue "truth," and he dismisses those who believe they can do the former. Fish argues, "No doubt, the practices of responsible citizenship and moral behavior should be encouraged in our young adults—but it's not the business of the university to do so."

Fish critiques a central tension in higher education about how to incorporate politically inflected conversations in the classroom. However, this tension can be used productively, as Nancy Welch describes in the article "Living Room: Teaching Public Writing in a Post-Publicity Era," in which students engage in public writing beyond the "stultifying 'letter to the editor' assignment" (475),[3] and as Patricia Bizzell contends in the *College English* opinion piece, "Composition Studies Saves the World!" in the genealogy of writing instruction as part of a liberal arts education that can "affect students' moral and political development positively" (186). Concern about the university's role in the production of healthy citizenship becomes even more urgent with current contentions over the influence of citizenship in the university setting. For instance, the aftereffects of the Patriot Act on international students have created a bureaucracy at universities in which (non-American) student citizenship is continuously scrutinized. Additionally, debates about the DREAM Act, which would allow the children of illegal immigrants to pay in-state tuition at state institutions as a way to increase their access to education and recognize the economic contributions of immigrant parents, represent another space where citizenship has an impact on access to higher education.

These instances mark but two of the ways that universities come into contact with citizenship. While Fish's *New York Times* op-ed depicts what I would call an institutionally internal view of citizenship, in which colleges and universities consider the influence they want to have on the citizenship of their anticipated student bodies, the Patriot and DREAM Acts trigger questions about how external factors impact the citizenship of students, particularly how legal dimensions interact with the intellectual work that universities want to do as they prepare students to be "citizens." Both of these pieces of legislation pointedly demonstrate how the broader legal and theoretical implications of citizenship within the university setting are not only about cultivating increased democratic participation but also the exercise of exclusion and control, particularly among those students with the most tenuous citizenship statuses. These concerns often exist on a parallel plane to the citizenship that is imagined to be cultivated within the classroom; from one perspective, universities are concerned with nurturing the citizenship of students, while from another perspective participating in its enforcement. These two approaches to citizenship within higher education demonstrate the conflicting practices within the institution; both emerge from anxieties about what students are being prepared to do in these educational spaces, with the construct of the citizen being used to establish explicit and implicit expectations of education's "product."

In chapter 1, I discussed the NCTE report "Writing in the Twenty-First Century." By articulating the stakes of teaching writing and connecting citizen-making to education, it is one of many documents that has circulated in the last decade about the role and impact of college education, illuminating current anxieties about what kind of citizen is supposed to be produced by higher education. Perhaps most influential of these reports is *A Test of Leadership: Charting the Future of U.S. Higher Education* from the U.S. Department of Education in September 2006, which depicts a domestic higher educational system at risk and outlines a plan to reinvigorate it. Better known as the Spellings Commission Report, after Bush-era Department of Education Secretary Margaret Spellings, the report was characterized in the news media such as the *New York Times* (Traub, 30 Sept. 2007) as a higher education No Child Left Behind and kicked off a flurry of concern about issues of "access, affordability, quality, and accountability" (Spellings xiii). The last paragraph of the report's preface tells readers that the strengthening of higher education (through the implementation of the commission's proposals, of course) would have numerous benefits for both the nation and individuals, highlighting the need for a highly educated workforce and raising the specter of global competition with statistics about how other countries have quickly surpassed the U.S. on a number of educational metrics. The preface concludes that "what individuals would gain is full access to educational opportunities that allow them to be lifelong learners, productive workers, and engaged citizens" (xiii). Providing a model of citizenship in which an engaged citizenry is inextricably linked at the individual level to both education and productivity, the Spellings report underscores the importance of accountability, much like No Child Left Behind and the K–12 Common Core State Standards implementation, asking colleges to find (presumably curricular) ways to achieve this model of citizenship for their students.

Moving away from an accountability model but still invoking productivity, the National Leadership Council for Liberal Education and America's Promise (LEAP), part of the Association of American Colleges and Universities, released its own report, "College Learning for the New Global Century," in 2007. Composed of a diverse cross-section of "educational, business, community, and policy leaders" (National Leadership Council vii),[4] As a counterpoint to the Spelling Commission's assessment-oriented vision of education, LEAP attempted to articulate the role of college education for a wide range of students in the United States. The report "spells out the essential aims, learning outcomes, and guiding principles for a twenty-first-century college education" and links higher education with the future of an American society "that will depend on graduates' future leadership and capabilities" (vii). For LEAP, these outcomes "should be fostered and developed across the entire educational experience, and in the context of students' major fields" (2). The report by LEAP underscores the essential idea that the educational aims, outcomes, and principles of a college education should prepare students for "work, life, and citizenship" (2) in order to build the foundations for their promising futures. The report's examination of these three intertwined goals makes explicit the increased attention to citizen-making and preparatory elements of higher education and reinforces a long-standing connection among these goals. No longer is "liberal education" the domain of the privileged, but rather a way to access "America's most valued economic asset" (13–14), the young citizens of the country. Through the frame of citizenship, this valuable economic asset is positioned as highly accessible, underscoring the need for both education and good citizenship in order for a college education to be worthwhile.

Instead of preparing a privileged few (see Berlin, Thelin), higher education, as posited in these reports, positions itself as a key component in the broad creation of a productive and satisfied citizenry. The original push for general education itself was a curricular reaction against specialization and vocationalization, a way to prevent students from "fall[ing] short of that human wholeness and civic conscience which the cooperative activities of citizenship require" (U.S., *Higher Education for Democracy* 49). With the Commission on Higher Education in 1946, arguably a moment that consolidated the work of higher education toward a common national goal, President Truman charged educators with the "task of examining the function of higher education in our democracy and the means by which they can best be performed" (Thelin 268). In the second half of the twentieth century and at the beginning of the twenty-first, higher education has seen the rise and fall of open admissions policies, growing student populations, and increased student diversity, all of which point to a growing number of institutions that have expanded educational opportunities and, as a result, offer the possibility of democratic citizenship to those who pass through them. The increase in access has tracked alongside increasing pressures for colleges to vocationalize or at least answer calls to make themselves relevant, which seems logical given that a broader population of students would result in a higher imperative for employable skills after graduation. The weight of citizen-making in higher education suggests that citizenship itself is the umbrella under which all of these different goals fall.

For instance, literacy teachers who hope to integrate literacy and citizenship production might choose to think of citizenship as increased civic participation and imagine students gaining better ways of communicating and expressing public opinion as a result of their classes. Critical literacy as styled by the university writing classroom is thus positioned as a tool that allows citizens to fully realize their citizenship by cultivating their participation skills. But for a student without legal residency or who feels like he or she has tenuous citizenship status, a class that calls for the promotion and cultivation of citizenship might mean that the student already has an impossible task to accomplish in the class, or such a class can even put a student in jeopardy by asking him or her to enter a public arena that they might prefer to avoid. Also, while participation through public writing introduces one way citizenship is cultivated through the distribution of literacy, literacy in the name of citizenship can also yield a citizenship that looks like the enforcement of certain values—an emphasis on self-improvement, an imperative of productivity, or a belief in civic responsibility. There seems to be a central tension between these two "brands" of citizenship, between a citizenship measured by the self-improvement and success of the individual versus a citizenship measured by the degree of participation and civic responsibility, with literacy playing a key role in both. Literacy educators must figure out how explicit civic goals like participation can and do fit in with varying definitions of legal and cultural citizenship, being aware and even wary of the potential disjuncture between the direct citizen-making that can be part of the classroom experience and the possible contradictions, particularly with certain student populations, such as those who cannot attain or perhaps do not desire legal citizenship.

A necessary part of understanding this dynamic means thinking beyond the individual classroom level and figuring out what role the writing classroom plays in accomplishing broader institutional goals. Consider, for instance, campuswide strategic plans that help to guide the changes and development at many institutions. These documents are aspirational in a sense; most discuss the same or similar ideas, particularly at public institutions—increasing the prestige of the institution, improving student success, preparing students for a globalizing world, addressing the diversity of students and faculty, and learning how to operate effectively with fewer resources or at least some nod to fund-raising. But from these abstract ideals, university policy presumably is created. The project or campuswide initiative that can associate itself with a key phrase like "student success," "excellence," "technology," or "globalization" often attracts money and administrative attention. University strategic plans and their associated buzzwords provide insight into how an institution imagines citizenship and the student-citizens that are being created at a particular school. The financial and institutional support of certain initiatives or programs over others illuminates the type of citizenship supported beyond the common phrasing often found in strategic plans such as goals to "prepare graduates for lives as educated and engaged citizens" (Pennsylvania State 21) or to "educate students to act as citizens of the nation and an ever-shrinking and interdependent world, cultivating through our curricula the idea that the betterment of humanity is our business" (University of Illinois at Urbana-Champaign 12).

Others might not invoke citizenship explicitly as a term, but will still include certain citizenship ideals and habits in their goals; for instance, Iowa State's strategic plan seeks to provide a diverse education that helps students to "create, share, and apply knowledge to make Iowa and the world a better place" and "prepare students for lifelong, productive participation in society."

Often, strategic plans such as these articulate an elaboration of the citizen beyond civic and participatory practices to one of more economic import, so that something like "global citizenship" defines students almost exclusively in terms of their productive capacities, invoking cultural understanding of the global that privileges skills that are salable on the marketplace and obscures the effects of the transnational movement of people. This emphasis on the employability of students can be attributed partially to the vocational turn in higher education, which Grubb and Lazerson attribute to the growth of education over the last century and the growing promise of education as job training at a range of institutions from community colleges to research universities. As a result, one implication of how citizenship is constructed through educational institutions is the subsequent deemphasis on the aspects of cultural citizenship that do not have an immediate economic payoff. For instance, it is telling that in the Pennsylvania State University strategic plan (as with many others, including at my own institution), there is a section on globalization that discusses the importance of internationalizing the faculty and student populations that is immediately adjacent to a section on addressing the challenges of the student body's growing diversity. But despite the common discourse of global citizens being the desired outcome of a college education, in which students would learn in college how to traverse languages, cultures, and nations toward a more cosmopolitan way of being, often the students who can already be considered "global" are doing so on a cultural level, on a familial level, rather than an economic one. So while achieving a sense of global citizenship is a marketable attribute, strategic plans such as these seem to imply that diversity is a problem that needs to be solved. As a result, the potential contributions students can make to those cultural dimensions of citizenship education somehow seem invisible in the higher education context.[5]

Documents such as these strategic plans show that in articulations about the goals of higher education, use of "citizen" as a commonplace term often channels tensions about growing vocationalism and anxieties about waning citizenship privileges. The plans portray the good citizen produced through higher education as someone with flexible literacy and the resulting capacity to be a global citizen, to operate between and among nation-state boundaries and presumably to use highly literate skills in order to negotiate among these different spaces to demonstrate qualifications for a future job and to compete in a global market. As Grubb and Lazerson assert, this transformation of education from liberal to vocational marks a central tension in educational policy today, as policy makers and educators (and even students) feel unable to reconcile civic and moral goals of liberal education with the goal of employable skills through vocational education, illustrated by the increase in majors such as business and the decrease in humanities and by the shift in "the purpose of education from collective goals—the maintenance of democracy, the preparation of moral leaders—to private goals like access to valued occupations" (150). Higher education thus establishes itself as an institution attempting to produce certain kinds of good citizens through curricular changes, although the efficacy of such changes is far from proven.

Emphasis on citizenship has become pervasive in discussions about the goals of both higher education and the goals of writing instruction, marking higher education and high functioning literacy as crucial components in the cultivation of the good citizen. Because first-year composition and other institutional writing courses serve a preparatory function and are a common element of most general education curricula, these courses become positioned as an integral part of student success and achievement through attempts to transform students into literate and engaged citizens. The writing classroom, a primary space for literacy distribution at the university level, often lies at the nexus of tensions between the higher education goals of vocation and citizenship. For example, in the "Goals for Student Writing" document that my own institution uses to guide all writing-intensive courses across disciplines, the second sentence asserts, "The professional success and personal satisfaction of twenty-first century citizens require fluency with a broad range of modes of communication," and that writing instruction "aims to enable students to take ownership of language and to develop a capacity for both critical analysis and considered reflection" (Queens College). Such statements make a common connection between critical literacy and citizenship, and represent citizenship as both work success and personal satisfaction, all made possible by the efficacy of one's literate communication skills. First-year writing classes function as a microcosm of the anxieties put upon the university; additionally, they represent what higher education seeks to accomplish and the expectations of what literacy can do. Thus, civic behavior will emerge from these traits and a certain level of writing skill and education can help individuals attain these economic goals and advance personal citizenship.

In many of these discussions about the role and goals of higher education, one term endures: citizenship. And underlying these discussions about citizenship and vocationalism are questions about the relevance of education. These questions about the importance of a college education have been asked both within academia, such as Gerald Graff's *Clueless in Academe* and Richard Arum and Josipa Roksa's *Academically Adrift*, and in the popular media like Kate Zernike's "Making College 'Relevant'" in the *New York Times* and "College Is Dead. Long Live College!" in *Time* magazine. Every question about assessment, general education, accountability, massive open online courses (MOOCs), and the like seeks the relevance of education in addition to its effectiveness. The integration of citizenship as a curricular goal has made education appear relevant beyond its instrumental goals, but as these examples demonstrate, institutions may also end up undertaking the risky task of measuring effectiveness only by the employability of their graduates, thus undermining the possibility of a fully realized political citizenship.

If, as Grubb and Lazerson claim, institutions of higher education have turned increasingly to preparing students for employment (5) instead of liberally educated critical thinkers, then it follows that the kind of citizen being created has also changed. Educational theorist David F. Labaree, in categorizing educational purposes into three goals—democratic equality, social efficiency, and social mobility (41), describes how "the democratic equality goal arises from the citizen, social efficiency from the taxpayer and employer, and social mobility from the educational consumer. The first goal expresses the politics of citizenship, the second expresses the politics of human capital, and the third expresses the politics of individual opportunity" (42). Like Grubb and Lazerson, Labaree argues that the increasing importance of social mobility as a goal of education allows vocational goals to dominate the other two. I contend, however, that in addition to being dominated by vocational goals, these conflicts are often obscured and subsumed by the concept of citizenship as seen in the pervasive use of the term. The communication-based skills described by Grubb and Lazerson as key characteristics of vocational higher education could also be used to describe the long-standing connection between literacy and citizenship. Because of this connection, citizenship has not been overshadowed by vocational goals or efficiency goals; rather, the citizenship constructed by higher education often simultaneously encourages civic behavior, productivity, *and* social mobility. And the use of the citizen to link these endeavors within general education reveals how debates about the goals of education in general can influence the work of the writing classroom and university-styled literacy, both implicitly and explicitly.

The use of "citizenship" as a term in relation to higher education and writing program goals offers weight and relevancy to curriculum. An unintended consequence, however, is the obfuscation of the economic influence on definitions of citizenship. Additionally, the pervasive conflicting messages about the kind of citizenship an institution aims to produce might also obscure the legal implications associated with citizenship, ones also tightly bound to economic conditions.

Legislating Citizenship

In spring 2006, protests calling for immigration reform sprang up in communities across the United States. Hundreds of thousands of people marched in the streets of large cities like Los Angeles, New York, Chicago, Washington, DC, as well as in smaller cities and towns and on college campuses across the nation.[6] At the heart of these protests were concerns about access to citizenship, immigrant work policies, and education. While these protests did not garner any widespread immigration reform, this movement articulated what has been at stake in contemporary battles over immigration policy. Immigrant workers and their supporters asked for more humane policies that, among other things, would recognize the contribution nonlegal immigrant workers were making to the U.S. economy by creating a pathway to citizenship for long-term residents of the United States and the possibility of increased access to resources like education for the children of these workers. These debates about immigration policy and citizenship boundaries cast citizenship as a status achieved by those who worked hard to earn it. In this section, I examine the rhetoric of work, opportunity, and language in legislative battles in the early twenty-first century that connect legal status to education and work, such as the debates over temporary worker policies and the proposed DREAM Act.

A familiarity with current immigration policy, particularly in light of proposed immigration reform by President Obama and by Congress in 2013, is important for educators who imagine themselves as participating in the production of citizens today. The legal landscape imposes the restrictions and boundaries put upon citizenship by determining who has access to legal status, a crucial component of citizenship that ensures access to the geographic space of the nation. Additionally, the contours of these legal debates may provide additional insights into the role of education and literacy for students who want to achieve not only cultural markers of citizenship but the legal status as well through such policies as the DREAM Act, which provides a pathway to citizenship and educational resources for high school graduates without current legal status. Work, education, and literacy are all significant tropes in the language of immigration reform, particularly in discussions about proposed pathways to citizenship. As discussed in chapter 2, legal policies help to shape the production of cultural citizenship habits by creating a set of conditions through which certain attributes like literacy and productivity are valued and ascribed to good citizenship. These characteristics are intended to be signifiers of an individual's citizenship potential. Contemporary immigration policy has been shaped by border control and deportation, with different categories of visas serving as characterizations of an immigrant's role—the student, the tourist, the short-term temporary worker, the highly skilled temporary worker, to name a few of the primary categories. These policies contribute to the shift in immigration policy away from familial reunification of the Immigration and Nationality Act of 1965 toward a continuing emphasis on jobs and intellect.[7]

Use of education and literacy as evidence of an individual's citizenship potential illustrates that laws and policies such as the DREAM Act and temporary worker programs do not simply enforce particular cultural habits and practices of citizenship for individuals; rather, the enduring rhetoric around these proposals also shapes broader beliefs about what it takes for immigrants to become worthy of citizenship. Additionally, habits like being literate make their way into arguments for changing the legal boundaries of citizenship, with "highly skilled" workers having more paths, more possibilities for legitimized mobility. This dialogic process indicates the complexity of understanding how citizenship influences and is influenced simultaneously by work and literacy.

Fear of the Immigrant in Temporary Worker Policies and Immigration Reform

At the start of his second term in 2013, President Obama proposed extensive immigration reform in the United States, which encompassed many of President George W. Bush's proposed policies about temporary work programs. Both the Obama and Bush plans called for a revamped temporary worker program under which undocumented workers already in the United States could gain temporary legal status. Such a program would address the tenuous living and working conditions of eleven million undocumented workers, granting certain protections and legal rights. Simultaneously, the proposals responded to anxieties about foreign workers entering the country illegally and taking jobs from citizens by putting a time limit on their presence in the country, becoming another addition to the sustained trend of fear-driven U.S. immigrant work policy.

Introducing this program marked the beginning of the Bush administration's efforts to solve the temporary immigrant work issue in 2004; yet immigration reform eluded his administration, culminating in nationwide pro-immigrant protests in spring 2006 and continuing in debates over the actions of the Minuteman Project, an anti-immigration citizen border patrol group, and local laws to prosecute businesses hiring undocumented workers (e.g., the Illegal Immigration Relief Act passed in Hazleton, Pennsylvania, in 2007, which was designed to discourage the hiring and housing of illegal immigrants). The state immigration laws passed in Arizona (2010) and Alabama (2011), based on enforcing immigration status, particularly in workplaces, underscore the trouble any presidential administration has with immigration reform and with continuing battles over who should be allowed to stay in the United States and who has access to particular resources while in the country. As of this writing, it is unclear if Obama's proposals will become policy, owing to continuing controversy over whether a temporary worker program would threaten jobs for U.S. workers.

Anxiety over jobs, among other societal resources including education and healthcare, fuels many of these debates. Sociologist Saskia Sassen describes this attitude as the "enactment of a series of dynamics usually associated with immigration" in Europe and the United States in which "anti-immigrant feelings, racialization, a crisis mentality about controlling immigration, [and] rapid fluctuations from periods of acute demand for foreign workers to mass unemployment [are] blamed on these same workers" (xiii). Illegal immigrants provide a ready supply of labor for a U.S. economy and standard of living that is reliant on cheap labor to perform behind-the-scenes, labor-intensive tasks. Even with movements in the United States toward exporting jobs in manufacturing and, more recently, clerical work and telemarketing, certain tasks cannot be outsourced such as restaurant work, housecleaning, child care, farm work, meat processing, construction, and others. The complex web of policies and laws surrounding immigrant work famously spawns loopholes and back doors, allowing an underground economy to thrive around these occupations, many based on cash payrolls. The economic downturn resulting from the financial crisis of 2007–08 also magnified the feeling that immigrants were taking jobs away from U.S. citizens.

Proposed temporary work programs such as President Bush's failed proposal and President Obama's 2013 proposal underscore the importance of productivity in evaluating immigrants and assessing how these kinds of policies categorize workers, particularly those who perform low-wage and low-skilled work, thus creating a permanent link between tenuous status and low-prestige work. Additionally, paths toward citizenship, for the most part, are driven by the logic that lies underneath temporary work policies and other work-oriented immigration policies: immigrant workers are measured by the economic contribution they are making to the country, one that weighs their worth against citizens who have primary ownership over resources like jobs. So even though temporary work programs have been fraught, the underground economy that thrives around certain kinds of work indicates a tacit approval of immigrants performing this kind of low-prestige work, even if temporary, as a way to prove themselves, despite their education level.

The legal terms of citizenship are quite clear—there are those who are citizens and those who are not. In the U.S. immigration system, noncitizens are made up of two large categories—immigrants and nonimmigrants. *Immigration and Citizenship*, a casebook on immigration law, makes this distinction: "Immigrants, as the label suggests, come to take up permanent residence, whereas non-immigrants enter for a specific purpose to be accomplished during a temporary stay—which might nonetheless last for many years" (Aleinikoff et al. 2003, 265). Nonimmigrants include workers with H-2A and H-2B visas admitted to the United States for quick and temporary entry—H-2B visas for agricultural workers and H-2A designating nonagricultural fields. The category of nonimmigrants also includes those with temporary visas like tourists or students who overstay their time limits. The group of low-wage workers addressed by temporary worker programs do not always fall within the legal boundaries of the permanent residency categories, which allows immigrants to legally reside and work in the United States, but in reality they cannot necessarily be considered "temporary" either.

The terminology used to draw nuances among these different categories of immigrants is telling. For example, "temporary worker" emphasizes the nonpermanent aspect of foreign-born labor. Simply put, they have come to the United States to work, but only on a temporary basis. Other terms used for this group of workers are similarly revealing. Nonnative residents, illegal aliens, noncitizens, immigrants, and temporary workers all differ in meaning and intention but generally refer to a group of people who live and/or work in the United States without having attained citizenship or legal residency, a contested group that is discussed in terms of what they can, but mostly what they cannot, contribute to the United States. The language itself reveals societal beliefs about the contributions and value of these noncitizen workers.[8] While recognizing that the categories of immigrants and nonimmigrants are legal categories distinguishing those who are formally recognized as residents of the United States, it is important to understand the impact of these categorizations beyond strict legal definitions. Supporters of progressive immigration reform have argued for the use of "noncitizen" or "noncitizen workers" in order to emphasize the unjustly diminutive status enacted upon this population, departing from legal uses of noncitizen to include both immigrant and nonimmigrant peoples. Use of the more common "illegal" reinforces the belief that (1) such workers should solely be identified as criminals, and (2) all low-wage, nonnative workers are in the United States illegally.

The shades of difference in this terminology emerge from the contradiction of fear-driven policy and labor needs, particularly in the workplace, which reveals the intersection of immigration, labor, and status. Since the term "illegal" is most often associated with low-wage workers, it foregrounds the illegal status of those individuals and enforces their illegitimacy while, in contrast, technology workers have been actively recruited in recent years. In *Examining the Importance of the H-1B Visa to the American Economy*, a 2003 hearing on the importance of the H-1B (the visa sponsored by U.S. employers for high-skilled workers) to the American economy, Senator Orrin Hatch asked, "whether the current anti-immigration sentiment is in the long-term interest of the American economy and American workers. If our Nation is to stay competitive, can we do without having access to the most talented individuals from abroad?" (2). Hatch's sentiments echo those of Warren R. Leiden, speaking about employment-based immigration on behalf of the American Immigration Lawyers Association. Leiden told the U.S. Subcommittee on Immigration during a 2001 immigration policy hearing that "in the increasingly global economy, [employment-based immigration] helps keep America competitive by attracting some of the best and the brightest, and international personnel are essential to developing products that will appeal to other countries and societies" (*Immigration Policy* 11). These sentiments about needing talented immigrants— the "best and brightest"—to fuel the American economy and keep the country competitive stand in stark contrast to the tropes of fear, dependence, and illegality used to discuss the low-wage noncitizen labor. This marked difference in terminology describing the two kinds of immigrant workers reflects disparate attitudes toward the work being performed and the type of worker in question. The legal distinctions between H-1B and H-2A/B visas, between those who are highly skilled and educated and those who are not, reinforce the notion that citizenship possibilities are not the same for all workers. By exposing this contradiction, the rationales for such boundaries begin to feel shaky.

Under a temporary worker program, undocumented aliens would work without fear of deportation, but both the Bush and Obama plans also clearly stated that such participation in the American economy would not help workers gain permanent status or citizenship. Unwillingness to recognize these initial "temporary" work periods in considerations of status changes brings to the forefront anxieties about the country's reliance on disposable labor. Not offering citizenship or more permanent legal status to such workers establishes an unsatisfactory system in which immigrant workers can remain nonentities, unwelcome as citizens or permanent residents but welcome to work within the borders of the United States; more permanent status would acknowledge their necessity and thus change the face of American citizenship. Attempting to ease anxieties by restricting access to citizenship creates and supports a rhetoric that establishes additional roadblocks immigrants must overcome in the process of establishing a viable life in the United States, whether as a naturalized citizen, permanent resident, or temporary worker.

Such dynamics affect how we look at citizenship, immigration, and labor laws involving nonnative populations. These anxieties are often exposed in deliberations about the distribution of societal resources such as employment or education among the population. For example, while introducing his proposed temporary worker program, Bush responded, with careful wording, to the belief that immigrant workers were a financial threat to U.S. citizens, requiring that "employers who extend job offers must first make every reasonable effort to find an American worker for the job at hand" ("Remarks"). The Obama administration extended the sentiment when he said that those who "grow our economy" will be welcomed, while those who were "living here illegally must be held responsible for their actions by . . . going to the back of the line" ("Streamlining Legal Immigration"). Rationales for policies like the temporary worker program are rooted in a common belief that illegal immigrants are a drain on the U.S. economy because they take our resources, live off of our welfare, and benefit from our schools. In truth, the U.S. economy relies on the labor of illegal immigrant workers, particularly in high labor/low status jobs. But the need for the labor of low wage immigrant workers still does not bring legitimate recognition, as represented by their lack of citizenship status.[9]

Both the Bush and Obama proposals attempt to establish careful boundaries around who can be a potential citizen. However, they ultimately break down when they strive to decriminalize some low-wage workers by allowing them to work in the United States legally for distinct periods of time while simultaneously refusing to legitimate their status (e.g., efforts to restrict access to public assistance and education). Noncitizens who make economic contributions but are not given access to societal resources blur the categories of citizen and noncitizen, revealing the contradictory ways that citizenship functions, particularly as a membership category. In response to this blurring of citizenship, it is useful to think about the terms of citizenship in two ways—the literal terms (i.e., terminology) used to make distinctions between citizens and noncitizens and the terms (i.e., rules) under which individuals are considered citizens and how these terms are established through various sites of citizenship production.

For young immigrants in particular, this means always having to deal with the burdensome association of being suspicious or a noncitizen. And in the case of those with noncitizen status, young immigrants are in a permanent space of illegitimacy, even while participating in the educational system that is supposed to help all young people advance. As I discuss in the next section, being literate and educated are supposed to help young immigrants gain legitimacy, which proponents of the DREAM Act have used as markers of productivity to argue for education-based immigration reform.

The DREAM Act and Being American

In addition to regulating work and the production of certain categories of worker, immigration policies and their attendant debates are often centered around the distribution of public resources—who can or cannot have access to services such as emergency rooms and privileges such as drivers' licenses. But more often than not, the resource most sought after and most contentious is education. In these debates, education and high literacy skills serve both as evidence for the potential or achievement of good citizenship and as a resource that must be protected from use by undocumented immigrants. In the DREAM Act debates, this dual tension is particularly fierce.

The DREAM Act has been part of various immigration reform proposals since its introduction to the Senate in 2001. The act proposes allowing undocumented minors who have GEDs or high school diplomas to begin a pathway to citizenship by rewarding them with permanent residency after two years of military service or college, as well as be eligible for in-state tuition at public universities. The DREAM Act would put into law the assumption that people already able to perform citizenship duties through participation in education or the military should be put on the path to becoming legal citizens, thus measuring citizenship potential through a person's potential for productivity. Like much immigration reform, it has been contentiously deliberated but never passed, with its most recent legislative defeat by filibuster in the Senate in December 2010. In 2011, Senator Harry Reid reintroduced the bill, but it stalled. Some legislators such as Senator Marco Rubio discussed the possibility of a noncitizenship version of the DREAM Act in which those proven undocumented minors can gain permanent residency but not a more expedient path to citizenship, a distinction that underscores the importance of enforcing boundaries between the citizen and noncitizen. The debates around the DREAM Act were subverted temporarily in June 2012 by President Obama when he enacted similar proposals with an executive action to halt deportation of young people who would qualify for residency through the DREAM Act (and until the act becomes law, this action could be reversed by Obama or any of his successors as easily as he enacted this policy change). In 2013, at the writing of this book, the debates continue in proposed immigration policy reform and probably will in perpetuity as long as a U.S. citizenry exists. Similar to the temporary worker policies discussed earlier, the DREAM Act puts nonlegal immigrants in a position to prove themselves worthy of citizenship. But instead of direct economic contributions such as the low-wage work discussed in the previous section, their economic potential is measured by success in high school, college, and military service. As legislation, the DREAM Act has the potential to change the legal boundaries of citizenship by recognizing some forms of cultural citizenship such as participation through education and military service and by transforming them to legal status.

There are no easy answers when it comes to immigration policy, but what legislation like the DREAM Act tries to do is to create an opportunity to legitimize hard-working, educated young people with a two-fold logic: first, the government has already invested resources into these individuals who never asked to be brought to this country in the first place. At a 28 June 2011 hearing on the DREAM Act, Secretary of Education Arne Duncan described how allowing such individuals in-state college tuition and a pathway to citizenship would be an "investment, not an expense" (Lennard), presumably in the face of critics of the DREAM Act who only see crowds of undocumented workers taking jobs from unemployed Americans. And again, as with university strategic plans, we see citizenship being constructed in terms of the economic contribution an individual can potentially make to the country. In both of these discussions, status is traded on whether a person will contribute to or drain society's resources.

Second, arguments often rely on narratives by those who say they are U.S. citizens in every way but legal status, as seen in the June 2012 *Time* magazine cover that pictured a group of young people with the headline "We are Americans" and an accompanying asterisk with "Just not legally." Such appeals are most evident in the narratives used in arguments to support immigration reform like the DREAM Act. They are often young people who were unwittingly brought to the United States by parents. Often touting the American dream as their motivation, they offer their success in school and their tenacity as evidence of their legitimacy. These stories reinforce the belief that education is an integral part of defining citizenship by relying on audience identification with educational success.

The idea of using formal education as a means to earn citizenship has endured, not just in the DREAM Act's numerous federal incarnations and numerous defeats, but also in states that have passed various versions of DREAM Acts with a focus on either in-state tuition for nonlegal immigrants or access to state-funded financial aid. In 2001, Texas passed the first law of its kind that provided in-state tuition for young, nonlegal immigrants who attended a Texas public school for three years, graduated with a Texas high school diploma, and could prove they were in the process of naturalizing (Rincón 89). Between 2001 and 2006, similar laws were passed in nine other states, including California, Illinois, and New York (2002),[10] with others that followed during the years since in Oregon, Colorado, and other states. In 2011, California and Illinois passed additional legislation allowing qualified nonlegal immigrants (those with diplomas and the requisite residency) access to state-funded financial aid. New York Senator Kirsten Gillibrand called on her local constituents to support a similar bill in New York, noting that "investing in the dreams of our immigrant youth is not only the moral thing to do. It is a social, academic and economic imperative" (27 Dec. 2011). This focus on students and increasing their access to higher education marks a perhaps not unremarkable contrast to other states-oriented immigration policies that are more restrictive, such as those in Alabama and Arizona. However, state-specific policies only add to the confusion about what makes a citizen, because while states provide their own legal boundaries over different resources, federal policy mandates the legal status of citizenship; no state can confer legal citizenship status (or take it away, for that matter), even if a young immigrant has gained access to certain citizenship resources like education.

In debates over the DREAM Act, immigration advocates have incorporated the economic into their emotional appeals. These two ways of characterizing a young immigrant as an investment and with potential for success though educational attainment reinforce a merit-based system for immigration policy and citizenship conferral, contributing to the rise of what Judith Shklar calls "economic citizenship" in which "a good citizen is an earner, because independence is the indelibly necessary quality of genuine, democratic citizenship" (92). This definition of citizenship is a departure from others that might privilege civic engagement or even ones that emerge from the legal arena such as the race privilege of the 1924 immigration act or the focus on family reunification that resulted from the 1965 immigration act.

The DREAM Act reinforces the long-standing appeal of education and literacy as components of defining citizenship. In it, education works as both evidence of citizenship potential as well as the payoff. Additionally, it codifies certain beliefs about citizenship in relation to education that, given the law's long time in limbo, are apparently somewhat controversial: (1) education and literacy can be used as a measure for who is worthy of receiving societal resources like education and legal status like citizenship; (2) legal status should follow cultural citizenship (not the other way around, as we might imagine with immigrants coming to Ellis Island, becoming citizens, and then becoming Americans in the cultural sense); and (3) to be a good citizen means you must first be a productive citizen. This intersection of multiple strands of citizenship issues speaks to the recurrence of DREAM Act proposals and the act's enduring appeal, even in the face of multiple defeats.

Such appeal is most evident in the narratives used in arguments to support immigration reform such as the DREAM Act. The highly public "coming out," so to speak, of the journalist Jose Antonio Vargas, who published an essay about his illegal status in the *New York Times Magazine* in 2011, serves as an apt example of how educational success, literate skills, and potential productivity are used as evidence for extending the boundaries of rightful citizenship. In his essay, Vargas documents his path upon arrival in the United States from an unknowing, twelve-year old, undocumented immigrant to a Pulitzer Prize–winning reporter, noting the importance of the mentors and sponsors who helped him go to college, earn internships, and get jobs, despite his illegal status. Vargas underscores one of the main tensions between cultural citizenship and legal status when he writes, "I convinced myself all would be O.K. if I lived up to the qualities of a 'citizen': hard work, self-reliance, love of my country." Individuals such as Vargas are taught that the first step to becoming a citizen is to act like a citizen; here he cites being a patriotic, economically independent, industrious worker as the key attributes to becoming a citizen. The DREAM Act not only emphasizes these attributes but also wants to codify them into law.

In many ways, Vargas's experience parallels that of other undocumented young people who have chosen to make themselves public figures in these heated immigration policy debates, trying to find safety in the public eye, rather than cower in the shadows. Earlier in 2011, the *New York Times* featured another less high-profile undocumented immigrant, Isabel Castillo, who has many of the same characteristics as Vargas—successful at school and diligent (Winerip A10). However, even though she was able to subvert the documentation needed to attend college, she was not able to do the same while looking for a job in social work. So instead of working as a social worker, she is now earning a living by working off the books as a waitress and working for the passage of the DREAM Act, which would allow her residency and the ability to work legally as a result of her successful completion of college.

What these two examples have in common are the characterizations of the individuals—hard working, literate, educated, innocent. They're cast not as criminals but rather as individuals who have had the status of illegality foisted upon them by parents who broke the law. In contrast to the rhetoric of the "anchor baby," which casts a suspicious eye on parents who come to the United States without documentation in order to produce an American citizen by birth, these immigrant narratives rely on the innocence of children who were brought here unknowingly, their diligent work habits that have led to success in school, and finally, their fear of discovery. They are worthy of citizenship status because they act like citizens. Individuals such as Vargas and Castillo already act like citizens and as a result they should become citizens, so the argument goes. They learned to act this way through the educational system; they have good grades, diplomas, and facility with the English language. Legislation such as the DREAM Act attempts to use education to legitimize industrious, educated young people who "never asked to be brought to this country in the first place" with the logic that success in school indicates an individual's potential to perform citizenship. Vargas has established a website, Define American, which is devoted to making public these kinds of narratives in an effort to bring the contributions of undocumented residents to light. What is compelling about these kinds of narratives is how they are being used to argue for the DREAM Act, to focus support on those who have the tenacity to make it through the gauntlet of the U.S. educational system on their own.[11] In both of these stories, there is a common thread of education, literacy, and language as proof of commitment to the United States. There is discussion of degrees earned, jobs that could have been. They are good students. And they are using the literacy they learned to explain how they are Americans in every way but their legal status.

However, the difference between the stories of these two individuals (and many of those who have written on Define American or other sites like United We Dream), is that one has been able to work through back channels with the help of sponsors and mentors to become a Pulitzer Prize-winning journalist and the other is getting paid under the table to waitress in the rural town where she grew up. This distinction seems to reflect an attitude about immigration that privileges individuals who can figure it out for themselves, with the implication that success depends on whether you can to work within the system to gain the necessary citizenship attributes. Admittedly, this is patently a U.S attitude in a pull-up-your-bootstraps kind of way and is reinforced by the construction of citizenship based on economic success that occurs both in places like higher education and in the legal realm through immigration policy. These messages about what makes a citizen through higher education and what makes a citizen through legal channels can result in a highly individualized process of citizenship acquisition. In this way, gaining citizenship seems almost like a gladiator-esque game in which only the strong survive. Only a few might make it to the end.

While the DREAM Act itself is laudable in its move to reward hard-working young people, the burden of earning citizenship becomes inextricably tied to those who can succeed in traditional school settings; in other words, the educational success and high literate skills of a nonlegal immigrant is supposed to guarantee their future economic contributions (or perhaps military service because you risk your life). In these narratives, learning English and becoming literate is often seen as proof for undocumented residents. If literacy is a measure of a person's productivity and also commitment to the United States, there is a sense in which English language learners are always suspect, always needing more, always at a deficit. These narratives highlight the authors' use of English language skills in an attempt to show that they are worthy of citizenship and demonstrate a loyalty that might be in question because of immigrants' possible hybrid allegiances. Vargas's relationship with the English language and the development of his literate skills play a significant role in how he became American. He underscores the importance of language instruction, explaining, "my first challenge was the language. Though I learned English in the Philippines, I wanted to lose my accent. From the moment I wrote my first article for the student paper, I convinced myself that having my name in print—writing in English, interviewing Americans—validated my presence here." He eventually became an award-wining journalist, using his literate skills for his job. In the essay, he uses these same literate skills to tell his story and prove that he is just like other Americans. The profile of Castillo also underscores the role of education and literacy, not just by her own estimation but also her mother's. When the reporter "asked how she felt about her daughter's education, she said, 'I'm very proud she has something to defend herself with'" (Winerip A10). The article describes how Castillo organized the Harrisonburg, Virginia, DREAM Act chapter, spending much of her time giving interviews and speeches to various community groups. Even though Castillo is not working in her chosen field, she can defend herself with her education, specifically her facility with language and literacy, in the eyes of her mother but also according to those who turn to her as an expert in immigration issues for young people.

Similar to the literacy test of the earlier twentieth century, education and literacy in English now operate as different kinds of gatekeepers, but instead of one test, the necessary level of education and literacy is elevated. The difference is that the DREAM Act facilitates a real integration of the importance of formal education into definitions of citizenship, particularly for those who are already in the country and acting like citizens. In the era of assessment, the aftermath of No Child Left Behind, and the advent of the K–12 Common Core, a public school curriculum that is test- and goal-oriented and competency-based also enforces a kind of citizenship that emphasizes productivity. While the DREAM Act itself is laudable in its move to reward hard-working young people, the burden of earning citizenship becomes inextricably tied to success in traditional school settings; in other words, the educational success and high literate skills of a nonlegal immigrant is assumed to guarantee their future economic contributions.

The common narratives about the "dreamers" that work to legitimize the citizenship of certain industrious and educationally successful young people (their narratives all say, look at me, I work hard, I get good grades, I'm an American, I'm legitimate), but I question the pressure to expand U.S. citizenship in a way that is increasingly reliant on educational success or, rather, evidence of productivity. The impact of these arguments about citizenship, such as those in the debates about the DREAM Act, have the perhaps unintended potential to force a neoliberal focus of citizenship that is just about individual activity and individual achievement rather than a larger, more meaningful overhaul of the way a nation defines its citizens. I want to suggest that such a redrawing (though it may benefit some immigrants like these successful yet undocumented students) might well undermine hopes for a less-punitive immigration policy as it ties access to U.S. citizenship so tightly to educational success, particularly because such success is increasingly less accessible as indicated by rising student debt and declining access to public institutions. The narrow definition of good citizenship as being based on school success obscures other kinds of economic contributions made by immigrants that are taking part in high labor and low-status jobs such as gardening, restaurant work, construction, and child care, creating a kind of class system within immigration policy debates where those who are following traditional school paths are at the top and those who do not—either because of desire or access—are shut out.

Taken together, these messages about what makes a citizen through higher education and what makes a citizen through legal channels can result in a highly individualized process of citizenship acquisition, one in which it becomes easy to reduce supports to help people through the process of acquiring citizenship. On a college campus this could translate to a reduction in programs such as instruction for English language learners or a debt-free education. It would be remiss, as educators, to not consider how we might help support such students or those who are not yet those students. Such an environment is not only hostile to students who are undocumented but also for many students of color and others who are at the periphery of the mainstream student body at many institutions. Work-oriented immigration policy in which an individual has to prove his or her productive potential creates an atmosphere that makes invisible the need for institutional support such as language learning support or reasonable tuition costs, particularly in light of the widespread belief in a citizen-producing education that basically makes citizenship an individual achievement.

This also concerns me because productive and economic activity increasingly defines citizenship, not the civic activity and engagement often promoted as citizenship. As a result, we risk ignoring the legal boundaries that have been put in place for those who look the part of the citizen, as many of these students do, but who do not hold the legal status of citizenship. I think this is of particular concern because of the trend in immigration policy that has moved toward reform at the state level, where some states like California and Texas have passed their own versions of the DREAM Act, providing access to resources without being able to confer any kind of legal status. This, of course, is in contrast to other states like Arizona and Alabama, where resources for those who are undocumented have been reduced to a further extreme. We can legitimize cultural, economic, or community citizenship—or even hybrid citizenships that acknowledge the transnational movement of people—but when it comes down to it, only the nation can confer the exact legal status of citizenship, the one that ensures an individual the ability to stay in a territory, the one with legal meaning. Thus, the rhetorical effects of something like the DREAM Act have the potential of eventually limiting who has access to citizenship.

On the surface, one of the implications of the DREAM Act is that it opens up citizenship as a legal status, but the accompanying debates also have implications for the concept of citizenship itself. The force behind the DREAM Act is to redraw citizenship boundaries, and while it may be a worthwhile revision of existing immigration policy, it keeps the status of citizen as a singular possession of a nation-state and also shifts the discussion away from illegality by casting the status of citizenship in terms of citizenly activity. Citizenship is thus being defined by activity; if you act like a citizen, then you are. But habits of citizenship, while still influential, should not be confused with citizenship itself.

If we recognize how Castillo, who possesses the typical habits of U.S. citizenship, slipped through the cracks as compared to Vargas because she was not able to locate similar kinds of mentors, then we also need to recognize the impact of allowing this to happen to a generation of young immigrants who might or might not be documented, who might or might not need resources for English language learning that are no longer available, who might or might not view citizenship as a pipe dream. It is generally easier to write off the need for these resources when it is assumed that they are for those who are not as legitimate as American-born citizens. For these reasons, we, as literacy instructors, also need to recognize how citizenship has become a channel through which to distribute all of these other values such as economic productivity and individual achievement, which potentially have more impact on students whose citizenship status is shaky and are at somewhat a remove from university culture such as first-generation college students, multilingual students, and students of color. We need to think about our own role in how these students, who are constantly being asked to prove themselves and their citizenship, may or may not be supported through a citizen-producing education.

The Promise of Citizenship and the Responsibility of the Teacher-Citizen

This book began with a series of questions about citizenship. Chief among them was why citizenship—namely, the need to fortify student citizenship—seems to be an almost naturalized and inextricable component of literacy learning. Yet efforts to ease anxieties about citizenship never seem to be satisfactory, as evidenced by a substantial history of citizenship production through literacy. The literacy training sites examined in the preceding three chapters were developed to address anxieties at a previous moment of tremendous economic and social change—the early twentieth century during the growth of a new mass manufacturing economy and subsequent changes in the nature of work and the population of workers. This change coincided with a foundational moment in the legal construction of American citizenship that saw a large influx of immigrants arriving in the United States in addition to the efforts of Americanization movements around World War I. However, the circumstances around citizenship production during this previous crisis are not simply a quaint relic of an earlier era from which contemporary readers can distance themselves because of how discriminatory, naïve, or hopeful past discourses seem to be.

Rather, this historical discussion can serve as a way to counteract the modern phenomenon of ambient citizenship, that pervasive but unspecific presence of citizenship discussed in chapter 1. Counteracting ambient citizenship means thinking more deeply about how citizenship is being defined, articulating clearly what we imagine is being achieved for an individual through citizenship, and understanding citizenship as a construct that operates alongside inequality and a stratified distribution of resources. Historicizing this process is useful because such moments are perpetual; the definition of citizenship, its production, and its boundaries are never and will never be permanent. There will always be anxiety about who is a citizen, how to become a citizen, and how to produce as many good citizens as possible. Definitions of the good citizen are fluid, based on what an individual, a group, or an institution might value at a specific moment in time. The historical case studies discussed in the foregoing chapters—Americanization efforts, labor education programs, English classrooms—underscore how anxiety invigorated literacy as a foundational habit of citizenship. And when a skill and trait such as literacy is used to try to resolve anxieties about citizenship, whether to ameliorate inequities or acculturate immigrants, its use becomes an enduring aspect of the production of citizenship.

The resulting foundational structures from this previous period have important implications for our practices today, specifically how the institutional constructions of education and literacy learning shape the literacy and citizenship of immigrants and working-class people. We live in a world still profoundly influenced by the legacies of this historical era—the mass educational system in which we teach was established, the groundwork was laid for increasing access to college (as well as its subsequent decline in value), unions intensified their struggle for power in the industrial economy, and the era's concerns about citizenship have persisted. While much of this book is historical, this project emerged from contemporary anxieties about citizenship and the college writing classroom and how we can attend to those concerns. The conflation of citizenship with other habits of citizenship such as productivity still resonates in current legal and educational policy discussions as legal and educational factors such as immigration policy and educational structure continue to shape our ideas about citizenship (e.g., evidence of who works hard, who has citizenship potential, and what should be done with literacy as a good citizen).

Our modern era could be characterized as another period of crisis for citizenship and the American way of life, much like the one the United States experienced around the First World War. Uncertainty still abounds. How will the United States respond to the global financial crisis, its various military interventions, and the specter of terrorism? In apartments and houses in cities and towns across the country, people are asking themselves how they will gain employment, how they will stay employed, how they will pay their bills. These concerns have trickled down into anxieties about the country and the protection of its resources, seen as finite and at risk of being depleted permanently without some type of imposed controls over who has access to them.

Citizenship is one important way to frame these concerns because it is a means to access multiple legal, cultural, and economic resources. Anxieties that immigrants will simultaneously erode the quality of the nation's citizenship while also taking its jobs have long influenced immigration policies. As a result, conversations about U.S. immigrant labor policy continue to attempt to determine who is rewarded for productive work, who contributes to society, and how citizenship acts as a synonym for productivity, patience, and obedience, as demonstrated by proposals for the DREAM Act and temporary worker programs. The lasting effect of such policies is that they do not so much extend citizenship, with its attendant rights and privileges, but rather harvest the labor out of a mobile, border-crossing population without the commitment of citizenship. Through these economic concerns, the construction and reproduction of beliefs about citizenship are informed by fears of the immigrant. This framework of citizenship is particularly important in the context of education because as educators we are part of the promise that our home institutions make, that higher education can help to create "educated and engaged citizens." While many of these legal and policy debates and decisions take place outside of the classroom, what the historical examples from earlier chapters and the more contemporary issues discussed here illustrate is the complex system of citizenship production in which literacy and education are a part.

Education has been used a way to mollify these anxieties by producing and rewarding particular habits of citizenship such as through the promise of success, the promise of "work, life, and citizenship" (National Leadership Council 2) after graduation. Thus, the precedents established almost a century ago provide a legal and cultural foundation for citizenship production, concerns that were evident even then about who could be considered a citizen and how education is used to make those determinations. These concerns still have immediacy and urgency for literacy instructors today, especially if the goal is the mindful production of citizens. As a result, it is important to continually and critically consider the ways that writing classrooms are situated as citizenship-producing spaces and how writing teachers take up and conceive of this notion. The invocation of citizenship in relation to literacy training produces a dialectical and mutually reinforcing relationship between these two concepts. Literacy training takes on certain urgency because it is part of the citizenship-producing process, acting as a gateway to status and resources. In turn, promotion of literacy as a habit of citizenship allows for literacy to be used as a measure of citizenship potential. For those who teach literacy, this dialectic relationship often produces hope—in literacy and in citizenship to make lives better. That potential is always present. But citizenship and literacy also converge to construct a system through which societal resources are channeled. For instance, in the 1910s and 1920s, the federal government used literacy training to illustrate to new immigrants how literacy could help potential citizens make economic gains, while unions like the ILGWU tried to harness literacy skills to gain political and economic power for worker-citizens. Meanwhile, public institutions of higher education, no longer just reinforcers of elite status but producers of a broader population of workers, were expanding their reach and refocusing curricula on the populist goal of creating useful citizens, acting simultaneously as a gateway and gatekeeper.

When an immigrant worker came to the United States in the early twenti-eth century and was confronted with different ways of acquiring literacy and achieving citizenship—through the union, through the nation, through for-mal avenues of education—he or she was also announcing citizenship potential through the attempted acquisition of literacy in English. The expectation of achievement then fell on individuals who could or could not use their literacy effectively to gain citizenship status. Today, literacy still operates in much the same way as evidence of who works hard and who has citizenship potential. Literacy instructors, among others, play an important role in determining how literacy acts as a marker of good citizenship.

If literacy is a critical element of achieving citizenship, as literacy educa-tors so often say, then literacy and the way we teach literacy are implicated in reinforcing citizenship values and definitions, spoken or unspoken. Literacy is a tool to measure citizenship potential but also a means through which to reinforce certain values about citizenship. And because citizenship itself has a myriad of definitions and values, literacy can be employed by a number of constituencies as a flexible tool to promote habits of citizenship contingent on other circumstances such as a person's productive potential. Legislative debates over *who* can be a citizen accompany cultural battles over *how* to define citi-zenship and it's in these battles that literacy instructors participate, both ex-plicitly and implicitly. We need to be clear about the different ways citizenship, in its flexibility, is promoted and cultivated through habits of citizenship such as literacy rather than assume a singular vision. Literacy programs of all kinds, including the ones described in this book, helped produce habits of citizenship that cultivated productivity, empowerment, or employability.

That connection between citizenship and literacy relies on economic defi-nitions in which habits of citizenship are measured by what is useful. I do not dispute the importance of civic behaviors such as an individual's ability to par-ticipate in civic discourse, but definitions of citizenship are not exclusive to these more explicitly civic habits. A good citizen can also be defined as a pro-ductive citizen, one that contributes rather than merely consumes resources. The historical case studies indicate the importance of work and the workplace in definitions of citizenship, whether for acculturating new immigrants to pro-ductive behavior, for attempts to use literacy to navigate a workplace deemed hostile to workers, or for educating young adults with an eye toward employ-ability in a changing economy. Literacy and education were used as tools to increase productivity and address inequalities during moments of crisis in this earlier era, and this continues to be the case. Historical studies such as those presented here are essential in order to trace a genealogy of how citizenship, literacy, and work have become implicated with one another and to develop a critical history of the relationship among these concepts, as they are realized today. The stories of Vargas and Castillo and discussions about the DREAM Act in this chapter echo previous tensions about how citizenship has been defined in terms of productivity. How educators choose to intervene in these tensions is dependent on whether we see ourselves as creating a citizenry or a group of individual citizens, how we decide to cultivate certain habits of citizenship over others, and how we imagine ourselves activating the citizenship of our students.

In order to make these decisions, literacy teachers and other educators need to consider their place in the process of the achievement of full citizenship, a particular fulfillment of citizenship that is not merely legal but also cultural, and that allows an individual full access to society's resources. Taking heed of Bryan Turner's contention that access to citizenship is shaped by juridical, political, economic, and cultural practices that work together to define who is a competent member of society, teachers need to understand how literacy plays a role in galvanizing these practices, necessitating attention to quests for citizenship and situating literacy-oriented citizenship production among broader practices of that production. The legal, cultural, and economic boundaries of citizenship are a critical part of what creates the value system for literacy, both how it should be used and what should be taught. Only when citizenship is understood to include its juridical, political, economic, and cultural practices can the influence of the writing classroom on the production of good citizens be evaluated fully.

However, as the previous examples have shown, citizenship as a concept can also obscure these practices because of its association with democratic participation. In the context of literacy learning, this "inherently progressive" association can be limiting, as Donna Strickland cautions in *The Managerial Unconscious* (18, 115–18). By uncovering the legal, cultural, and economic motives that animate the production of citizenship, we must seek to answer what specific kind of citizenship we hope to produce through literacy, or risk situating citizenship as simply another assessable learning goal in our curriculum. Clearly this is not a simple task: an education that works to create "educated and engaged citizens" might seem at odds with the more vocational goals of gaining a college degree when the issues of cost, relevance, and employability are all quite important. But rather than trying to resist vocational goals of literacy when such economic influences are inextricably connected, educators might consider the influence of legal boundaries and economic conditions of citizenship and focus on finding ways to engage with the resulting individualistic definitions of citizenship that so much citizenship production seems to enforce, such as those that put citizens in categories of either obedience or participation.

Finding ways to engage with concepts of individually based citizenship achievement means that we must question how our pedagogies might comply or resist these different narratives. Such questions should be answered individually in our classrooms and in our scholarship in order to make the crucial turn outward so that the answers can become institutional curricula, educational policy, and laws. We need to recognize the multiple ways citizenship definitions and beliefs are produced and can be achieved and also how these beliefs act on our students as well as how their access to and desires about education affect the ways they might be defining citizenship for themselves. In other words, how do they view education as a component of their own achievement of citizenship? We do not necessarily have to enact all of these imperatives, but we should be aware of how the system is working to create, limit, and complicate the understandings of citizenship we currently possess.

One avenue through which we can begin answering some of these questions is to consider our role not just as educators, but as teacher-citizens. If we imagine our students as student-citizens, then we must also see ourselves as teacher-citizens, regardless of how visible citizenship production is in our classrooms. Students arrive with their own ideas about goals and expectations for both class and citizenship, but so do teachers. The role of the teacher-citizen is not one in which the teacher awards or judges the citizenship of students, but rather a more delicate one in which the teacher recognizes his or her role, both implicit and explicit, in a larger process of citizenship production. Returning to Danielle Allen's "habits of citizenship," the habits taught in a classroom speak to the multilayered way citizenship gets formed, practiced, and enacted, and teacher-citizens participate in that process. By looking at the work we do through this framework, we can find ways to recognize where we can, where we cannot, and where we already do affect the citizenship production of students.

Whether or not we make direct connections between the advanced literacy we teach and habits of citizenship, we need to understand how our own citizenship and obligations as a citizen can affect how we conduct classroom work. We should try to understand how our own enactment of citizenship impacts the citizenship of those we teach and where certain responsibilities might lie. Allen's insight on the collaborative work of citizenship production lends itself to how we might approach this task as writing teachers: "On the same page or in the same city, alongside each other without touching, citizens of different classes, backgrounds, and experiences are inevitably related to each other in networks of mutual benefaction, despite customary barriers between them, and despite our nearly complete lack of awareness, or even disavowal, of these networks" (45). As teacher-citizens, we participate in decisions that are dispersed through these networks, such as how we ask students to interact with one another, the kinds of literate activity we privilege through the readings and assignments we give, and how we imagine and value how students will use literacy after they leave our classrooms. The citizenship training that we provide exists within the other kinds of lessons about citizenship that students might encounter and how citizenship is defined depends on how we all take up these different lessons in our interactions with one another, in person or mediated through law. Allen reminds us that the relationships among citizens "*is* [what constitutes] citizenship, and a democratic polity, for its own long-term health, requires practices for weighing the relative force of benefactions and for responding to them" (45–46). Citizenship, therefore, isn't charity to be doled out by sponsors, but rather a collective practice, one that relies on the relationships among citizens. As literacy educators, we can move toward making those relationships more visible and tangible to students as part of the citizenship production that takes place in our own classrooms.

If universities wish to create citizens, as their strategic plans often state, examining the connection between classroom practices and the habits of citizenship they engender in concert with participating in critical conversations about what makes a citizen (legally and culturally) may help advocates in higher education create spaces for, and have more nuanced understandings of, the citizenship being produced in our classrooms. Such connections could be made by becoming mentors or sponsors for students like Vargas or Castillo, working at the policy level at our institutions, or becoming more active in changing (or at least being more knowledgeable about) immigration and citizenship policy that affects the legal boundaries of citizenship. As teacher-citizens, for example, we might work to support certain kinds of immigration policy to change legal boundaries, but also try to understand how habits like literacy and productivity that emerge from these legal boundaries can impact our pedagogies.

Current attempts to redefine citizenship have particular resonance within the post-Fordist shift from a mass manufacturing economy toward service or knowledge work. Attempts to use literacy to shape citizenship, by writing teachers and other kinds of sponsors, are part of an ongoing process, one that subsumes some of the many external influences and anxieties that leave their mark on the writing classroom. It is vital that we discuss the implications of these changing economic realities on our current expectations for citizenship and, subsequently, how we manage those expectations in the writing classroom. In order for the writing classroom to enact citizenships that matter, we need to recognize the ways that our idealized notions of citizenship are complicit in the citizenship that already exists.

The arguments I present here are not conclusive and, in fact, are ongoing. In many ways the drive toward equality, the desire to create learning spaces where people can think and analyze, make these efforts to produce citizenship seem futile but noble. While legal boundaries continue to define citizenship in important, tangible ways, citizenship is also an idealized state where cultural values are constantly being produced and reproduced. And where there is production, there is potential for intervention and change. The focus of this book has been on individuals who are on the margins attempting to gain access to this idealized state, the location where literacy seems to have a powerful influence on the hope for social mobility. Literacy often reinforces two narratives of equality and individualism; thus, literacy can be used both as a habit of citizenship and a marker of productivity. This produces a particular kind of citizenship that allows for the distribution of resources to some but facilitates the exclusion of others. Examining the state of these ideas is a fundamental element of making citizenship matter.

To that end, I ask literacy instructors to pause and reconsider what is behind the often rote invocations of citizenship that provide the backdrop for so much of the work we do—in the classroom, on the curricular level, in the institution, and even on a national level. Reflective deliberation about citizenship has the potential to refocus and broaden the common disciplinary discussion about citizenship, making more concrete the aspiration for a robust citizenship in relation to our own practices. Rather than a simple call to action in name only, we need to deliberate on the habits of citizenship that are being cultivated through our actions so that we may respond more effectively to current and continuing changes in the concept and reality of citizenship, whether caused by globalization, transnational migration, law, or public policy. We should acknowledge the limitations of what citizenship can do for students, as well as the limitations put upon students by not only the idea of citizenship, but also its legal, political, and cultural boundaries. And we should create spaces where our citizen-making through the teaching of literacy is a more deliberate activity, one that enlivens the concept of citizenship by connecting classroom practices to other instances of citizenship production that happen outside of the classroom, such as those in the legal, political, and economic realms. At its core, the citizenship that we create through literacy is aspirational, a promise. And it's a promise that we must consider how we keep.

NOTES

Introduction

1. Stephen Diner traces the distinction between the mature industrial society and the industrializing society of the nineteenth century. He writes, "Many factories, mills, and mines from the mid-nineteenth century on required workers with considerable skill to perform complex tasks. Skilled craftsmen themselves determined the manner and pace of their jobs" (50). Even though the nature of work may have changed with the advent of industrialization, workers themselves still felt like they had some control over the work they did. But in the late nineteenth and early twentieth century, "most of American industry moved in the opposite direction, reducing the skill and therefore the autonomy of workers" (51).

2. See Stanley Fish on higher education in the *New York Times*; Richard Arum and Josipa Roksa's *Academically Adrift: Limited Learning on College Campuses*; Andrew Delbanco's *College: What It Was, Is, and Should Be*; Gerald Graff's *Clueless in Academe*; Andrew Hacker and Claudia Dreifus's *Higher Education?: How Colleges Are Wasting Our Money and Failing Our Kids*; Richard P. Keeling and Richard H. Hersh's *We're Losing Our Minds: Rethinking American Higher Education*; or even the Spellings Commission report on higher education.

Chapter 1. In the Name of Citizenship

1. According to the U.S. census, only 62 percent of the population between fourteen and seventeen years of age were attending school in 1920, as opposed to 97 percent in 2010 (U.S. Census Bureau). While colleges saw some growth, fewer than 5 percent of Americans between eighteen and twenty in 1917 attended college, compared to an increase to 15 percent in 1937 (Thelin 205). In 2012, over 50 percent of the population over twenty-five had some college education.

2. This report marked an important moment when the federal government wanted to unify the efforts of "individual institutions, local communities, the several States,

the educational foundations and associations . . . toward the same general ends" (U.S., *Higher Education* 85).

3. Eberly introduces the term "citizen critic" as distinct from public intellectual to describe "a person who produces discourses about issues of common concern from an ethos of citizen first and foremost—not as expert or spokesperson for a workplace or as a member of a club or organization" (1). Her book about public discussions of controversial books over the course of the twentieth century explicitly responds to "publics theory" and reflects a wider response to the 1991 English translation of Habermas's *Structural Transformation of the Public Sphere* in speech communication and English studies scholarship. In the field of rhetoric and composition, see Berlin (*Rhetoric and Reality* and *Rhetorics, Poetics, and Cultures*); Faigley; and Spellmeyer.

4. Wells warns against seeing writing instruction as a way to "fix" students' deficiencies (or the perception of these deficiencies). She describes the difficulties of trying to use the writing classroom to bolster the public discourse of students: "As compositionists, we apply a deficit model to public discourse: it is one more thing students don't know, one more thing we have trouble teaching. . . . But public space is not available, at least not in the form we have imagined it" (327). Explicit in these discussions are themes of the public sphere and paucity of public discourse, implicitly equating healthy citizenship with participation in these arenas. Wells rethinks this deficit model by complicating the discussion about public discourse in writing classrooms, laying out four important considerations in the organization and execution of public writing in composition classes: First, the classroom is a "version" or "model" of the public sphere by incorporating rhetorical strategies that emphasize persuasion. Second, students analyze public discourse as the main text of the class. Third, the class should "produce student writing that will enter some form of public space"; and fourth, the class should engage in disciplinary interventions with the public (339).

5. Kettner explains that the thirteen colonies developed a "modern view of citizenship, based on voluntary allegiance to a community defined by a territory, instead of the medieval concept of personal allegiance, involuntary because it was acquired by virtue of birth" (31). In his view, "the status of 'American citizen' was the creation of the Revolution. . . . Americans came to see that citizenship must begin with an act of individual choice" (208).

6. Steve Lamos's study of the Educational Opportunity Program at the University of Illinois at Urbana-Champaign demonstrates the movement of responsibility from institution to the individual. He writes how a proposal for the program places "primary responsibility for change and reform not upon the institution in general or the EOP program in particular, but rather upon students themselves: it is students who will need to 'additively learn' this superior standard English" (53).

Chapter 2. Literacy Training, Americanization, and the Cultivation of the Productive Worker-Citizen

1. The different versions of federal citizenship textbooks carried slightly different names with each iteration (*Student's Textbook, Federal Citizenship Textbook, Federal Textbook on Citizenship Training, Teaching Our Language to Beginners*). Additionally,

some texts list the U.S. government as the author, while others name Lillian Clark. In an attempt to distinguish these different versions from each other, I refer to specific titles and years of publication as often as possible.

2. This chapter is not intended to be a complete legislative and legal history on immigration and Americanization, but rather offers a short background to contextualize the texts I study here. For a comprehensive account, see Desmond King's *Making Americans: Immigration, Race, and the Origins of the Diverse Democracy*, Mae M. Ngai's *Impossible Subjects*, and Vernon Briggs's *Immigration Policy and the American Labor Force*.

3. These two fears are somewhat contradictory since any socialist effort would presumably include a desire to raise wages. For a more detailed discussion of these nativist groups, see King 74; Roediger 14.

4. Within the federal government, the work of immigration and naturalization was housed in offices, bureaus, and divisions with different names over the period of time covered here. According to Marian L. Smith, the Office of the Superintendent of Immigration was created by the Immigration Act of 1881 and was housed within the Treasury Department. The Immigration Act of 1885 changed the name from Office of Immigration to Bureau of Immigration, and in 1903 the Office moved to the newly formed Department of Labor, which is of particular interest to my research. The Bureau of Immigration became the Bureau of Immigration and Naturalization in 1906, only to be split into two separate bureaus in 1913.

5. James R. Barrett defines Americanization as "the broader acculturation of immigrants, the day-to-day process by which they come to understand their new situation and to find or invent ways of coping with it." He goes on to assert that "Americanism was a contested ideal. There were numerous understandings of what it meant to be an American, divergent values associated with the concept, and so, many ways that an immigrant might 'discover' America" (997). Barrett's explanation of Americanization complements my discussion of habits of citizenship and the varying ways they develop. In this chapter, I offer literacy programs as one way among many that Americanism was learned.

6. The Bureau of Immigration reports that 1907 marked a high point during the fifty-year period between 1880 and 1930 with 1,285,349 immigrants. In 1900, 448,572 individuals immigrated to the United States, which steadily increased or at least maintained until restrictions dropped immigration rates from 1,218,480 in 1915 to 326,700 the following year. Numbers rose again until the passage of the National Origins Act in 1924 (706,896 in 1924 and 294,314 in 1925). Again, I point to King, who cites that between 1882 and 1907 the numbers of European immigrants doubled from 648,186 to 1,207,619, and I note the importance of the percentage of eastern Europeans that increased during that time from 13.1 percent to 81 percent (51). Additionally, the U.S. Census Bureau recorded that in 1893, the United States received 2,392 immigrants from Asia (which included "Turkey in Asia," China, India, Japan, Korea, and the Philippines); this number jumped to 23,533 by 1919. This growing numbers of non-European immigrants fed the anxiety that the newer immigrants were of a low quality and potential.

7. Historian Herbert G. Gutman writes that post-1843 America held a "profound

tension" between "the older American preindustrial social structure and the moderniz-
ing institutions that accompanied the development of industrial capitalism. After 1893,
the United States ranked as a mature industrial society," one that embraced scientific
management and the incorporation of businesses, overshadowing previous agrarian
and craft-oriented economies (13).

8. Sidney Kansas offers an excellent contemporary account of immigration policy
before 1928 with *U.S. Immigration: Exclusion and Deportation* (1928). Kansas writes
about the establishment of the position of commissioner of immigration in 1864; the job
was to institute national regulations, but also to encourage immigration to the country.
Because this law was repealed two years later, Kansas discusses how restrictions were
passed only on the state level until two Supreme Court decision in 1876 (*Chy Lung v.
Freeman* and *Henderson v. Mayor of New York*) charged Congress with the responsibility over immigration matters. The year 1882 saw the first immigration restriction with
a ten-year suspension of Chinese labor, which got extended for another ten years in
1892. The 1891 Immigration Act formed further restrictions on others who were deemed
unacceptable because of mental or physical illness.

9. Cleveland justified the veto by saying, "limiting immigration to those who can
read and write in any language twenty-five words of our Constitution . . . would not
protect our country against degeneration from imported turbulence and disorder, and
that it was far more safe to admit a hundred thousand immigrants who, though unable
to read and write, are coming to our shores to establish a home and seeking an opportunity to work, than to admit one of those unruly agitators and enemies of government
control, who cannot only read and write, but delights in arousing the illiterate and
peacefully inclined to discontent and tumult" (qtd. in Kansas 8).

10. On the 1915 veto, Wilson said, "it would exclude those to whom the opportunities
of elementary education has been denied without regard to their character, purposes,
or natural capacity; that these are not tests of character or personal fitness, but tests of
opportunities in the countries from where the immigrants came" (qtd. in Kansas 13).

11. In addition to the legislative activity over the conferral of citizenship to immigrants, this moment was charged with anxiety over citizenship as seen by the aftereffects of *Plessy v. Ferguson*, the development of the worker education movement, and
the rise of mass manufacturing and corporatization, not to mention the continuing
growth of citizen-making institutions such as libraries, settlement houses, and universal public schooling. The publication of the citizenship training texts coincided with
the progressive education movement and increased attention to the literacy of the public at large, which imbued literacy with its value and made it logical for immigrants to
be literate in English.

12. In *Immigration Policy and the American Labor Force*, Vernon Briggs Jr. provides
an extensive discussion of nonimmigrant labor policy in the United States, which enforced a temporary labor force from Mexico and the British West Indies. The Bracero
program, which lasted from 1917 to 1922, was a way to bring cheaper labor from Mexico
into the United States without conferring citizenship (Briggs 98). The United States
established a Mexican Labor Program from 1942 to 1964, and a similar program for

workers from the British West Indies (1942–47). Aleinikoff, Martin, and Motomura cite these programs as providing necessary labor during wartime while ensuring workers' stays in the United States were temporary (160). The Bracero program was revived from 1942 to 1964, temporarily bringing between four and five million Mexican workers to the United States (397). Interestingly, stricter guidelines existed for those workers from geographically distant locations like Asia, who could not so easily be "returned." Despite the use of Chinese and Japanese workers in industries like sugarcane plantations in Hawaii and railroad construction, the 1917 Immigration Act formalized the previous restrictions of immigrants from the Asian-Pacific triangle, such as the 1882 Chinese Exclusion Act (see King 79; Takaki 29, 209).

13. In "Americanization from the Bottom Up," James R. Barrett writes about the perpetuation of anti-immigrant suspicions: "Older immigrants and natives passed their own prejudices onto newcomers. Irish immigrants, who had been in job competition with Asians and blacks for more than a generation before eastern European immigrants arrived and who themselves suffered discrimination and violence at the hands of nativists, often developed racist attitudes and repertoires of behavior" (1001).

14. The ease of assimilation for previous immigrants is somewhat an illusion, as documented by David Roediger's *Wages of Whiteness*. Roediger's text and Matthew Jacobson's *Whiteness of a Different Color* provide a more detailed analysis of the formation of race and whiteness and the racialization of new immigrants.

15. The 1907 Immigration Act established a joint House-Senate commission to study issues surrounding immigration. The committee was commonly known as the Dillingham Commission, after the head of the commission, Senator William Paul Dillingham (R-Vermont).

16. Historian Stanley Aronowitz traces the "myth that the socialist and communist movements were essentially importations from Europe" (142), citing a high anti-immigrant bias within the Socialist Party and the radical movement in the early twentieth century. He writes, "the overwhelming majority of members of the Socialist Party in the United States in the early twentieth century were native-born Americans" (142). Yet the association of immigrants with radicalism was still prevalent and motivated attitudes, legislation, and Americanization programs.

17. Additionally, Higham writes about how "Americanization was another indication of the growing urgency of the nationalist impulse. Americanization brought new methods for dealing with the immigrants; it significantly altered the traditions of both nativism and confidence" (235). For a very detailed description of the range of these programs, see his chapter, "Crusade for Americanization," in *Strangers in the Land* (234–63).

18. Constance Kendall uses the term "(il)literacy test" instead of more common "literacy test," because "the phrasing 'illiteracy test' as opposed to 'literacy test' or 'educational test,' which was primarily used by Lodge and the other restrictionist legislators, implies its underlying purpose, i.e., to identify a 'defect' rather than to certify possession of a skill. The phrase 'illiteracy test' appears more frequently in the earlier Congressional Records (pre-1900); whereas, the phrase 'literacy test' appears more regularly

after 1900. My use of the phrase '(il)literacy test' is meant to emphasize the ongoing tension between the two phrasings" (116).

19. The debates over the literacy test provide an interesting parallel discussion to these citizenship training classes and texts, ones that also address the literacy of immigrants. Arguments for the literacy test often fell back on assumptions that linked literacy with the quality of personhood. For example, in the Dillingham report, numerous parties questioned the quality of the new immigrants who were entering the United States by citing their lack of literacy and then the literacy rate among prisoners as evidence of how you could judge a person on his or her literacy. Reverend Lichiter, representing the Junior Order of United American Mechanics, told the commission, "I beg to say in passing that over one-fifth of all the alien felons now confined in our state and federal jails and prisons are illiterate, every one of whom and their offspring would have been excluded . . . by the illiteracy test" (27). In this same report, the Immigration Restriction League cites the growing numbers of foreigners in prison in the United States (103). The link between illiteracy and criminality as it pertained to immigrants served as a warning, as if to say that allowing illiterate immigrants into the country was the equivalent of opening the doors to criminals. Suspicion of immigrants to a lesser degree surrounded the citizenship and literacy training discussed here.

20. Ngai reports that after the Immigration Act of 1924, "ineligibility to citizenship and exclusion applied to the peoples of all the nations of East and South Asia. Nearly all Asians had already been excluded from immigration, either by Chinese exclusion laws or by the 'barred Asiatic zone' that Congress created in 1917" (37).

21. The Bureau of Education also promoted their own Americanization campaigns and the two bodies, Education and Naturalization, were sometimes in conflict. Because the two worked both together and separately, the combined efforts were "undoubtedly confusing," according to King. Generally, the Bureau of Education's programs were "less concerned with the political pressures" (King 96).

22. The five-year residency period could be seen as a kind of waiting or probationary period in which potential citizens had five years to show what kind of citizen they would become. While the practices of each individual were not scrutinized, immigrants were expected to hold steady employment and learn English during this period of time. Today, a similar five-year waiting, or "continuous residence," period still exists for permanent residents who seek naturalization.

23. Variations were published throughout the 1930s, 1940s, even into the 1950s but with decreasing frequency and few changes until another large-scale revision of these kinds of texts in the 1960s, presumably around the next wave of significant immigration law changes.

24. These texts often assume a male audience, perhaps because the citizenship of women was connected to their husbands until the 1922 Cable Act (Daniels 50).

25. Deputy Commissioner Raymond Crist left a robust paper trail of his mostly form letter correspondence in the Bureau of Immigration and Naturalization papers in the National Archives. The files include letters to hundreds of cities, towns, and organizations across the country, yet most letters don't ask anything more than the number of

textbooks needed, indicating a heavy reliance on the textbook to do the work of train-ing instructors and shaping these different programs.

26. Both the American Legion and the Daughters of the American Revolution have origins as nativist groups that would have an investment in Americanizing (certain groups of) immigrants.

27. Although the texts somewhat unified the large number of classes taught across the country, at least in terms of content, the decentralized organization of these cours-es makes it difficult to create an accurate tally of students who enrolled during this period. A 1920 Department of Labor report cites the distribution of 98,958 textbooks to public schools that held classes for naturalization candidates accompanied by other documents like naturalization information forms and school announcement posters, reaching around 2,000 communities (King 88). It is not entirely clear whether these textbooks correspond one-to-one with the number of students. At the Citizenship Convention, the University of Wisconsin extension division director Andrew Melville reported in 1917 that the school had 35,000 students enrolled in these classes (U.S., "Pro-ceedings" 84), and J. M. Berkey, director of special schools and extension work for pub-lic schools in Pittsburgh, reports in that same year an enrollment of 60,000 students; in the three years following, these classes increased in number rather than decreased (U.S., "Proceedings" 39). In 1921, Massachusetts reported 20,745 students, 750 evening classes, 327 factory classes, and 248 neighborhood and club classes (State of Massachu-setts 7); the numbers for just one state are so large that a one textbook to one student ratio seems unlikely. It seems that in some classrooms, every student was getting a text-book while in others, teachers were using these textbooks as guides to run their classes. While these books represent the federal government's effort to impose uniformity on citizenship training efforts, pinning down an exact number of students is unlikely due to the indeterminacy of these numbers.

28. The use of the name Angelo implies that the main character of this lesson is Italian. Names vary with the lessons, some such as Angelo, but also some that are more "neutral" (Anglicized) like Mr. White, Mr. Brown, or George, or seemingly biblical, like Joseph and Mary. Because there is no overt naming or association of stereotypical ethnic or racial traits of the characters through these lessons, I understand the use of various names as an attempt to imagine the audience of the texts, perhaps a kind of precursor to multiculturalism.

29. Melvyn Dubofsky writes that between 1917 and 1920, "union membership grew by more than 2 million (from 2, 976,000 to 5,034,000) for a total gain of almost 70 percent," with almost 20 percent of the civilian nonagricultural labor force in unions (*The State* 74).

30. Because of the ongoing racial categorization of immigrants, this erasure was acceptable within certain boundaries. As already discussed, the target for these lessons were certain groups of southern and eastern European immigrants who were deemed as having citizenship potential (as opposed to just temporary labor potential like many Mexican and Asian workers).

31. Steven J. Diner describes how the development of an extensive railroad network

in the post–Civil War era enabled "corporations to ship goods produced in one place to a national and international market" (15). He describes growth in industries like iron, steel, and textiles (31–33). Additionally, the increase in the manufacture of consumer and agricultural machinery like sewing machines, typewriters, and harvesters and the development of retail corporations that sold food and other household goods at the turn of the century created their own sprawling networks of labor and production (42). As Diner notes, this new corporate model of production depended on large numbers of workers (34).

32. The process of citizenship still involves the five-year waiting period and the demonstration of competency in English established in the 1906 Naturalization Act. More recently, the Patriot Act's mandate for extra screening, the 30 July 2007, increase in citizenship application fees (from $400 to $675), and recent debates on immigration reform all point to an increasingly more difficult atmosphere to gain entry into and citizenship in the United States. For example, this process was extensively debated, particularly through widespread immigration marches in spring 2006 and the eventual defeat of the immigration reform bill in the Senate. In addition to a temporary guest worker program, one of the main issues was a proposed shift away from family reunification toward a more work- and education-oriented point system to determine who was eligible to enter the country. In recent years, these debates have continued, although often on a state level, like in Arizona, in the absence of a national push for reform. President Obama proposed extensive immigration reform in 2013 that included a temporary worker program, increased border control and revisions to permanent residency and citizenship policies, but as of this writing, it has not been passed.

Chapter 3. Class Work: Labor Education and Literacy Hope

1. For this chapter, I also examined papers from the Women's Trade Union League (WTUL), the American Federation of Labor (AFL), and the Amalgamated Clothing Workers' Union, but they played a less prominent role in comparison to the union-driven ILGWU and WEB materials. By contrast, publications like *Life and Labor*, published by the WTUL, took up the labor education movement from the perspective of the female workers and the upper-class and middle-class activists who constituted the organization's membership.

2. The moment when these worker education programs were emerging in force converged with a widespread citizenship crisis in which various parties debated over what makes a citizen. In the early twentieth century, laws and conditions surrounding citizenship and naturalization were certainly in flux. As discussed in the previous chapter, a growing number of immigrants coming to the United States led to various immigration reforms, including the 1917 Literacy Test Act and the development of citizenship training classes, the success of the women's suffrage movement, and the public school movement, which sought to train citizens at a young age. The First World War also led to broad Americanization movements that discussed and debated the quality of all citizens. Additionally and even more importantly, workers faced the increasing power of industry and growing economic inequality in the workplace. The development of

worker education programs was part of this landscape of anxiety about citizenship, and attempts to sort out the cultural and social meanings of American citizenship alongside labor struggles that highlighted growing inequality among American citizens

3. Socialism in the United States had enough support that the Socialist Party candidates won 1,150 offices in thirty-six states in 1911, including eighteen mayoral elections and a seat in Congress, and Socialist Party candidate Eugene V. Debs carried 6 percent of the vote in the 1912 presidential election (Diner 223). But by the end of the 1910s, that support had waned, partially due to its association with foreign revolutionaries and the rising nationalism around the First World War.

4. These organizations had ties to the Working Men's College in England and to the Working Men's Party in the United States. In the United States, they were closely affiliated with Thomas Skidmore's agrarian movement, which held that workers should move out of the industrial world and back to the land. This sentiment later became enshrined in law in the Homestead Act, according to Bruce Laurie (67). The Working Men's Party used education as well as a focused political agenda, with "planks designed to bridle monopoly and speculation and preserve the small shop and independent farm" (Laurie 80) to promote their philosophy.

5. For a more detailed historical treatment of labor conflicts during this period, see Altenbaugh, Dubofsky, Montgomery, and Nelson.

6. The use of intelligence here becomes loaded with eugenics in the background during this period. Yet, it seems clear that the term "industrial intelligence" is used to refer to a quality that one can develop, rather than one that is innate.

7. From the proceedings of the WEB conferences on workers' education, one might come to the conclusion that Cohn's involvement and leadership points toward a mix of male and female members. WEB included male leaders such as Spencer Miller Jr. and Alexander Fichlander. Yet Tarr cites that the 80 percent of the ILGWU's members were female, and thus the union with the strongest presence in the workers' education movement was also the union with a female majority. Rather than focus on the pervasive feminization of education, the focus of my chapter is mainly on the large number of immigrants within the unions where WEB was most active. For more focused gender studies, see rhetorical scholar Karyn J. Hollis's *Liberating Voices: Writing at the Bryn Mawr Summer School for Women Workers* and Ruth Milkman's edited collection, *Women, Work and Protest*. In the collection, Alice Kessler-Harris writes that the male leadership of the ILGWU wanted "unity, discipline, faithfulness," while "the female rank and file searched for community, idealism and spirit" (129). Kessler-Harris cites this gender tension as a key to the internal ideological struggles within the union. What Kessler-Harris labels as "mistrust" of female leadership, I would characterize, in addition, as a mistrust of immigrants within the labor movement.

8. Unlike the federal immigrant literacy programs discussed in the previous chapter, textbooks and teaching materials are not prevalent in the archives of union programs.

9. In addition to being the author of many of the articles in *Justice* (most likely penning many of the often anonymous "Educational Notes and Comment"), her papers at the New York Public Library include correspondence from various unions around the

country, asking for her advice on how best to bring workers' education to local unions. For example, a letter from John P. Frey, who served as the editor of the *International Molders' Journal* in Cincinnati, wrote to Cohn about the strength of the ILGWU's work in education: "I wish that every international union contained an educational department. If all of them did and these departments were conducted by intelligent directors, then our movement would more speedily occupy the position in the nation's affairs which it should" (John P. Frey letter to Fannia Cohn, 22 July 1921, Fannia Cohn papers, New York Public Library).

10. Hollis writes about the effect of funding for full-time summer programs at Bryn Mawr, noting that the funding "made it possible for 'American-born' cotton mill girls from the South to study alongside immigrant Jewish dressmakers from Eastern Europe or Italian Catholics from the Northeast" (16). Yet such full-time study and time off from work was not possible for many immigrant workers.

11. The Workers' University was held on the weekends at Washington Irving High School in New York City and taught a similar slate of classes.

12. Often these articles were published without authors and not all were labeled editorials. However, given that the staff of the ILGWU or *Justice* was not particularly large, it is not an illogical assumption that Cohn or one of her close associates was authoring the editorials and anonymous articles. Incidentally, not everything in *Justice* ran with bylines, seemingly as a matter of course, rather than an indication of inflammatory content.

13. Such discussions relied on emphasizing the distinction between mainstream and workers' education, while maintaining the value and importance of separate training. Perhaps the most telling and explicit comparison to colleges and universities is the naming of labor education programs as labor colleges or universities, such as the ILGWU's use of the name Workers' University and the naming of Brookwood College, particularly in contrast to the lengthy efforts to make the two kinds of institutions distinct from one another. The term "labor college" was also used by many educational programs in various cities around the country. This kind of self-valuation of the extra-curriculum offered by labor unions demonstrated how labor colleges and educational programs wanted to position themselves as equally valuable as established and formal institutions of education, primarily colleges and universities. The comparisons to higher education served to give value to labor education programs in two distinct (and possibly paradoxical) ways—by appearing to offer the same caliber of education to its students and by making it clear that programs were distinct because they provided a curriculum not to be found in more institutionalized venues. Through these distinctions, unions acknowledged the growing value of educational institutions while simultaneously devaluing formal institutions in order to show their worth.

14. Altenbaugh writes, "The Evening School Department of the New York City Board of Education supplied the teachers—about forty during the 1922–23 school year—and public school facilities free of charge" (37).

15. By using Gompers's earlier words, the article itself, published in 1925, seemed

intended to demonstrate support of the movement while simultaneously pushing for a less radical curriculum.

16. Altenbaugh describes how public opinion against socialism and the labor movement contributed to drops in union membership throughout the 1920s. Between 1920 and 1923, union membership dropped from 5 million to 3.6 million with only 2.9 million workers as unionists by 1930. He writes, "Put another way, union membership in 1930 amounted to a paltry 10.2 percent of the more than thirty million nonagricultural employees counted in the census, a marked drop from 19.4 percent in 1920" (40).

17. Of course, references to "intelligent citizenship" become particularly loaded in the age of eugenics. It is not entirely clear whether proponents of workers' education saw themselves as tapping into a latent intelligence among all workers or among a select few, or if workers' education was simply a way of overcoming a lack of intelligence with literacy serving as a way to visibly demonstrate an intelligence that may or may not exist.

18. And some, like Mailley, promoted the development of a socialist citizenry over the republican citizenry found in the United States as a way to address the growing inequality. A complicated political landscape remained in the background of the development of workers' education, including the growing strength of the Socialist Party and the subsequent schism and founding of the Communist Party in the United States in 1919. Although the radical IWW lost much steam in 1917–18 after federal repression (Dubofsky, *Hard Work* 66), Marvin E. Gettleman suggests that the split between the Socialist Party and Communist Party spurred the development of schools to "teach Marxism and the party line" (261), such as the New York Workers School, which existed from 1923 to 1944. These schools were decidedly more explicit about their political stances in comparison to those of the WEB and ILGWU.

19. This idea of "collective identity" became a loaded belief in the post–Bolshevik revolution world. This reference to the "great labor army," which recalls Marx's discussion of the "labour-army" (639), is probably explicitly (and efficiently) referring to revolution. Whether Cohn carefully veiled her references or felt that education as part of a revolutionary movement was only one of many possibilities for workers' education is unclear, and its lack of clarity is indicative of how workers' education straddled the line between radical and accommodation policies in order to appeal to the broadest number of workers.

20. In *Wages of Whiteness*, David Roediger outlines a detailed genealogy of the phrase "wage slavery," particularly in the chapter, "White Slaves, Wage Slaves, and Free White Labor." He talks about how "wage slavery survived the Civil War in much wider currency and continued to be a phrase used by Marxist writers (and soapboxers) into the twentieth century" (72). Roediger cites Norman Ware's *The Industrial Worker* to trace the origins of the phrase back to the mid-nineteenth century when "some highly skilled and relatively well-paid artisans [saw] their own wage labor as a kind of slavery" (71).

21. Wong makes clear that Cohn did not consider herself a Marxist and tried to keep

"workers' education above politics" (51). While Cohn was a member of the Socialist Party in Russia, by the time she immigrated to the United States in 1904 she saw socialism as "a basic creed, an article of faith . . . she eschewed doctrine and formal party affiliations. As a result, she was able to work with both Socialists and Communists within the ILGWU" (Wong 40).

22. This sense of urgency tracks throughout many of the documents. For instance, in *Justice*, an article titled "The Function of Labor Education" describes how "activities of all kinds—lectures, forums, classes, social and recreational functions, *must* be organized" (10; emphasis added). The imperative for labor education emphasized the necessity of literacy and educational training, giving the sense that there were few other options that would be as effective.

23. There were, in fact, many roadblocks to a young person's access to higher education, which prevented most people from attending college during this time. John R. Thelin writes that "college enrollments represented less than 5 percent of the American population of eighteen- to twenty-two-year-olds" (169), citing tuition costs and also the need for young adults to work.

24. Unions rarely published comprehensive lists of all classes and their enrollments, instead favoring articles that talked about different classes. Even so, they tended to downplay the English classes and really emphasized the other classes. However, English classes were offered more than any other class and remained a constant presence in the printed materials, and they seem to be the ones with the highest enrollment in the few records that exist.

25. Of course, whether this underbidding was done knowingly or unknowingly is up for interpretation. It is also important to note that many union materials were published in Hebrew, Italian, and other languages in order to reach non-English speakers.

26. Because of the use of the first initial, the gender of the writer is not visible. Often ILGWU unions had male and female members, causing this difficulty in determining gender of the author for many of their publications.

27. *Justice* would occasionally publish letters to the editor, providing firsthand testimonials of the benefits and importance of workers' education. They served as constant reminders of the importance of literacy and education for the movement. This document, of course, brings questions about authorship and its authenticity. Was it written by a student? Or perhaps Cohn or Fichlander? An assignment in a course?

28. The distinctions among categorizations were not uncommon, even in the federal citizenship texts. The *Teacher's Manual* that accompanies the 1922 version of the federal text suggests that teachers divide their classes up into beginners who speak English but are literate in their home languages and those who are illiterate in their home languages (U.S., *Teacher's Manual* 2). *Teaching Our Language to Beginners* offers the rationale that "the illiterate pupil presents a special problem in any classroom, since it is impossible to learn to read or write as quickly as the literate pupil" (Clark 5).

29. Cohn herself ended up being a casualty of these battles, losing a fifth term as the ILGWU vice-president in 1925 (Wong 50). While she remained the union's

executive secretary, she was "increasingly relegated to marginal activities" by the 1930s (Wong 54).

30. Altenbaugh traces how the AFL executive council advised "affiliated unions to withdraw their support from Brookwood" (182), which led to a public battle between Brookwood and the AFL in the pages of the *New York Times* (184) and culminated at the AFL national convention in New Orleans in November 1928.

31. This tension between native-born and "foreign" workers (in every sense of the word, so this included African Americans) is the main argument of Roediger's *Wages of Whiteness*.

32. One notable exception is the Highlander Folk School, which was founded in 1932. John M. Glen describes Highlander as a training ground for "labor, civil rights, and Appalachian reform" (19), but its roots were in Danish folk schools (Glen 4) rather than solely worker and industrial education.

33. Altenbaugh admits that it was clear that "labor colleges did not achieve their larger dream of broad social change. A new social order, as they—and the noncommunist left—envisioned it, did not come into being" (256). They "successfully altered the structure of the American labor movement" (256) but through the establishment of labor colleges, not the after-school programs. Brookwood, a full-time institution, educated leaders on the labor movement who ended up playing key roles in the 1929 Southern textile workers' strike and the 1936 autoworkers' strike (256).

Chapter 4. English and Useful Citizenship in a Culture of Aspiration

1. Rapeer described the educational aims of education as a reflection of the "principal problems of the American people" (381). He wrote, "These seven aims, stated as phases of social efficiency, are as follows: 1. vital or physical efficiency—health; 2. vocational efficiency; 3. domestic efficiency; 4. civic efficiency-citizenship; 5. moral efficiency—morality and religion; 6. a vocational efficiency—right use of leisure; 7. social-service efficiency—social service" (381).

2. I would argue that the history of higher education in the United States is one of continuous expansion punctuated by spurts of growth that were encouraged by events like the passage of the Morrill Act in 1862, the culture of aspiration, as Levine describes, the GI Bill, the civil rights movement, and the growth of for-profit institutions, among others.

3. With his focus on the late Progressive, World War I period, Levine also disrupts the commonly held view, initially forwarded by Laurence R. Veysey, that "the major innovations in higher education ended with the professionalization of the elite university around the turn of the century" (Levine 15).

4. Lynn Bloom made a contemporary version of this argument in "Freshman Composition as a Middle-Class Enterprise."

5. See James Fleming Hosic's *Reorganization of English in Secondary Schools* for a contemporary understanding of how these questions about the connection between high school and college animated curricular discussions. This 1917 report, by the Na-

tional Joint Committee on English Representing the Commission on the Reorganization of Secondary Education of the National Education Association and the National Council of Teachers of English, was published by the Bureau of Education to understand the new role of high school as a common school.

6. Or at least the perception of an increasing number of kinds of students. While the idea that education was expanding to serve a greater part of the public and thus had its imprint on many of the policies and attitudes, as Levine describes, much of this was aspirational, laying the groundwork for future expansion after World War II. He talks about "the myth of democratic education," believing that it was an illusion to think that college students were not mostly privileged, even though there were some exceptions. Even in state universities that "permitted greater access to higher education, the children from less privileged socioeconomic backgrounds were still terribly underrepresented there" (130). He provides statistics from the University of Minnesota from the mid-1920s to show that one student for every 21 professionals in the state, one child of clerical workers for every 185 clerical workers, and one laborer's child for every 1,583 laborers (130). So while the numbers of students increased, the diversity of those students was still quite low.

7. Levine writes, "Fearful of the rise of the city, with its huge concentrations of ethnic Americans, fearful of the increasing number and visibility of the children of immigrants in American economic, political, and social institutions, many WASPs scrambled for the means to preserve their cultural hegemony. Higher education was not immune to this climate of intolerance" (148).

8. Other students of color, to use a contemporary term, were already excluded from most mainstream higher education either in earlier years of education or, in the case of African American students, in such a wide swath that they established institutions of their own. Levine states, "The treatment of black students provides an even more dramatic example of how WASP educators and their traditional constituencies clung to their racist views. While the number of students at black colleges and universities leaped six times from 2,132 in 1917 to 13,580 in 1927, the number of black students at predominantly white colleges increased barely at all" (158–59).

9. Levine describes the distinction between the two periods in which "in 1915, less than one in twenty young people went to college; the 1947 [Truman] commission insisted that free and universal access to at least two years of postsecondary work be the major goal" (217).

10. In addition to these public goals, one of the key reasons for the formation of NCTE was to keep the high school course from becoming solely college preparatory.

11. One of the first tasks of NCTE was to figure out what they wanted the uniform requirement to look like and to provide recommendations. They examined issues such as the population of high schools and colleges; most high school students would not go to college, yet their curriculum was being unnecessarily influenced by it. The exam probably reflected the collegiate goals for the English classroom but an anxiety about "teaching to the exam" also existed, resulting in a National Conference on Uniform Entrance Requirements and various committees that addressed this issue. An early

issue of the *English Journal* published an excerpt from *English Problems* by James Hosic, a document that came out of a committee on the entrance requirement by the National Education Association. The excerpt, titled "The Influence of the Uniform Requirements in English," exemplified the tensions regarding the changing nature of institutions of higher education. Hosic discussed how high schools ended up teaching to the exam and that

> the problem of the articulation of the high school with the college is a natural result of our educational development. It has arisen from the overlapping of the older system of endowed colleges, with their self-developed preparatory schools, and the newer system of public high schools and universities, organized and supported by the state. The academy was not originally but soon became a preparatory school. The public high school, on the other hand, is intended to provide an increased opportunity of education for the children of the people. With the development of the state universities, it [the public high school] has come to be thought of as the necessary stepping-stone from the elementary school to the college of liberal arts, the college of science, or the professional and technical school. (103)

Hosic described a change in the population of school-aged teenagers and the anxieties that became associated with that shift.

12. Previous scholarship has explored this relationship between the high school and college. In his history of the NCTE, J. G. Hook describes how the organization "originated in protest by public secondary schools against curricular domination by colleges" (3) by the Uniform Reading Lists (also Applebee 51; Berlin, *Rhetoric and Reality* 33). Because of the continuing influence of college demands on high school curriculum, I think it's important to consider the way that high school and college composition instruction worked together as a site of literacy training and citizenship production and discover how the structures of education, college requirements, high school courses, and so on, influence the kind of advanced literacy that becomes certified through educational institutions. Also, Thelin suggests that the large amount of construction and campus-building between 1890 and 1910 "signaled a transformation in access to American higher education—a shift away from being a scarce commodity and an elite experience. The nation was edging toward a commitment to mass higher education, a goal that was fueled by the expansion of public secondary schools" (205).

13. Raymond Macdonald Alden from the University of Illinois was one who worried about composition courses taking over English departments. In 1913, he wrote,

> the huge courses which have arisen for the correction of faults and the establishment of elementary ability in writing on the part of those who have not acquired it at the age when they should have done so—is undoubtedly a problem by itself. This is the work which now requires so large a staff, apart from all other English work, and distorts the whole market for "English" instructors. The simple fact is that the demand for teachers of strictly collegiate English is not so large as it has been made to appear through the development of this one type of course, and the sooner this is realized the better. (355)

To those like Alden who felt that English departments should get out of the composition business, the work of composition teaching should not be the "whole market" or even a large portion of what English instructors do, but instead indicates an aberration in the market that should be corrected or else English departments will suffer the consequences (presumably by having to do more composition teaching and less literary study).

14. Incidentally, Cohen is cited as teaching at Washington Irving High School, which is a space where many workers' education courses took place at night. She reported, "In the evening classes, then, in which English is taught to foreigners, the language, after the rudiments are mastered, is studied in connection with the duties and privileges of citizenship. Civics is taken up, however, not in a technical academic way but in relation to the experience of the immigrant in the city" (618).

15. For example, the influx of immigrant populations and nonstandard English speakers into the public schools fed the attention to correctness during this period. Many writers cite the home language of students as a way of explaining how the English classroom could not solve all "problems" with writing. For example, Charlotte Herr, a high school teacher from Cicero, Illinois, said in 1913, "When many children in school come from homes where ignorant or foreign-born parents struggle with the grammar and vocabulary of a comparatively unfamiliar language, picking up, because it is the easiest way, the expressions of the uneducated people who are their fellow-laborers and neighbors, knowing little and caring less that the forms of speech they thus acquire are not good English, and their children hear this kind of language for many hours a day at home, the short period spent at school can do little to counteract such an influence" (185). Herr talks about the responsibility of the school to attend to these issues while simultaneously relieving the school of its culpability. Instruction in English was absolutely necessary, particularly with students who came from "uneducated" or "foreign-born" families, but at the same time schools had a limited influence on students who did not hear "good English" in their homes.

16. In *City College and the Jewish Poor*, Sherry Gorelick refutes the common belief about City College as a "Red" institution around World War I. Citing Stephen Duggan's characterization in his memoir, *A Professor at Large*, that such a reputation was "unjust," Gorelick contends that while communism was a presence at City College, it was not necessarily a "Bolshevik heaven" (181).

17. Published critiques include "Is the College Making Good?" by Edward Bok, and Thomas R. Lounsbury's "Compulsory Composition in Colleges."

18. This same concern about the power provided through the curriculum is found in discussions during the National Conference on the Uniform Entrance Requirements and subsequent attempts to balance writing, analysis, and literature in the English curriculum. The whole point of the conference was to try to shape the requirements in a way that would satisfy the colleges but also give teachers the power to provide a course still relevant to noncollege students. The reading list remained a particular point of contention, and in a May 1912 issue of the *English Journal* Arthur Willis Leonard re-

ported that the conference agreed that the colleges should test the "power to write, power to think, power to read and appreciate" (298), rather than a prescribed list of books.

19. Earle illustrates this point: "Nevertheless, anyone who is going to use a language intelligently needs not only skill but also knowledge of its mechanics that he may understand why it works as it does, just as certainly as one who is going to run an automobile needs not only skill but also knowledge of the machinery" (480).

20. According to the U.S. Census Bureau, in 1890, 33,400 people worked as stenographers and typists, jobs that required a certain level of literacy and training; by 1920, that number had risen to 615,100. In 1910, it was only 326,700, and 154 in 1870 (Banta; see also Kittler).

21. Bruce Laurie describes the turn of the century as a time when "machine-driven production eclipsed the hand labor of the sweating system, all but completing the transformation of artisans into industrial workers" (215), and a time that saw private ownership of industry and business surpass public ownership. Also, Samuel Bowles and Herbert Gintis cite that by 1890, two-thirds of all "economically active" people in the United States were employees (182). Additionally, they discuss the growing numbers of management between 1890 and 1930, from 90,000 to 336,000 (182).

Chapter 5. Teaching Literacy and Citizenship in the Twenty-First Century

1. The persistence of citizenship anxieties can be seen in the difficulties of making changes to U.S. immigration policy. The United States imposed immigration restrictions in 1921 and 1924. Its resulting quota systems remained relatively in place until the Hart-Celler Act of 1965, which marked significant reform (Daniels 134). In the time since, no comprehensive immigration reform has been passed, although family policies, refugee status, and temporary work policies continued to be tweaked. The protests around immigration reform in 1996, 2006, and 2013 focused on the maintenance or expansion of the boundaries of citizenship, whether through access to citizenship resources such as employment and education or the creation of boundaries through increased border controls and penalties for those without legal residency.

2. Thelin describes how this mid-twentieth-century period saw "the shape of American higher education . . . simultaneously altered in two contrasting ways. On one front, its base was extended so as to move significantly closer to providing mass access to higher education. On another front, the tip of the pyramid was pushed upward as American colleges and universities showed increasing capacity to add advanced, academically selective programs, from the undergraduate level on up through the professional schools and doctoral programs" (260). Enrollments soared, with under 1.5 million college and university students in the United States in 1939–40 to over 7.9 million by 1970 (Thelin 261).

3. For a book-length treatment of public writing in the composition classroom and a study of writing as social action, see Welch's *Living Room: Teaching Public Writing.*

4. Members include Derek Bok (interim president of Harvard University), Myles Brand (president of the NCAA), Barbara Lawton (lieutenant governor of Wisconsin), Stephen Mittelstet (president of Richland College, Dallas County Community College

District), Keith J. Peden (senior vice president of Human Resources, Raytheon Company), Deborah Traskell (senior vice president, State Farm Mutual Automobile Insurance Company), and Jack M. Wilson (president, University of Massachusetts system). The diversity of stakeholders in the future of college education seems to speak to the importance of shaping all kinds of higher education to the intellectual, political, and economic future of the country.

5. One profound example of this kind of tension can be found in the University of California system and the response of the institution and the student body to the influx of Asian students. Despite stated efforts to create global citizens, the reality of harnessing the ready group of global students in the Asian American population has been sidelined by racial tensions, admissions questions, and even cultural questions about the racial makeup of the student population. In spring 2011, UCLA confronted this issue after an undergraduate student, Alexandra Wallace, posted a video blog entry that mocked the Asian student population, questioning their familial ties and non-English language use. OiYan A. Poon observed that "even though the great majority of Asian students at UCLA are either 1.5 or second-generation Asian Americans overwhelmingly from California, Wallace views them as an un-American and monolithic horde." Wallace's alienation and othering of such a large part of the student population calls into question whether Asians and Asian Americans can actually be included in the process of citizenship production by the University of California system. Is global citizenship possible when the citizenship production on campus seems to exclude such a large part of the population? In the UCLA case, the racial differences produced cultural discomfort, not marketable attributes.

6. During this period, many people mobilized around proposed immigration reform in the United States. While the movement began specifically as a response to HR 4437, making illegal immigration or aiding illegal immigration a felony, supporters called for extensive immigration and naturalization reform, particularly for those already working in the United States. Protests culminated on 10 April 2006 with an estimated 102 cities organizing demonstrations (see Newman).

7. As chapter 2 makes clear, there has been an economic component to immigration, but I'm specifically talking here about the way policies have been argued for and discussed.

8. On 2 April 2013, the Associated Press dropped "illegal immigrant" from its stylebook, asking that "illegal" only refer to behavior, not people.

9. Of course, not everyone who enters the United States wishes to become a citizen, but debates around immigrant work rely on the assumption that everyone who comes wants to stay.

10. In addition to California, Illinois, and New York, the other states include Kansas, Nebraska, New Mexico, Oklahoma, Utah, and Washington (Rincón 109). Rincón reports that California, New York, and Texas are "home to almost half of the nation's undocumented residents" (109).

11. Unless you are willing to risk your life for citizenship through military service, as some undocumented residents do.

WORKS CITED

Adams, Katherine H. *Progressive Politics and the Training of America's Persuaders.* Mahwah, NJ: Lawrence Erlbaum, 1999.

Alden, Raymond Macdonald. "Preparation for College English Teaching." *English Journal* 2 (1913): 344–56.

Alden, Rose. "On Teaching American." *English Journal* 3 (1914): 182–83.

Aleinikoff, T. Alexander, and Douglas Klusmeyer, eds. Introduction to *Citizenship Today: Global Perspectives and Practices.* Washington, DC: Carnegie Endowment for International Peace, 2001.

Aleinikoff, Thomas Alexander, David A. Martin, and Hiroshi Motomura. *Immigration and Citizenship: Process and Policy.* 5th ed. St. Paul, MN: Thomson West, 2003.

Allen, Danielle S. *Talking to Strangers: Anxieties of Citizenship since Brown v. Board of Education.* Chicago: University of Chicago Press, 2004.

Altenbaugh, Richard J. *Education for Struggle: The American Labor Colleges of the 1920s and 1930s.* Philadelphia: Temple University Press, 1990.

American Federation of Labor. "Labor and Education." New York: American Federation of Labor, 1910.

Applebee, Arthur N. *Tradition and Reform in the Teaching of English: A History.* Urbana, IL: National Council of Teachers of English, 1974.

Aronowitz, Stanley. *False Promises: The Shaping of American Working Class Consciousness.* New York: McGraw-Hill, 1973.

Arum, Richard, and Josipa Roksa. *Academically Adrift: Limited Learning on College Campuses.* Chicago: University of Chicago Press, 2011.

Baker, Franklin T. "The Teacher of English." *English Journal* 2 (1913): 335–43.

Banta, Martha. *Taylored Lives.* Chicago: University of Chicago Press, 1993.

Barnes, Walter. "The Reign of Red Ink." *English Journal* 2 (1913): 158–65.

Barrett, James R. "Americanization from the Bottom Up: Immigration and the Remaking of the Working Class in the United States, 1880–1830." *Journal of American History* 79 (1992): 996–1020.

Berlin, James A. *Rhetoric and Reality: Writing Instruction in American Colleges, 1900–1985*. Carbondale: Southern Illinois University Press, 1987.

———. *Rhetorics, Poetics, and Cultures: Refiguring College English Studies*. Urbana, IL: National Council of Teachers of English, 1996.

Berndt, Michael, and Amy Muse. *Composing a Civic Life: A Rhetoric and Readings for Inquiry and Action*. New York: Pearson/Longman, 2004.

Bizzell, Patricia. "Composition Studies Saves the World!" *College English* 72 (2009): 174–87.

Bloom, Lynn Z. "Freshman Composition as a Middle-Class Enterprise." *College English* 58 (1996): 654–75.

Bok, Edward. "Is the College Making Good?" *Outlook*. 16 August 1913, 16.

Bosniak, Linda. "Denationalizing Citizenship." In Aleinikoff and Klusmeyer, 237–52.

Bowles, Samuel, and Herbert Gintis. *Schooling in Capitalist America*. New York: Basic, 1976.

Brandt, Deborah. *Literacy in American Lives*. New York: Cambridge University Press, 2001.

Breck, Emma J. "A New Task for the English Teacher." *English Journal* 1 (1912): 65–71.

Briggs, Vernon M., Jr. *Immigration Policy and the American Labor Force*. Baltimore: Johns Hopkins University Press, 1984.

Buel, Elizabeth C. Barney. *Manual of the United States: For the Information of Immigrants and Foreigners*. Washington, DC: The National Society, Daughters of the American Revolution, 1924.

Bush, George W. "President Bush Proposes New Temporary Worker Program." 7 January 2004. http://georgewbush-whitehouse.archives.gov/news/releases/2004/01/20040107-3.html.

Callan, Eamonn. *Creating Citizens: Political Education and Liberal Democracy*. New York: Oxford University Press, 1997.

Campbell, Kermit E. "There Goes the Neighborhood: Hip Hop Creepin' on a Come Up at the U." *College Composition and Communication* 58 (2007): 325–44.

City College. *College Bulletin*. New York: City College, 1911–22.

———. College of Liberal Arts and Sciences (CLAS) Faculty Council. Minutes, 23 September 1920, City College Archives.

Clapp, John M. "Oral English in the College Course." *English Journal* 2 (1913): 18–33.

Clapp, John Mantle, ed. *The Place of English in American Life: Report of an Investigation by a Committee of the National Council of Teachers of English*. Chicago: National Council of Teachers of English, 1926.

Clark, Evans. "Workers' Education." *Nation* 113 (1921): 670–73.

Clark, Lillian P. *Federal Textbook on Citizenship Training, Part 1, Our Language*. Washington, DC: Government Printing Office, 1924.

———. *Federal Textbook on Citizenship Training, Part 2, Our Community*. Washington, DC: Government Printing Office, 1924.

———. *Teaching Our Language to Beginners*. Washington, DC: Government Printing Office, 1924.

Cohen, Helen Louise. "The Foreigner in Our Schools: Some Aspects of the Problem in New York." *English Journal* 2 (1913): 618–29.

Cohn, Fannia. "Classes Begin at International Unity Centers." *Justice,* 17 September 1920, 1.

———. "Education and the American Labor Movement." *Justice,* 20 August 1920, 5.

———. "Labor Day Thoughts." *Justice,* 2 September 1921, 6.

———. "Our Workers' University." *Justice,* 30 April 1920, 3.

"Colleges for Workers." Editorial. *New York Evening Post,* 20 July 1921, 6.

Committee for Americanism of the City of Boston. *A Little Book for Immigrants in Boston.* Boston: City of Boston Printing Department, 1921.

Connors, Robert J. *Composition-Rhetoric: Backgrounds, Theory, and Pedagogy.* Pittsburgh: University of Pittsburgh Press, 1997.

———. "Mechanical Correctness as a Focus in Composition Instruction." *College Composition and Communication* 36 (1985): 61–72.

"The Constituency of the English Journal." *English Journal* 2 (1913): 392.

Cremin, Lawrence A. *American Education.* New York: Harper & Row, 1988.

Crist, Raymond. *Report of the Commissioner of Naturalization to the Secretary of Labor.* Washington, DC: U.S. Department of Labor, 1928.

———. *Report of the Commissioner of Naturalization to the Secretary of Labor.* Washington, DC: U.S. Department of Labor, 1929.

Crowley, Sharon. *Composition in the University: Historical and Polemical Essays.* Pittsburgh: University of Pittsburgh Press, 1998.

Cruikshank, Barbara. *The Will to Empower: Democratic Citizens and Other Subjects.* Ithaca, NY: Cornell University Press, 1999.

Cushman, Ellen. *The Struggle and the Tools: Oral and Literate Strategies in an Inner City Community.* Albany: State University of New York Press, 1998.

Daniels, Roger. *Guarding the Golden Door: American Immigration Policy and Immigrants since 1882.* New York: Hill and Wang, 2004.

Danish, Max M. "Topics of the Week." *Justice,* 12 November 1920, 2.

Dawson, Charles A. "Two Experiments in Experience." *English Journal* 2 (1913): 437–44.

Delbanco, Andrew. *College: What It Was, Is, and Should Be.* Princeton, NJ: Princeton University Press, 2012.

Delli Carpini, Dominic. *Composing a Life's Work: Writing, Citizenship, and Your Occupation.* New York: Pearson/Longman, 2005.

Dillingham Commission. *Statements and Recommendations Submitted by Societies and Organizations Interested in the Subject of Immigration.* U.S. Dillingham Commission Report. Vol. 41. Washington, DC: Government Printing Office, 1911.

Diner, Steven J. *A Very Different Age: Americans of the Progressive Era.* New York: Hill and Wang, 1998.

Dubofsky, Melvyn. *Hard Work.* Urbana: University of Illinois Press, 2000.

———. *The State and Labor in Modern America.* Chapel Hill: University of North Carolina Press, 1994.

Duffy, John. "Letters from the Fair City: A Rhetorical Conception of Literacy." *College Composition and Communication* 56.2 (2004): 223–50.

Duncan, C. S. "A Rebellious Word on English Composition." *English Journal* 3 (1914): 154–59.

Earle, Samuel Chandler. "The Organization of Instruction in English Composition." *English Journal* 2 (1913): 477–87.

Eberly, Rosa A. *Citizen Critics: Literary Public Spheres.* Urbana: University of Illinois Press, 2000.

"Educational Comment and Notes" *Justice,* 29 January 1921, 6.

"Educational Comment and Notes." *Justice,* 22 July 1921, 6.

"The Educational Work of the International." *Justice,* 7 May 1920, 4.

Ervin, Elizabeth. "Encouraging Civic Participation among First-Year Writing Students; or, Why Composition Class Should Be More Like a Bowling Team." *Rhetoric Review* 15 (1997): 382–99.

Faigley, Lester. *Fragments of Rationality: Postmodernity and the Subject of Composition.* Pittsburgh: University of Pittsburgh Press, 1992.

Farrington, D. Davis. "Oral Work and Democracy." *English Journal* 13 (1924): 478–82.

Feinstein, Irving Norman. *The Growth and Development of the Study of English Language and Literature in the College of the City of New York, 1847–1934.* Master's thesis, Department of English, City College of New York, 1934.

Fish, Stanley. "Why We Build the Ivory Tower." *New York Times,* 12 May 2004.

Flower, Linda. *Community Literacy and the Rhetoric of Public Engagement.* Carbondale: Southern Illinois University Press, 2009.

Ford, Jon, and Marjorie Ford. *Citizenship Now.* New York: Pearson/Longman, 2004.

Freire, Paulo. *Literacy: Reading the Word and the World.* New York: Routledge, 1987.

Friedland, Louis S. "The Bases for Our Educational Work." *Justice,* 6 February 1920, 5.

———. "In Our Educational Department." *Justice,* 5 March 1920, 4.

"The Function of Labor Education." *Justice,* 21 April 1922, 10.

Genung, John Franklin. *Handbook of Rhetorical Analysis: Studies in Style and Invention.* Boston: Ginn & Company, 1902.

Gere, Anne Ruggles. *Intimate Practices: Literacy and Cultural Work in U.S. Women's Clubs, 1880–1920.* Urbana: University of Illinois Press, 1997.

Gettleman, Marvin E. "The New York Workers School, 1923–1944: Communist Education in American Society." In *New Studies in the Politics and Culture of U.S. Communism,* ed. Michael E. Brown, Randy Martin, Frank Rosengarten, and George Snedeker, 261–80. New York: Monthly Review, 1993.

Gillibrand, Kirsten, and Lillian Rodriguez Lopez. "If the Feds Can't Pass the DREAM Act, New York State Must Do Its Part." *New York Daily News,* 27 December 2011. http://www.nydailynews.com/opinion/feds-pass-dream-act-new-york-state-part-article-1.996283.

Gilyard, Keith. *Composition and Cornel West: Notes toward a Deep Democracy.* Carbondale: Southern Illinois University Press, 2008.

Giroux, Henry. *Schooling and the Struggle for Public Life: Critical Pedagogy in the Modern Age*. Minneapolis: University of Minnesota Press, 1988.

Glen, John M. *Highlander: No Ordinary School, 1932–1962*. Lexington: University Press of Kentucky Press, 1988.

Gold, David. *Rhetoric at the Margins: Revising the History of College Writing Instruction, 1873–1947*. Carbondale: Southern Illinois University Press, 2008.

Goldblatt, Eli. *Because We Live Here: Sponsoring Literacy beyond the College Curriculum*. Cresskill: Hampton Press, 2007.

Goldin, Claudia, and Lawrence F. Katz. *The Race between Education and Technology*. Cambridge, MA: Harvard University Press, 2008.

Gompers, Samuel L. "Workers Education Bureau." *American Federationist* 32 (November 1925): 1080.

Gorelick, Sherry. *City College and the Jewish Poor: Education in New York, 1880–1924*. New Brunswick, NJ: Rutgers University Press, 1981.

Gosling, T. W. "How the High-School Teacher of English Can Assist in the Exploitation of Pupils' Powers." *English Journal* 2 (1913): 513–17.

Graff, Gerald. *Clueless in Academe: How Schooling Obscures the Life of the Mind*. New Haven, CT: Yale University Press, 2003.

Graff, Harvey J. *The Literacy Myth: Literacy and Social Structure in the Nineteenth-Century City*. New York: Academic Press, 1979.

Grubb, W. Norton, and Marvin Lazerson. *The Education Gospel: The Economic Power of Schooling*. Cambridge, MA: Harvard University Press, 2004.

Gutman, Herbert George. *Work, Culture, and Society in Industrializing America: Essays in American Working-Class and Social History*. New York: Vintage Books, 1977.

Habermas, Jürgen. *The Structural Transformation of the Public Sphere: An Inquiry into a Category of Bourgeois Society*. Trans. Thomas Burger. Cambridge, MA: MIT Press, 1991.

Hacker, Andrew, and Claudia Dreifus. *Higher Education?: How Colleges Are Wasting Our Money and Failing Our Kids*. New York: Henry Holt, 2010.

Harris, Joseph. "Beyond Community: From the Social to the Material." *Journal of Basic Writing* 20 (2001): 3–15.

———. "The Idea of Community in the Study of Writing." *College Composition and Communication* 40 (1989): 11–22.

Hathaway, Esse V. "The Building of an English Course of Study." *English Journal* 7 (1918): 526–32.

Heater, Derek. *Citizenship: The Civic Ideal in World History, Politics, and Education*. Manchester: Manchester University Press, 2004.

Heath, Shirley Brice. *Ways with Words: Language, Life, and Work in Communities and Classrooms*. Cambridge: Cambridge University Press, 1983.

Herr, Charlotte. "Co-Operation in the Teaching of English Composition." *English Journal* 2 (1913): 185–87.

Higham, John. *Strangers in the Land: Patterns of American Nativism, 1860–1925*. 2nd ed. New Brunswick, NJ: Rutgers University Press, 1988.

Hill, Herbert Wynford. "The Problem of Harmonizing Aesthetic Interests with the Commercial and Industrial Trend of Our Times." *English Journal* 2 (1913): 609–12.

Hollis, Karyn J. *Liberating Voices: Writing at the Bryn Mawr Summer School for Women Workers*. Carbondale: Southern Illinois University Press, 2004.

Hook, J. G. *A Long Way Together: A Personal View of NCTE's First Sixty-Seven Years*. Urbana, IL: National Council of Teachers of English, 1979.

Hopkins, Edwin M. *The Labor and Cost of the Teaching of English in Colleges and Secondary Schools with Special Reference to English Composition*. Urbana, IL: National Council of Teachers of English, 1923.

Hosic, James Fleming. "The Influence of the Uniform Requirements in English." *English Journal* 1.2 (1912): 95–121.

———. "Reorganization of English in Secondary Schools." *Bureau of Education Bulletin* 2. Washington, DC: Government Printing Office, 1917.

Hutcheson, Philo A. "Setting the Nation's Agenda for Higher Education: A Review of Selected National Commission Reports, 1947–2006." *History of Education Quarterly* 47.3 (2007): 359–67.

Hutcheson, Philo A. "The Truman Commission's Vision of the Future." *Thought and Action: The NEA Higher Education Journal* (Fall 2007): 107–15.

"In Our Educational Department." *Justice,* 9 January 1920, 6.

International Ladies' Garment Workers' Union. *Garment Workers Speak*. N.p., N.d.

Iowa State University. "The Iowa State University Strategic Plan: 2005–2010." Ames: ISU University Relations, 2005. http://www.public.iastate.edu/~strategicplan/.

Jacobson, Matthew Frye. *Whiteness of a Different Color: European Immigrants and the Alchemy of Race*. Cambridge, MA: Harvard University Press, 1998.

Kansas, Sidney. *U.S. Immigration: Exclusion and Deportation*. New York: Holland Publishing, 1928.

Kates, Susan. *Activist Rhetorics and American Higher Education, 1885–1937*. Carbondale: Southern Illinois University Press, 2000.

Katz, Michael B. *The Price of Citizenship: Redefining the American Welfare State*. New York: Owl Books, 2002.

Keeling, Richard P., and Richard H. Hersh. *We're Losing Our Minds: Rethinking American Higher Education*. New York: Palgrave Macmillan, 2012.

Kendall, Constance. *The Worlds We Deliver: Confronting the Consequences of Believing in Literacy*. PhD dissertation, Department of English, Miami University of Ohio, 2005.

Kerr, Clark. *The Uses of the University*. 5th ed. Cambridge, MA: Harvard University Press, 2001.

Kessler-Harris, Alice. "Problems of Coalition-Building: Women and Trade Unions in the 1920s." In *Women, Work and Protest: A Century of U.S. Women's Labor History,* ed. Ruth Milkman, 110–38. New York: Routledge, 1985.

Kettner, James H. *The Development of American Citizenship, 1608–1870.* Chapel Hill: University of North Carolina Press, 1978.

King, Desmond. *Making Americans: Immigration, Race, and the Origins of the Diverse Democracy.* Cambridge, MA: Harvard University Press, 2000.

Kittler, Friedrich A. *Gramophone, Film, Typewriter.* Trans. Geoffrey Winthrop-Young and Michael Wutz. Stanford: Stanford University Press, 1999.

Kivisto, Peter, and Thomas Faist. *Citizenship: Discourse, Theory, and Transnational Prospects.* Malden: Blackwell, 2007.

Kornbluh, Joyce. *A New Deal for Workers' Education.* Urbana: University of Illinois, 1987.

Labaree, David F. "Public Goods, Private Goods: The American Struggle over Educational Goals." *American Educational Research Journal* 34 (1997): 39–81.

"Labor Seeks Education." *New York Times,* 10 July 1925, 16.

Lamont, Hammond. *English Composition.* New York: C. Scribner's Sons, 1906.

Lamos, Steve. "Language, Literacy, and the Institutional Dynamics of Racism: Late-1960s Writing Instruction for 'High-Risk' African American Undergraduate Students at One Predominately White University." *College Composition and Communication* 60 (2008): 46–81.

Laurie, Bruce. *Artisans into Workers.* Urbana: University of Illinois Press, 1997.

"Learn English." *Justice,* 18 February 1921, 6.

Lennard, Natasha. "Trying Again with the DREAM Act." *Salon,* 28 June 2011. http://politics.salon.com/2011/06/28/dream_act_senate_hearing/singleton/.

Leonard, Arthur Willis. "A Report of the Proceedings of the National Conference on Uniform Entrance Requirements in English." *English Journal* 1.5 (1912): 294–301.

Levine, David O. *The American College and the Culture of Aspiration, 1915–1940.* Ithaca, NY: Cornell University Press, 1986.

Lewis, W. D. "The Aim of the English Course." *English Journal* 1 (1912): 9–14.

Lindemann, Erika. "How Well Are We Listening? Lessons from the Founding of NCTE and CCCC." *College Composition and Communication* 62 (2011): 504–39.

Lounsbury, Thomas R. "Compulsory Composition in Colleges." *Harper's,* November 1911, 866–80.

Mactavish, J. M. "The Education of Class Conscious Workers." *Justice,* 23 September 1921, 10.

Marshall, T. H. *Citizenship and Social Class.* New York: Cambridge University Press, 1950.

Marx, Karl. *Capital.* Trans. Samuel Moore and Edward Aveling. Ed. Friedrich Engels. New York: International Publishers, 1947.

McKitrick, May. "The Adaptation of the Work in English to the Actual Needs and Interests of the Pupils." *English Journal* 2 (1913): 405–16.

Miles, Dudley. "Composition as a Training in Thought." *English Journal* 2 (1913): 362–65.

Montgomery, David. *Workers' Control in America: Studies in the History of Work, Technology, and Labor Struggles.* New York: Cambridge University Press, 1979.

National Leadership Council for Liberal Education and America's Promise (LEAP). "College Learning for the New Global Century." Washington, DC: Association of American Colleges and Universities, 2007.

Nelson, Daniel. *Managers and Workers: Origins of the Twentieth Century Factory System in the United States, 1880–1920*. Madison: University of Wisconsin Press, 1995.

Newman, Maria. "Immigration Advocates Rally across United States." *New York Times*, 10 April 2006. http://www.nytimes.com/2006/04/10/us/10cnd-rallies.html?pagewanted=all&_r=0.

"News and Notes: Association of High-School Teachers of English of New York City." *English Journal* 2 (1913): 530–33.

Ngai, Mae M. *Impossible Subjects: Illegal Aliens and the Making of Modern America*. Princeton, NJ: Princeton University Press, 2005.

Obama, Barack. "Streamlining Legal Immigration." 29 January 2013. http://www.whitehouse.gov/issues/immigration/streamlining-immigration.

Ohmann, Richard. *English in America: Radical View of the Profession*. New York: Oxford University Press, 1976.

Ong, Aihwa. "Cultural Citizenship as Subject-Making: Immigrants Negotiate Racial and Cultural Boundaries in the United States." *Cultural Anthropology* 37 (1996): 737–62.

Otte, George, and Rebecca Mlynarczyk. *Basic Writing*. West Lafayette, IN: Parlor Press, 2010.

"Our English Classes." *Justice*, 14 October 1921, 10.

Paine, Charles. *The Resistant Writer: Rhetoric as Immunity, 1850 to the Present*. Albany: State University of New York Press, 1999.

Pendleton, Charles S. "The New Teacher of English." *English Journal* 6 (1917): 575–83.

Pennsylvania State University. University Strategic Planning Council. *Priorities for Excellence*. May 2009.

Poon, OiYan A. "Ching Chongs and Tiger Moms: The 'Asian Invasion' in U.S. Higher Education" *Hyphen*, 27 September 2011. http://www.hyphenmagazine.com/node/3472.

Prendergast, Catherine. *Literacy and Racial Justice: The Politics of Learning after Brown v. Board of Education*. Carbondale: Southern Illinois University Press, 2003.

"Prof. Egbert of Columbia and Labor Education." *Justice*, 2 June 1922, 10.

Queens College. "Goals for Student Writing." City University of New York, 2007. Brochure.

Rapeer, Louis W. "The Outside of the Cup: Relative Values in High-School English." *English Journal* 5 (1916): 379–91.

Recht, Charles. *American Deportation and Exclusion Laws*. New York Bureau of Legal Advice, 15 January 1919, rept. by the National Civil Liberties Bureau, 1919.

Rincón, Alejandra. *Undocumented Immigrants and Higher Education*. New York: LFB Scholarly Publishing, 2008.

Ritter, Kelly. *Before Shaughnessy: Basic Writing at Yale and Harvard, 1920–1960*. Carbondale, IL: Southern Illinois University Press, 2009.

Roediger, David. *Wages of Whiteness*. 2nd ed. New York: Verso, 1999.

Roll, M. Letter. *Justice*, 6 May 1921, 6.

Rudolph, Frederick. *Curriculum: A History of the American Undergraduate Course of Study since 1636*. San Francisco: Jossey-Bass, 1977.

Rutland, J. R. "Tendencies in the Administration of Freshman English." *English Journal* 12 (1923): 1–10.

Sassen, Saskia. *Guests and Aliens*. New York: The New Press, 1999.

"Says Workers' Bureau Has No Radical Aims." *New York Times*, 6 March 1923, 23.

Schneider, Dorothee. "Naturalization and United States Citizenship in Two Periods of Mass Migration: 1894–1930, 1965–2000." *Journal of American Ethnic History* (2001): 50–81.

Shklar, Judith. *American Citizenship: The Quest for Inclusion*. Cambridge, MA: Harvard University Press, 1998.

Simmons, W. Michele, and Jeffrey T. Grabill. "Toward a Civic Rhetoric for Technologically and Scientifically Complex Places: Invention, Performance, and Participation." *College Composition and Communication* 58 (2007): 419–48.

Smith, Dora V. "The Danger of Dogma concerning Composition Content." *English Journal* 15.6 (1926): 414–25.

Smith, Marian L. "Overview of INS History." In *A Historical Guide to the U.S. Government,* ed. George T. Kurian, 305–8. New York: Oxford University Press, 1998.

Smith, R. R. "Increasing Satisfactory Production in Composition." *English Journal* 14 (1925): 466–74.

Spellings Commission Report. U.S. Department of Education. *A Test of Leadership: Charting the Future of U.S. Higher Education*. Washington, DC: Government Printing Office, 2006.

Spellmeyer, Kurt. *Common Ground: Dialogue, Understanding, and the Teaching of Composition*. New York: Prentice-Hall, 1993.

State of Massachusetts. Department of Education. "Adult Immigrant Education in Massachusetts, 1920–1921." Report, July 1921.

Street, Brian. *Literacy in Theory and Practice*. Cambridge: Cambridge University Press, 1985.

Strickland, Donna. *The Managerial Unconscious in the History of Composition Studies*. Carbondale: Southern Illinois University Press, 2011.

Stuckey, J. Elspeth. *The Violence of Literacy*. Portsmouth, NH: Boynton/Cook, 1991.

Takaki, Ronald. *Strangers from a Different Shore*. Boston: Little, Brown, 1989.

Tarr, Elvira R. "Union-Based Labor Education: Lessons from the ILGWU." In *The Re-education of the American Working Class,* ed. Steven H. London, Elvira R. Tarr, and Joseph F. Wilson, 63–70. New York: Greenwood, 1990.

Thelin, John R. *A History of American Higher Education*. Baltimore: Johns Hopkins University Press, 2004.

Thomas, J. M. "Training for Teaching Composition in Colleges." *English Journal* 5 (1916): 447–57.

Thompson, Clive. "Brave New World of Digital Intimacy." *New York Times Magazine,* 5 September 2008.

Traub, James. "No Gr_du_te Left Behind." *New York Times Magazine,* 30 September 2007.

Turner, Bryan S., ed. Introduction to *Citizenship and Social Theory.* Newbury Park, CA: Sage, 1993. 1–18.

United States. *Higher Education for Democracy: A Report of the President's Commission on Higher Education,* vol. 1, *Establishing the Goals.* New York: Harper Collins, 1947.

U.S. Bureau of Naturalization. *Federal Citizenship Textbook Part 1, English for American Citizenship.* Washington, DC: Government Printing Office, 1922.

———. *Federal Textbook on Citizenship Training.* Washington, DC: U.S. Department of Labor, 1924.

———. "Proceedings of the First Citizenship Convention." U.S. Department of Labor. Washington, DC: Government Printing Office, 1916.

———. *Student's Textbook.* Washington, DC: Government Printing Office, 1918.

———. *Teacher's Manual (to Accompany Part 1—Federal Citizenship Textbook English for American Citizenship).* Washington, DC: Government Printing Office, 1922.

U.S. Census Bureau. *Current Population Survey, 2010 Annual Social and Economic Supplement,* 2010.

———. *Fourteenth Census of the United States.* Vol. 2. 1920.

U.S. Subcommittee on Immigration, Border Security and Citizenship of the Committee on the Judiciary. *Evaluating a Temporary Guest Worker Program.* 108th Congress. Washington, DC: Government Printing Office, 2004.

———. *Examining the Importance of the H-1B Visa to the American Economy.* 108th Congress, Washington, DC: Government Printing Office, 2003.

U.S. Subcommittee on Immigration of the Committee on the Judiciary. *Immigration Policy: An Overview.* 107th Cong., Washington, DC: Government Printing Office, 2001.

University of Illinois at Urbana-Champaign. *University of Illinois at Urbana-Champaign Strategic Plan.* January 2006.

Vargas, Jose Antonio. "My Life as an Undocumented Immigrant." *New York Times Magazine,* 22 June 2011, MM22.

Veysey, Laurence R. *The Emergence of the American University.* Chicago: University of Chicago Press, 1970.

Ward, Cornelia Carhart. "The Opportunity of the English Teacher." *English Journal* 7 (1918): 364–70.

"We Are Americans." *Time,* 25 June 2012, front cover.

Weiss, Bernard, ed. *American Education and the European Immigrant.* Urbana: University of Illinois Press, 1982.

Weisser, Christian R. *Moving beyond Academic Discourse: Composition Studies and the Public Sphere.* Carbondale: Southern Illinois University Press, 2002.

Welch, Nancy. "Living Room: Teaching Public Writing in a Post-Publicity Era." *College Composition and Communication* 56 (2005): 470–92.

———. *Living Room: Teaching Public Writing in a Privatized World*. Portsmouth, NH: Boynton/Cook, 2008.

Wells, Susan. "Rogue Cops and Health Care: What Do We Want from Public Writing?" *College Composition and Communication* 47 (1996): 325–41.

White House. "Building American Skills through Community Colleges." 4 October 2010.

Winerip, Michael. "Dream Act Advocate Turns Failure into Hope." *New York Times*, 21 February 2011, A10.

Woll, Matthew. "Matthew Woll Issues Statement and Correspondence with 'Railway Review' about Attack on Workers' Education Bureau." *The Paper Makers' Journal* 21–22 (1922): 8–13.

Wong, Susan Stone. "From Soul to Strawberries: The International Ladies' Garment Workers' Union and Workers' Education, 1914–1950." In *Sisterhood and Solidarity: Workers' Education for Women, 1914–1974*, ed. Joyce L. Kornbluh and Mary Frederickson, 39–74. Philadelphia: Temple University Press, 1984.

Workers' Education Bureau. *First National Conference on Workers' Education in the United States*. New York: Workers' Education Bureau, 1921.

———. *Reports of the Executive Committee from the National Convention, 1921–1925*. New York: Workers' Education Bureau, 1926.

———. *Sixth National Convention*. New York: Workers' Education Bureau, 1929.

"Workers Twice Ban Radical Policies." *New York Times*, 20 April 1925, 12.

Wozniak, John Michael. *English Composition in Eastern Colleges, 1850–1940*. Washington, DC: University Press of America, 1978.

Yancey, Kathleen. "Writing in the Twenty-First Century." Urbana, IL: National Council of Teachers of English, 2009.

Young, Morris. *Minor Re/Visions: Asian American Literacy Narratives as a Rhetoric of Citizenship*. Carbondale: Southern Illinois University Press, 2004.

Zernike, Kate. "Making College 'Relevant.'" *New York Times*, 29 December 2009, ED16.

INDEX

CPSIA information can be obtained
at www.ICGtesting.com
Printed in the USA
LVHW030244130821
695223LV00019B/1825